Björn Rombach & Rolf Solli

Constructing Leadership

Reflections on film heroes as leaders

Santérus
Academic Press
Sweden

www.santerus.com

ISBN 10: 91-7335-002-8
ISBN 13: 978-91-7335-002-0
Cover profile: Sven Bylander
Layout and cover: Santérus Academic Press Sweden
Cover photo: ©AP/Scanpix; Bonasera, portrayed by Frank Puglia, asks Don Vito Corleone, portrayed by Marlon Brando, right, for a favor in a scene from the 1972 movie *The Godfather*.
Santérus Academic Press is an imprint of
Santérus Förlag, Surbrunnsgatan 56vi, SE-113 48 Stockholm, Sweden
academicpress@santerus.se
www.santerus.com
Printed by Lightning Source, UK 2006

Contents

Foreword

It is normally said that texts should have a beginning, middle and an end if they are to be readable. This is the end of our text. After years of study, watching films, analysing what leaders in films do and writing this book, we will soon close the file and send it to be printed. Our hope is that reading it will be useful and enjoyable for managers, managers-to-be and all students who are interested in theories about leadership. For us a good theory is something that we can use to understand and reflect on our everyday experiences.

We believe that managers will find this book useful if they start to wonder how they should manage. Not because we can tell them, as researchers, what they should do but because what we write will enable them to reflect over their own practices. Both managers and managers-to-be have every reason to play with ideas about different ways of doing what other managers does. This book will provide something they can base these ideas on. We know that films are used in teaching from the primary classes all the way up to universities and other forms of education, but we also know that not enough use is made of films. Films offer an opportunity to analyse behaviour that appears to be realistic both in terms of breadth and depth without therefore creating disturbances in the real reality.

Initially we thought that this book could be sold in a box together with the nine films we analyse. A book and nine DVD's would have made an attractive presentation. But this came to nothing because of the regulations about distributing films. However, we recommend readers to get hold of the films. This will make it possible to alternate between reading and watching films, even if not all the films have to be watched or watched again. There is a lot to be said for watching and discussing the films with others, it is more enjoyable and adds new perspectives.

Finally we would like to thank our colleagues at the School of Public Administration and Göteborg Research Institute for the opinions they have expressed on earlier versions of our texts. Our special thanks go to Patrik Zapata Johansson, who is the constructively critical reader all authors long for, and to Elisabeth Ravenshorst for the excellent improvements she proposed for the chapter on Elizabeth. Monica Kostera at Växjö University threatened to write the book herself if we did not get a move on. And our gratitude also goes to all those who have shown interest and patted us on the back without really knowing what we were trying to do. We believe that this work is in English. David Jones, Rhetorica AB, has seen to this and without him it would probably have been yet another book in Swenglish.

As usual, our thanks to our families as well for their persistence in pointing out that you cannot work all the time. Thank you Eva, Merja, all the boys, and everyone else involved. And note that from now on watching film is not something that we can classify as work any longer, although it may well become so for you.

January 2006

Björn Rombach and *Rolf Solli*

CHAPTER 1

A Steven Spielberg

Films are like motorways into people's heads. There was a good reason for the sudden increase in BMW sales in the USA or why children started to fight with light sabres. Films influence us. When James Bond began to drive a BMW in *GoldenEye* in 1995 this led to runaway sales. The Z3 Roadster sold out immediately. And by the next film he had already switched to an inferior vehicle anyway. And we Star Wars fans would probably never have seen the missing instalments if peripheral sales had not been so profitable.

Films cannot only give products a push. Ideas can be marketed as well. Adolf Hitler bought Leni Riefenstahl, who made her masterpiece *Triumph des Willens (The Triumph of Will*, 1935). This was great art and also effective propaganda. In a number of interviews (with Borg for instance in 1995) Leni Riefenstahl says that she was interested only in aesthetic creation. Not without justification, her political naivety has been condemned by posterity.

But the opportunity offered by film to influence people is not entirely unproblematic. As Eva Blomberg points out in her article 'Professor Film in the service of popular education' (2001) it is not at all simple to educate the electorate with the help of films. We venture to conclude that non-fiction films about how leadership should be exercised will have difficulties in contributing to the improvement of leaders. Feature films get across – the question is whether they actually give rise to what can be called education.

Our interest in this book is in leadership in films. In this first chapter we describe why and how leadership in films can be important for leaders now and in the future. We want to convince you that it is worth going on reading it (that the book is a Steven Spielberg – the Mozart of our day). In other words this book does not suffer from lack of ambition. In the first chapter we will also focus on some of the problems that the study has caused us.

> The Maestro says it's Mozart
> but it sounds like bubble gum
> when you're waiting
> for the miracle to come.
>
> (Leonard Cohen 1992, *Waiting for the Miracle*)

Many studies of leadership have shown that leaders are patterned to a very high degree on their models. These may be mentors – managers end up resembling what their own managers were like. They may also model themselves on individuals or situations encountered when they were young. The imitation may be either deliberate or unaware. But fashionable trends may also serve as models, communicated for instance by consultants. What consultants in the management field do and how they do it is not without interest. Here Barbara Czarniawska's classic *To Coin a Phrase* (Czarniawska-Joerges 1988) is well worth reading – it deals in actual fact with the managers and not those who shape them.

This work has been written in the context of a research project in which we analyse feature films from a leadership perspective. Similar approaches have been adopted with great success to novels (for example by Czarniawska-Joerges and Guillet de Monthoux 1994, March and Weil 2003) and the television series *Absolutely Fabulous* (for instance by Höök 1998). The question we ask is whether film has not been underrated as a bearer of the norms for the behaviour of adults in the labour market. Popular films have a wider circulation than books. We, two middle-aged men, have seen at least 4,000 films each. No small proportion of these films was, admittedly, repeats. Reading books is part of our work, but even so we do not believe we have read 4,000 books. Several action-oriented studies show, moreover, that managers rarely read books – it takes too long (Mintzberg 1973, Kotter 1982, Tengblad 2005).

It may also be the case that we adopt a less critical approach to films than to inter-office memos and journals. The message is driven home because we open up to it voluntarily, indeed even pay for it. If we fail to identify with films their only impact is to expose us to flickering light, voices and sounds while simple music is playing. But even so the melodies will play inside our heads for decades. Many of us have been hearing Ennio Morricone (see for instance *The Good, the Bad, and the Ugly*; 1966) as we walk alone along a long, straight, sun lit asphalt road.

When a viewer finally dozes off clutching the remote control a great deal has happened in one way or another. He or she has been entertained by seeing how sultry and disagreeable or cool and delightful various places can be. Sometimes a lesson in leadership has also been offered. It is not unlikely that, like Colonel Nicholson in *The Bridge on the River Kwai*, a manager will briefly walk with her hands behind her back on the day after seeing the film. She may consider it necessary to take an overall approach, and may even use these words during the first meeting of the day. But if the film shown on television was not *The Bridge on the River Kwai*, then different thoughts may arise and different words used.

We are not claiming that people become just like the characters they see in films. On the whole a composed and critical distance is preserved to the roles we view. But it is not always that this distance is maintained and sometimes we want to be influenced. This applies not only to ordinary people – it applies to leaders as well.

The surface of the film is analysed

Films can be seen in different ways just as other forms of cultural expression can be approached differently. Our youthful idol among Swedish declamatory poets, Bruno K. Öijer, claimed in a radio programme some time ago that what a lot of other poets produced was pretentious crap. That is possible, but the last time his *Photographs of the Smile of End of the World* (1974) ended up on the coffee table crap was the epithet that young people agreed on. And the anthology compiled by Rolf Aggestam and Gunnar Harding in 1974 entitled *Anarchistic Songs by 20 Young Poets* is definitely pretentious. But not for that reason unnecessary. Anyway, if we had no pretensions whatsoever, we would not have referred here to Bruno K. either.

Film can be read at various depths. The pretentiousness in the poetry of others was, according to Bruno K. Öijer, what could only be construed by other poets or critics. Poetry of good quality (but these are not his words) was more immediate; more exposed and could be read by everyone. We are claiming that all films can be interpreted and that good films have several levels that are relatively accessible for interpretation. Krzysztof Kieslowski, who knew more about film than we do, claims in *Kieslowski on Kieslowski* by Danusia Stok (1995) that film virtually always has merely a surface. It would have been more damning for our argument if he had said that film had only depth.

We have read films in the same way as case studies are read in programmes in the social sciences, but like the novels used by Czarniawska-Joerges and Guillet de Monthoux (1994, Introduction), films are not cases at all. One difference is that films, like literary texts, provide us with information about the kind of things we cannot normally grasp when we read academic studies or journalism. For instance we can learn exactly what people are thinking and what they do in secret or without realising it themselves. We can be presented with a whole. In our readings we have looked for explicit lessons for leaders or future leaders who watch the films. We have focused on how leaders lead, but we also have an interest in the totality that includes their private lives.

Fiction is characterised by the fact that it is invented but not by its mendacity. Scientific accounts of reality are also invented – but in them certain assertions may be false and others true. In the case of fiction truth and falsehood are irrelevant issues. Borderline cases may be found in narratives of the lives of historical individuals like *Elizabeth* and *Nixon* later on in this book. In these, deviations from the truth are not false but instead become interesting. In the same way incongruities are interesting in descriptions of the future like the film *Matrix*. For our purposes invented fiction has one advantage over other forms of narrative in being simple and structured (cf. Cohn 1999).

Our practical analyses have been inspired by David Altheide's useful guide *Qualitative Media Analysis* (1996). With his refreshing mix of traditions he has produced a serviceable approach rather than a tool. We have also been influenced by the semiotic trends that have been the latest fashion in organisational research for some time (and are perhaps therefore on the wane). Generally speaking, this means that we consider the receiver's interpretation to be equally justifiable as the sender's. In other words, we are interested in the surface rather than what lies beneath it. If there are subtexts, they are not our concern.

The surface of a film consists of images and in many of our films subtitles in English. When we quote from the films we use the subtitles throughout. The one exception is *Nixon*, which was only available in a VHS version without subtitles. We have decided to quote the subtitles because this makes our work easier and gives the text greater stability – even though the subtitles do not in some cases agree with what is being said in the film.

We have manuscripts for many of the films and we have also had access to the books on which some of them were based. One argument for minimising our use of material like this is that our interest is in the models presented in the films. If a film is based on a book, the manuscript never reproduces it exactly and in its entirety, nor does any film ever reflect the manuscript precisely. Mark Glassy makes the same distinction when he analyses *The Biology of Science Fiction Cinema* (2001), as does Lawrence Krauss in *The Physics of Star Trek* (1997). Both of these works are, by the way, extremely entertaining for all of us who persist in regarding discrepancies between real reality and the reality of film as nothing more than errors. Nevertheless – when we use sources in addition to the films and subtitles we say so.

> I focus only on what actually made it to the screen. After all, this is what the paying public actually saw, and this is what has stuck in their minds, for better or worse. (Glassy 2001, p. 4)

Subtitles allow themselves to be incorporated into our text without problems. One text can be cited in another text without being altered. What is said in dialogues can also be quoted relatively exactly. When we turn speech into text we lose features like tone of voice, pauses and facial expressions. But these are minor problems when compared to converting what we see into words in a book. If an image is to become written text it has to be translated. In translating images into text our ambition has been to produce descriptions rather than interpretations. We are deliberately trying, therefore, to stay on the surface. We cannot help the fact that every translation of an image into text also involves interpretation.

The problems in translating images to text indicate that all who read this book should themselves see the films we analyse. This does, however, not completely solve the problem – it merely increases the number of translations. We do not intend, however, to exaggerate the problems our readers and we encounter in translating what we see to our superficial understanding of what happens. Whenever we see something this process begins – so it is something we are good at. In an interview, Pär-Anders Granhag, who has studied the psychology of lying, went so far as to advocate video recordings of interrogations of suspected criminals 'as it is easier to see when someone is lying on film than when you see them in real life' (Asklöf 2001, p. 17; see also Strömwall 2001).

Anyone watching a film with others can read into it one thing where those next to him will see something else. But once they have shaken the popcorn out of their clothes and left the auditorium there are also things that they have all seen. This obviously also applies if we have been lying alone in front of the television. It is not the case that depth is more sophisticated or requires special training. On the contrary, too much education can narrow our vision. We find it easier to agree that we have seen the same thing if it presented directly to our view without requiring too much of our analytical powers.

When we discuss the influence of film here, it is precisely what is explicit on the surface that interests us. One justification for this superficial reading is that it is most usual for certain audiences in certain situations. The audience we are referring to consists of managers in mid-career or who have at least made some progress. They watch films on television until the small hours. Often in hotel bedrooms, or lazing in the sofa after putting the children to bed. They have not actively selected the film but have rather rejected pornography, golf and conversation to become involved in a narrative that has already started. When it gets late enough, or another Cola Light would taste good, they switch the box off, not caring whether the director has had his say or not.

Even the surface of a film offers a great deal to look at. The youthful car or the jogging hero's attractive butt can easily make the greatest impact on the viewer. One fine day we will go jogging ourselves. The surface displays objects or deals with behaviour – how actors do what they do. Films have a great deal of surface and therefore lend themselves readily to imitation. Complex structures and what lies deeper are much more difficult to copy. It is easier to look like Madonna by next week than to sell over a 100 million records and influence the world through the music you have made. Imitation can be looked upon as a way of testing what it is like to do this or that. If our imitation leads to success, the behaviour deepens and survives as a norm.

Choice of films

In this book we analyse what leaders do in nine films. In other words, we are not interested in the entire contents of the films. The question of what leaders do in films and how they are described is an interesting one. In the Swedish medical journal *Läkartidningen* (issue 15, 2001) we saw a brief preliminary report from Gena Weiner's project on the roles of physicians in films. It turns out that these can be epitomised as the stereotypical roles of hero, villain or seducer. The question of the roles they play could be asked about the leaders in films. We have opted not to do so. Without going into a lengthy discussion of this topic, it will suffice to say that we do not consider it fruitful and that there already exist innumerable role typifications.

In *MCM*, one Swedish bikers magazine among many that we read more frequently than the Medical Journals, we found an article (Jonsson 2001) that presented the ways in which motorbikes have been presented in Swedish films through the ages. This metal steed and its riders have had to symbolise alienation, freedom, criminality, power, speed and perversion. If we focus on the roles assumed by doctors, Peter Jonsson sees heroes and villains on Swedish motorbikes as well. And Zac on his black Harley-Davidson (in *House of Angels* from 1992) was a seducer. Roles are like jeans – if you make them big enough everyone will find something to suit them. And what's more, many of us have no objection if they (roles and jeans) are slightly too tight so that they contain and restrict what really is us. Heroes, villains and seducers exist in films irrespective of whether there are any doctors or not.

Someone is bound to ask why we did not choose ten films. It is after all a nice round figure, as long as you do not want to divide it by three. And then there must be some people who would have preferred seven. It is after all a sacred number. But it was nine. They are:

Any Given Sunday (1999)
Matrix (1999)
Elizabeth (1998)
Beck – Decoy Boy (1997)
Nixon (1995)
The Mozart Brothers (1986)
Life of Brian (1979)
The Godfather (1972)
The Bridge on the River Kwai (1957)

Every time we describe our project to somebody (including both our publisher and our children's friends) the response has been the same. After having established that it sounds like an interesting book, they go on to suggest what films we should analyse. In other contexts we ourselves have asked colleagues what films they think would suit our purpose. We have looked for films in which leadership is in fact exerted. This is not at all as common as we originally believed it was.

We eliminated those films that were difficult to get hold of. Almost every film is available but not always without difficulty. To begin with we intended to use *Fitzcarraldo*, the 1982 film by Werner Herzog, but it turned out that it had to be ordered specially. We have not included any television series either as they can be hard to obtain on video. As we happen to be Swedes, we could not resist choosing the best Swedish leadership film we know of – even though it cannot be found in a standard video boutique. We should be grateful that there is a version of *The Mozart Brothers* directed by Susanne Osten with English subtitles. We also included *Beck – Decoy Boy* (*Beck – mannen med ikonerna*), which is one of the films in a series originally based on the novels by Maj Sjöwall and Per Wahlöö about Inspector Beck (such as *Roseanna* 1965/1993). This film does not have subtitles but on the whole it is not difficult to understand anyway ...

Apart from visible leadership and availability we had two more criteria. The films we selected had to be good in the sense that people knew about them and recognised them. Whether or not they really are good films is something we cannot decide. We do not know anything about film. This may be a good opportunity to stress that we know nothing about film theory either, nor are we attempting to analyse film from a film studies point of view. Having read a few introductory texts in this field, we have been able to piece together that film analysis is interesting but differs in essence from our goal in writing this work. Have we made this sufficiently clear?

The films on which we were going to base the analyses used in this book also had to be different in character. We did not want only North American films but preferably some from Europe and Sweden as well. They were not to have only male leaders as their protagonists. This last consideration was, by the way, a tricky criterion. We have determined, as have many before us (and one that does so interestingly is Grint and Case 1998, p. 559), that management is masculine. There are many war films and sports films to choose from, but we did not want only to include this kind of film. Not more than one film could present a dour detective with his team. We could happily include a film that was historical, one set in the present and any period in between them. We were even able to include the future. No film was to be unwatchably disgusting. And so on.

This variety was intended to sustain the interest of anyone who wanted to watch the films in parallel with their reading of the book. If films differ, you can always find something interesting and you can also watch several films without tiring. We also hoped that variation in the empirical material would enable us to broaden our analysis. If the films were different, it was likely that several themes would emerge when we analysed them. This turned out to be true. In the eyes of some maybe too true. A lot of themes come up in the films and are therefore dealt with in this book.

It should also be pointed out that we have allowed the differences between the films to play a role in structuring each of the chapters as well. The films are different and therefore so are the chapters. We do not see this as a problem. On the contrary, we ourselves are easily bored by section headings that recur chapter after chapter.

As everybody can see, we have opted to discuss the films in chronological order, the most recent first and the oldest last. We experimented with different sequences but chose this one in the end for relatively arbitrary reasons – some order is required. But our choice does not have to be the reader's choice. We believe that the chapters can well be read in any order at all, although the last chapter should be saved until the end. If you do not like films about sport or action films, it might be a good idea to begin with the chapter on *Elizabeth* before reading the others.

All our data are available

Books that purport to be final research reports usually have a section on methodology. We have written about selection and interpretation above. The following section will describe how we collected our data.

The data collection, the empirical material, the subject of the analysis in this book, or whatever you prefer to call it, comprises the behaviour of managers or leaders in nine feature films. The films that we have studied are also available in their entirety for anyone reading this book. In this way we have reduced the methodological problems dramatically in comparison with other studies of managerial behaviour.

Normally collecting and presenting data causes major problems. Case studies cannot be replicated. Researchers have to convince the readers that they have observed what they claim. It is also necessary to demonstrate to what extent what is reported is a result of the researcher's presence while conducting the study. We have no problems of this kind in this book. In our case the data survives in its entirety in exactly the same form it had prior to the study. Anyone who reads this book can also watch the films. It may even be that more enjoyment can be found in watching the films than in reading a book about them ...

It is unlikely that our playback equipment has resulted in any significant differences between the films we have seen and those seen by the readers of this book. Nevertheless life is not so simple that there are no methodological problems concerning the data at all. Together we have watched each film more than ten times. This means that the film we saw last contains more details than when we saw it for the first time. During our first and perhaps second viewing of the film we saw it as a whole. Since then we have concentrated on specific elements to a great extent. We have also stopped the films on many occasions to make notes and wound them backwards and forward to look for events or dialogue.

We have both seen nearly all of these films at the cinema. The viewing on which our work in this book is based has, on the other hand, almost entirely taken place at home or in our offices. Most often we have watched them in solitary concentration. We have watched a lot of the films on a computer screen. The normal cinemagoer does not see the same number of repeats as we have. To some extent, as well, the way we watch the films is not the normal one. We have concentrated on them for their entire length and watched them on our own. If we had been watching idly at home we might possibly have zapped from scene to scene or film to film or to other programmes. If the films had been screened on a commercial channel we would certainly have zapped somewhere else during the commercials and then failed to return to the channel in time for the film to continue. Where and how you watch films affects what you see.

The prevailing problems related to the influence on what we see of our preconceptions and knowledge applies to this study as well as to other studies. What we see is affected by what we know. As we have pointed out earlier, there are also difficulties implicit in the way we translate images from the screen into words in this book. We attempt to restrict our descriptions to the surface of the films but we are forced to translate the images into words. This last factor is one reason why we persist in presenting fairly thorough accounts of the surface of the films.

Choice of themes

In the various chapters we take up different themes or aspects of leadership. At times we are certain to repeat ourselves. Some messages are too short to rank as themes. We could be said to have used our films as the basis for analyses that follow a number of central approaches. A few words on how these have been selected are appropriate here.

In choosing the themes we have first watched the films a few times and then described the way in which we see the leaders acting. In several cases these descriptions provided the themes then used to analyse the film. In *The Godfather* the focus is on decision-making and *Beck* deals with middle management. *Elizabeth* spotlights action and *Nixon* the issue of accountability.

Certain analytical themes were chosen more actively. For instance we considered it important in a book on leadership to deal with decision-making, the situation of middle managers, actions and accountability. We write and you read – so we decided what to deal with and you decide how long you will read for. Keep going – this introduction only has two more short paragraphs to go.

A book about nine films in which we take up a couple of themes per film and do not avoid the sidetracks that appeal to us will be pretty broad. We use a wide brush and feel that it is reasonable to do so. From day to day, leaders encounter a multitude of questions and problems that are linked to each other. It is merely ridiculous when good leadership is reduced to a few simple rules of thumb.

We have written this book for managers in mid-career or those who are thinking about becoming managers. This is by no means a small group. We have also written for those who, like ourselves, are interested in the nature of leadership. Hopefully its format will also make this book suitable for our constant companions – citizens with an interest in society. We have made great endeavours to balance breadth and depth to avoid writing a book too thick to read. Our ideal has been a work that you can read lying on your back and that will cause no injury if you happen to doze off and it drops on to your face. Enjoy it!

CHAPTER 2

Any Given Sunday – motivation is everything

You should be interested in challenges – that is what it says in advertisements for managerial positions. On the other hand it rarely says what is meant by challenges. Most people's thoughts will turn to the capacity to adapt an organisation to prevailing market conditions or something similar. Challenges can involve this or completely different things; they can also come from within the organisation. Internal challenges come from others who want to take over your responsibilities. They can be younger colleagues 'who want to get ahead', but they can also be older members of the staff who feel that they have been overlooked. Workplace intrigues are by no means uncommon.

Intrigues, challenges, a fall and also restitution – sometimes known as revenge – all of this can be found in the film *Any Given Sunday* (1999). On its uppermost surface, if we can think of it in terms of layers, the film is about a legendary 55-year-old coach, Tony (Anthony) D'Amato (excellently acted by Al Pacino) who runs the Miami Sharks. Tony is described on the film's official web site as 'a man more in love with the game than anything else in life, including himself' (Internet reference 1). The subject is American professional football and there are many shots from matches and training. One of the points of sport is that the results are often definite and clear. Team sports are particularly interesting. A link can be assumed between the actions of the team managers and results, which means that immediate evaluation is never far away. In individual sports the link with coaches and managers is presumed to be weaker.

Why does the film begin with this particular quotation from Vince Lombardi? 'I firmly believe that any man's finest hour – his greatest fulfilment to all he holds dear is that moment when he has worked his heart out in a good cause and lies exhausted on the field of battle – victorious.' How can you struggle for 'a good cause' in football or any other sport? There are masses of other quotations from Vince Lombardi to choose from, which is not surprising when a Latin teacher becomes a successful coach – he won five league championships (NFL) in the USA in ten years with his team The Green Bay Packers! Before Vince Lombardi took them over the Packers were a no-win team. We have allowed Vince (1913–1970) to formulate most of the headings we use in this chapter. (Internet reference 2)

Where winning is concerned, one of Tony D'Amato's guiding principles is that really wanting to win is important. The leader's (coach's) task is to give the players self-confidence, motivate the group and keep it together. Without self-confidence or motivation the team cannot win. Cohesion is so important that even the best player can be sacrificed if this is needed to keep the team together. But Tony also says: 'This game has got to be about more than winning'. Both power and motivation are immediately present in the film – and it would be difficult to envisage leadership without these ingredients.

Wanting to win is everything

Things are not going well for Tony D'Amato when the film begins. As the film opens, his quarterback, Cap Rooney – 38 years old and nominated as best player in the league three years running – goes into a tackle and is severely injured. This is serious. The importance of the quarterbacks cannot be overrated; they function in more or less the same way as line managers on the field. The quarterbacks lead and the rest of the team follow. This is all based on a complicated social agreement in which the quarterbacks earn their authority. During a lively dinner Tony explains this to the future star Willie Beamen.

TONY D'AMATO:

> You're a goddamn quarterback! You know what that means?! It's the top spot, kid. It's the guy takes the fall. It's the guy everybody's looking at first, the leader of a team. Who will support you when they understand you? Who will break their ribs and their noses and their necks for you because they believe? Because you make them believe. That's a quarterback.

Not all leaders constantly require so much support or face such high expectations as they do in football. That would be unbearable. But in periods of adaptation there are similarities between a quarterback and managers in companies and public administration. Even the unexpected can become routine as Dan Kärreman shows in his study of a newspaper company (1996). But this does mean that it is not interesting to see what happens to leadership in situations that managers consider 'difficult' (Lind Nilsson 2001). It is for instance clear that colleagues and management groups become more important in situations like this.

In a good team there are good reserves. Tyler Cherubini may be sound but he is not yet ready. 'All right, nice and easy. We're up. See? 21-17. Just hold on. Steady', Tony tells him. Tyler has hardly walked on to the field before he too is injured. A television commentator exclaims: 'Two quarterbacks in a row. I have not seen this since '88. Or '78?' Real bad luck. The reserve could not cope. This is partly because he has not been able to spend enough time on the field. The regular quarterback has been too good to replace. Perhaps Tony was also a little niggardly about giving the reserve a chance to show what he could do. This was basically the coach's error. He selects the team. Tyler Cherubini should have been trained for his role.

Today's slimmed organisations often lack reserves. When people on staff quit, are ill or take parental leave there is nobody to take their place. Organisations are not as robust as they once were. Even though some degree of turnover and time off work can be predicted, it seems as if organisations no longer dare have individuals with genuine capacity sitting around on the subs' benches leafing through magazines. As a result, panic recruitment solutions involving relatively expensive manpower companies and massive workloads have become more and more frequent. But the slimmed organisations also impact on the social ambitions endorsed by many organisations. For instance, how can you have a positive approach to parental leave and the recruitment of women of child-bearing age if there is nobody else in the organisation able to take over their tasks?

In the film we now see the team's director and also one of its co-owners, Christina Pagniacci (acted by Cameron Diaz) in the VIP stand. That's right, a woman! With two injured quarterbacks she starts phoning in an attempt to buy a new one. A crisis is approaching for the team and work starts immediately to ward it off – almost as a reflex. Similar crises have probably threatened or even occurred for the team previously, while Christina has been its director or when she was her father's apprentice.

One alternative to maintaining reserve capacity for normal operations (staff in the substitute box) is extra managerial capacity (a director in the stand). If this exists, crises can be staved off and managed with no disturbance of the work in other respects. However, slimming down at middle-management level for the sake of horizontal structures has been even more extreme than the slimming down of operations in many organisations (cf. Ohlsson and Rombach 1998). This means that normal crises that occur as a matter of course may jeopardise an entire organisation.

On the pitch it is now a case of fielding a reserve for a reserve. Next in line is the unknown Willie Beamen, aged 26. Willie has not been near a match ball for a long time. His role in the team is to sit on the subs' bench. He is reading a magazine and does not even notice that his turn has come to go on to the field. The assistant coach gets him moving by bawling him out. Tony grabs hold of him: 'Okay, Beamen, you're up. Left Deuce Zig 22 Tomcat.' This is a coded instruction telling Willie what to do. A simple pass to Julian Washington. Willie looks up at the stands. 'Look at me!', Tony says. 'You're gonna do fine. You hold it all inside. There. Stay focused. Okay? Stay there.'

Things do not start well for the greenhorn, Willie Beamen. When he is going to tell his teammates what tactics to adopt he is so nervous he throws up. Things go really badly for the team as well. Willie reacts to this by changing the game plan – all on his own. This is about as probable as Ford telling his subordinates that they were now going to begin building BMW's. Things do not go much better as a result. A television commentator, played by the film's director Oliver Stone, explains that Willie Beamen is passing too soon because he is nervous.

Willie's deviations from the game plan are adaptations to the opposing team's defence. In reality it is odd that this is presented as being so remarkable. He is a manager with a great deal of responsibility, but according to his boss, the coach, and his assistant, the strategist, he always has to comply with the detailed script given to him by the coach. Willie does not do so – he devises his own strategies. Even when they lead to success, Tony gets angry. 'What the hell was that? I called a Regular 22 Fox. You know what that is, son?' Willie knows. 'You run the plays I call.' And Tony says flatly: 'You with me, son?' The message cannot be misunderstood. Willie does the only thing to do – he agrees.

Mental toughness is essential to success

During a break Tony gives the team a pep talk using a lot of four-letter words and at the same time claims that he can tolerate mistakes. 'You gotta do something out there. … If you make mistakes, make them big. I won't eat your lunch for that.' But he does not want to lose and neither do his players. We see motivation being created and also an attempt to increase the acceptance of risk.

Tony makes it clear that the team can and should win. 'We're only down by three. We can win this. … Gentlemen! This is where we live! We're not gonna let them fuck with us in our house, are we? Let's go out there and kick some second-half ass!' Motivating them means pointing to the possibility of winning and suggesting some sort of obligation to succeed. This seems to get through to all of them except Willie Beamen, who is standing alone in a corner contemplating his fate.

The attempts by the leader to increase the group's acceptance of risk recur throughout the film. This behaviour differs from the prevailing impression of the role of the manager as a buffer against surrounding uncertainties (Thompson 1967, cf. as well Cyert and March 1962). If uncertainty can be reduced there are no risks that can or need be taken. The message in the film is instead that acceptance of risk requires a certain basic security that does not occur spontaneously. Encouragement is one method used by the leader in the film. Rosabeth Moss Kanter (1977) has shown in her feminist classic *Men and Women of the Corporation* that readiness to take risks increases if people regard themselves as members of a homogenous group. Tony's words 'this is where we live' help to create this homogenous feeling.

Not only leaders tend to act to reduce acceptance of risk, but also this is regulated by the organisations themselves in the sense that they restrict the repertoire of actions open to their staff (cf. Brunsson 1985). Protecting employees from perceiving risks and preventing them from taking risks is easy. It is as if this is what organisations are made for. Tony, like leaders in general, is taking on a much more difficult task when he wants to persuade the players that 'You gotta do something'.

After some time the Sharks are down by ten points. This is quite a lot but not insuperable. Tony asks for time-out and asks Willie what is wrong with him. Willie thinks everything is happening too quickly. Tony calms him down: 'Believe me when I tell you this. You can only get better. And you don't have to worry about getting the hook because I got no one left.' Willie remains unconvinced and feels himself that he is playing very badly. Tony launches the operation of raising his self-confidence by simplifying his task. The courage he wants to get at demands some basic security. During his pep talk with the group in the changing room Tony did not get through to Willie. Now he makes a second attempt.

TONY D'AMATO:

> You played this game your whole life. You know what I'm saying? You grew up in Dallas, right? So maybe you're back in Dallas right now. You're home you're enjoying yourself. You're back in the hood just before your mama calls you in for dinner. I say 'Go to the Buick. Turn

around, I'll throw it to you.' ... What I'm saying is, you gotta forget it all. The crowd, the audibles, the goddamn playbook. Just focus on this next one pass. Go to the Buick. Turn around. Enjoy it. That's what you're here for.

The personal approach has its impact. Willie believes in himself and finally gets a pass that leads to a touchdown. That's positive, but not positive enough for the Sharks. Instead of booting the ball in, the team loses. And it is not only Willie's fault. Tony did not have the courage to follow through and Julian Washington focuses too much on his individual bonus. Besides, it is odd for such generous rewards to be offered for individual achievements in a team game by anyone but the team managers.

Timidity in companies and administrations can also sometimes be explained by individual bonus agreements that professionals have outside the organisation. For researchers, for instance, it can be a waste of energy to seek success in or for their own organisation. Success outside the organisation, in having articles published in international specialist journals or securing appointments of various kinds, may, for example, become more important. The bonus may consist of money, a better post or higher status. This all compares more than favourably with the rewards for success within the organisation.

A television commentator points out: 'And now D'Amato's lost four games in a row.' After the match Tony rapidly gathers the team together. Willie is tired of losing. Tony tells him he 'played strong' and that he personally has reached the age when 'you get used to it'. Tony says to the team: 'All right, everybody, listen up! Played your hearts out there today. No blame, nobody.' Then the team's priest takes over and one of the things he says is 'there are no atheists in foxholes'. If not before, that is, surely, when they emerge.

Christina, the director who inherited the team from her father, Art, is consoled by her mother (Margaret), who obviously knows very little about football – she refers to the ball as 'that thing'. But her mother knows something that Christina has forgotten. She knows that 'it's just a game'. Christina realises that she now has a lot to do and tells her husband that she will not be home until late.

A few marginal events take place before the next match. We learn for instance that the regular quarterback will not recover quickly, if he ever will. Willie is told off by his mother for not telling her that he would be on television and also because he is not a regular quarterback. Tony gets a scolding from a television reporter and is almost picked up by Mandy Murphy – if he is ready to pay five thousand dollars for the whole night. She is attractive and Tony is over the hill, but he still declines. Because of this, and perhaps also because he has lost four matches in a row, Tony begins to wonder whether his coach's instincts are going. 'All I got are my instincts. I lose those, I got nothing.' Tony is not particularly sober and ends the evening as last man in the bar. When he gets home he rings his ex-wife Jeanette and talks to her answering machine about their children and grandchildren. Again an example of a hopeless male manager.

Success has a price

Next day there is training as usual and it is also time for meeting at Christina's home. Before Tony arrives in his elegant sports car we learn that Christina is considering moving the team to Los Angeles. One of her advisors thinks she should sell the team for 250 million dollars. Christina really wants to tell Tony off properly but she is not very successful. He has an answer to everything and is on the side of the players. Points in his favour. Although she insists on and wants renewal. And victories. Points there too. Finally Christina suggests that Tony may not get a new contract.

Quarterback number two, Tyler Cherubini, has recovered sufficiently for the next match. This does not help – he screws up immediately and Willie Beamen has to be fielded. Willie is quite successful, but still throws up at times during the match. One of the reasons for his success is that he suddenly alters tactics without asking the coaches. This makes Tony really angry. 'Following the script' seems to be more important than winning points. This is also true in many work places. Willie gets the team behind him because he is the quarterback. Initially, therefore, it is his position that gives him the authority he needs. The Sharks win the match and the reporter taps into his keyboard: 'A new breed of athlete and man. The future. Welcome to the 21st century.' He can see the result but does not seem to realise that the new quarterback's authority is based on an uncertain foundation.

At a party, and these are numerous in this film, we hear a great deal of tittle-tattle. Willie's girl friend, Vanessa Struthers, finds it difficult to become one of the gang, and she does not get any help from Willie either. The team's young and expensive strategist and statistician, Nick Crozier, complains to Christina that Tony does not listen to him. He does not want to go on working with Tony. Christina calmly tells him that he will not have to in the following season. She works hard during the party. Among other things, she finds time to threaten the mayor by saying that she will move the team if he does not make sure a proper new stadium is built. Christina is unhappy that the team is losing money. According to the film's official web site she goes in for a 'take-no-prisoners style of management' and brooks no opposition (Internet reference 1).

Christina shows that leadership is not something exclusive to the official workplace. It is just as important to organise and manage things in other arenas as well. Research has demonstrated that this is generally applicable (Sjöstrand et al. 2001). Most things are decided outside boardrooms and council chambers. This can be a problem in the public sector as it weakens representative democracy. Shareholders could experience corresponding problems. But discussions about increased focus on 'shareholder value' indicate the opposite (see Brodin et al. 2000). 'In the light of history, however, all enhancements of an ownership perspective appear favourable from an industrial, dynamic perspective' (op. cit. p. 12).

It seems unlikely that any organisation could be managed profitably from a room that is cut off from everyday circumstances and operations. It may be possible to keep owners satisfied for a while. Nevertheless, if this is detrimental for long-term positive development nothing has been gained. We will also find it unsatisfactory from the point of view of the communities in which we live. There is a lot to suggest that a gradual shift is required of the strategies we invoke to shape events. A functioning democracy needs to adapt to the restrictions that limit the scope for voters to exercise any real influence.

Time for the next match. Now the Sharks do better and this is because Willie is feeling increasingly secure. But still he throws up now and again. Willie is in command of the game and is becoming more and more of a star. The team follow him. Willie is asked to make commercials, express opinions on television and take part in talk shows. He is paid increasing attention and he becomes more and more self-assured. During one talk show he goes so far as to refer to Tony as 'Coach Stone Age'. It should be noted, by the way, that this film is patently free of advertising in the form of product placement – in spite of the fact that sport is an area in which advertising is very common. It could be imagined that the director wanted to emphasise that this is culture and not … sport.

They will love you later

At regular intervals Tony seeks Willie out. He tries to talk about Willie's role in the team. Tony sits next to Willie in the plane taking them to the next match but does not succeed in getting the conversation to flow easily enough for anything significant to be said. He invites Willie home to dinner so that they can discuss the rules of the game. Tony tries to teach Willie humility, respect and that football is a team game. The discussion ranges backwards and forwards and we catch regular glimpses of *Ben-Hur* on the television in the background.

After some time Tony and Willie get on to the heavy leadership issues. Tony claims that leadership means sacrificing oneself: 'Sacrifice. The times he's gotta sacrifice because he's gotta lead by example. Not by fear and not by self-pity.' You could almost believe that Tony has read David McClelland's books. Because David McClelland (1985) claims that an effective leader is good at motivating others to perform well, rather than at performing well himself. Willie does not like what he is hearing, he wants to leave and makes no bones about saying so.

Willie is having problems with himself after all his success. He quarrels with his nice girl friend, Vanessa, who moves out. He is unnecessarily pushy with Christina when she tells him how well he has done and he is surly to a television reporter who gives him a great deal of coverage. Willie's contacts with his teammates develop really badly. He makes enemies of virtually all of them. They think he is too full of himself, especially on television. Their disagreements become obvious on the field. Nobody helps Willie unless they have to. In football this means that you get really knocked around and that you lose. Finally Willie is struck by one of his own team. Tony thinks that Willie can learn that the team will not play for him if he behaves as he does. Nevertheless, after the match he bawls out the whole team: 'Thirty years in football I never seen something stinks like this! Today out there you embarrassed yourselves. Today I'm ashamed to be your coach.' He rubs salt in the wounds.

Tony is not the only one who tries to get Willie back on course. The gigantic defender Luther Shark Lavay makes his attempt in the sauna. 'The game's taught you how to strut, how to talk shit, how to hit. But what else?' Julian J-man Washington also has difficulties in being a member of the team and is taught a lesson. A small boy asks how much he earns and is really impressed. But he also says: 'My dad says you won't take passes up the middle because you might get hurt.' What the boy means, as his body language shows, is that J-man is quite simply a coward. It is not pleasant to hear the truth even if you are a superstar.

Tony visits the injured Cap Rooney at home. Cap is seriously disturbed by his injuries and does not believe he will ever succeed as a quarterback again. Tony takes control of the situation and speaks reflectively and unemphatically to Cap. 'You know these things you're saying are all in your head, Rock (Cap). They're not real. You understand?' Cap claims that his body is finished, not his head. Tony continues in the same tone as before. 'I wouldn't let you get hurt. I need you, Rock, to lead this team. Come on. One more time. You and me. You and me, together. Trust me.'

Cap gives in. (Persuasion and establishing a common purpose – see actions that inspire motivation later.) At the training session that follows it turns out however that things are indeed coming to an end. Cap has become frightened.

In the next scene Cap tries to explain to his wife, Cindy, that he is thinking of giving up soon – she becomes furious and hits him. Mysterious in some way. Or perhaps this is what he has needed many times before – someone who really says that he is a stupid idiot and worthless when he does not want to struggle any more. Who knows – what has always been right becomes wrong in the end. The difficulty is knowing when it is going to happen. Another theory is that Cindy is not doing this for his sake at all, but for her own. At one of the parties it was obvious that her importance lay in being the quarterback's wife. She was able to keep Willie Beamen's girl friend out in the cold. If Cap retires, his wife will have to as well.

The breach between Tony and Christina becomes deeper and deeper. When she finds out that Tony is considering starting the play-off with Cap as quarterback, she is very upset. Their altercation ends with Christina explaining to Tony that her father made her the team's director because he did not think Tony was up to it. He thought quite simply that Tony was too old. Tony has nothing to counter this last argument with, and he evidently begins to doubt himself. His problem is that the pep talker needs to find some way to pep himself.

If you aren't fired with enthusiasm ...

Just like real reality, film is crawling with experts. There can be no doubt that we are living 'in an age of experts' (Brint 1994). Experts have important functions in and around the team in *Any Given Sunday*. In an industry, which is fundamentally based on blocking competitors by using force injuries will be sustained – they are included in the calculations – and doctors have an important function. The doctor's job is to tell the coach how long an injured player will be injured for. The doctor can provide important information that can be decisive in choosing which strategy to use during a game. The Miami Sharks have two doctors and one of them takes care of stomach disorders, fluid intake and the like and his name is Ollie (Oliver Powers). The other, Harv (Harvey Mandrake) deals with bones, and this is the most important task.

The function of the experts is to assist the coach. What the doctors can offer is based on their professional skills. There are real conflicts. In choosing between the health of the players, what is best for the team and their own best, it is the team that counts – most of the time. Harv has difficulties in knowing what priorities to make. It gets really difficult when he starts to take orders from Christina. She wants to see Willie and the injured demon-tackler Shark on the field, but not Cap. One way of achieving this would be for Harv to say that Cap is injured and unable to play, whereas Shark could be declared fit. Christina convinces Harv with the observation 'what you help save us now, we won't forget at contract time'. If you have a wife, a mistress, and other expensive habits, it is easy to accept arguments like this.

Experts are dangerous individuals whose presence is only useful when they do what they are supposed to. Disloyal experts – like those who are not working for the coach – disrupt the organisation and the game. One solution to this problem is to get rid of them. When Tony finds out that Harv switched the X-ray plates of the leading tackler to conceal the truth he is enraged. He seeks out Harv as he walks around the plane talking on the phone to his daughter. There is a brief exchange of words about the matter and Tony makes, or perhaps announces, his decision. 'I want you out of here! … I never wanna see you near one of my players again!' Harv makes a clumsy attempt to set things to rights, but it does not work – the coach decides and in this case he does so rapidly and effectively. And here it must be remembered that Harv and Tony have been working together for many years, perhaps too many? Recruiting is difficult, firing even more difficult. For Tony both processes are fairly easy. The game is what matters and the individuals involved subordinate to it. That is the way things can be in films. The reality outside film is often more complex even though it appears similar to the surface of the film.

People who work together will win

Before the last match of the season Tony talks to the players.

TONY D'AMATO:

> I don't know what to say, really. Three minutes till the biggest battle of our professional lives. All comes down to today. Either we heal as a team or we're gonna crumble. Inch by inch, play by play, till we're finished. We're in hell right now, gentlemen. Believe me. And we can stay here, get the shit kicked out of us or we can fight our way back into the light. We can climb out of hell one inch at a time. Now, I can't do it for you. I'm too old. I look around, I see these young faces, and I think I made every wrong choice a middle-aged man can make. I pissed away all my money, believe it or not. I chased off anyone who's ever loved me. And lately, I can't even stand the face I see in the mir-

> ror. You know, when you get old in life, things get taken from you. I mean that's part of life. But you only learn that when you start losing stuff. You find out life's this game of inches. So is football. Because in either game, life or football the margin for error is so small. I mean, one half a step too late or early, and you don't quite make it. One half-second too slow, too fast, you don't quite catch it. The inches we need are everywhere around us. They're in every break of the game, every minute, every second. On this team, we fight for that inch. On this team we tear ourselves and everyone else around us to pieces for that inch. We claw with our fingernails for that inch because we know when we add up all those inches that's gonna make the fucking difference between winning and losing! Between living and dying! I'll tell you this. In any fight it's the guy who's willing to die who's gonna win that inch. And I know if I'm gonna have any life anymore it's because I'm still willing to fight and die for that inch. Because that's what living is! The six inches in front of your face! Now, I can't make you do it! You gotta look at the guy next to you! Look into his eyes! I think you're gonna see a guy who'll go that inch with you! You're gonna see a guy who will sacrifice himself for this team because he knows, when it comes down to it, you're gonna do the same for him! That's a team, gentlemen! And either we heal now, as a team, or we will die, as individuals. That's football, guys. That's all it is. Now, what are you gonna do?

At the beginning of his speech Tony is calm and hesitant but then it gradually builds up to a strident climax before concluding calmly and expectantly. Undoubtedly rhetoric is his thing. His speech takes effect. The players run out on to the field with more fire than ever before.

Tony's low-key; intimate conversations with the individual players have their counterparts in most kinds of organisation. Management involves a great deal of talking (Rombach 1986, Ekman 1999). But the major speeches are different. Admittedly speeches are made at jubilees and other festive occasions in many organisations, but they do not form part of the day-to-day management routines in the same way. The role played by speeches has been taken over by documents like evaluations, quarterly reports and statistics of various kinds. The presentation of these documents at meetings or conferences can resemble speeches in many ways.

The score doesn't mean a thing

The match starts and there is a lot of tackling. Vince Lombardi once said: 'You never win a game unless you beat the guy in front of you. The score on the board doesn't mean a thing. That's for the fans. You've got to win the war with the man in front of you. You've got to get your man.' The results are not that encouraging for the Miami Sharks. They are soon behind the Dallas Knight by the equivalent of a goal, by one 'touchdown'.

In the VIP stand Christina talks during the match to a representative of the owners' association. He is played by Charlton Heston (who happened to have the main role in *Ben-Hur* – he was younger in 1959) and is relatively uninterested in both the game and Christina's desire to get more television coverage. Their meeting finishes with him urging Christina to come to a meeting of owners in New York. Other owners do not like the way she is talking about moving the team. Charlton claims that this would be against the rules.

We hear Charlton say, 'I honestly believe that woman would eat her young', when Christina is out of earshot. This is part of her leadership strategy, in a man's world, to act the man. At times she also opts to play deaf or to overlook what has been said. Talking about an offer that has been made for the team, the older advisor, Ed, says: 'You're like your dad. You're a dreamer. Take the money! You're still young, darling. Start over. Start a family. You don't love football any way.' He certainly never gave her father similar advice. She asks Ed to shut up. She only listens to her mother when she wants to as well.

On the field the Sharks are not doing well, they are behind with the score at 21 to 10. Suddenly Cap cannot find anyone to pass the ball to. He goes for a touchdown and makes it, but is tackled heavily as he reaches the end zone.

At half-time Tony and Cap quietly agree that Willie will be fielded in Cap's place. Just after Tony has told Willie that he is going to lead the team on the field, Christina storms into the changing room. She is furiously angry and begins to yell at Tony in front of the players. She wants to see Willie on the field and says that Cap is finished. Tony is just as angry. He drags Christina into a storeroom and they scream hysterically at each other until Willie comes in to say that he has already been told that he is being fielded. This takes the wind out of both their sails. And here Willie shows us that things are beginning to turn for him. He is taking responsibility for the team and risking a slap in the face. If the team is going to win, its coach and manager cannot spend half-time standing in a storeroom screaming at each other.

Willie has already apologised to his girlfriend by now and been given a chance to start over. In his anxiety he even followed her into the ladies room. Heart-warming for romantics like us with long-standing marriages.

The second half begins unpromisingly. Willie throws his first pass badly so that the other team gets the ball. One of the opposing players loses an eye – which confuses us more than it amazes us. The match turns. Willie gets one play on the move after the other. He has understood that he has to lead the team and the others have to believe in him when they look him in the face. He apologises to his teammates on the field. They accept. Luther goes in for a tackle that will probably cripple him. Cap provides intensive support from the sidelines all the time. Even the cowardly diva Julian makes his sacrifice. With only 55 seconds to go Willie throws up, and this does wonders. He is lucky enough to have the chance of a final try that can win the match and he succeeds. But the officials do not award him the try.

In the VIP stand Christina tells her mother that she is under pressure from the other owners, the players and Tony. She feels that she has lost control totally. She too apologises to her mother and is reconciled with her.

With only nine seconds of the match left Willie asks for time-out. He has realised that the other side have worked out how the Sharks intend to play. During the pause Tony and Willie talk about their dinner at Tony's. They joke with each other, in spite of everything. Willie and his team have managed to move the ball some distance but not all the way. They get a new chance when only four seconds are left. Willie's last attempt involves leaping right over his opponents. This sequence takes 35 seconds on film even though it deals with no more than 4 seconds! But anyway, Willie and his teammates succeed; they win the match in the absolutely final second.

Tony meets Willie in the stadium after all the others have left. Willie says that he has learnt more from Cap during the first half of the match than during the previous five seasons. Tony explains that he approves of humility but still believes that Willie should be given all the credit possible for his contribution. Tony tells Willie about a recent meeting with a retired quarterback he used to hang around with in the 70s. Although he retired a long time ago the quarterback told him what he missed most of all: 'What he missed were those other guys looking back at him in the huddle. Those eleven guys every one of them seeing things the same way. All of them looking downfield together. That's what he missed.' When Tony tells him that this is his last season with the Sharks, Willie has already worked it out for himself. When Tony says that he is all washed up as a main coach, Willie is not so sure.

The power to inspire others to follow

Tony's leadership technique is to motivate the people working with him. He has methods for many different situations. He motivates the team with the aid of the major, stirring speech intended to arouse enthusiasm and team spirit. One approach is to make the team feel ashamed; another is to appeal to their sense of belonging. One significant background variable is that Tony has access to the power of being able to decide whether a player will stay on the team or not. By extension this means that he can decide if a player will become rich or not. Tony does not need to demonstrate his power, everyone is aware of how the system works.

But Tony does not only make impressive speeches. He 'manages' important players by talking to them. On the whole he does so quietly and obviously puts a great deal of thought into what he says. He talks them round, and on the surface it looks pretty simple. He frequently acts like any other teacher and talks about the way things are, for instance what leadership on the field involves. The trick is to get his players to see things his way, self-evident, but no less true for that. We are also given examples demonstrating this truth.

We do not believe that the scriptwriters, Daniel Pyne and John Logan, have devoted too much time to leadership theory, but they could well have done so. Of course they know a little. They must surely have heard about Abraham Maslow's ideas on motivation. Maslow's hierarchy of needs is still being taught in high school.

Abraham Maslow (1954) claimed that our five fundamental needs are the physiological needs, safety needs, the need to belong, the need for esteem and the need for self-actualisation. It is easy to criticise the idea of a hierarchy in which subordinate needs have to be satisfied before higher ones can take over and motivate us. It is possible that Abraham Maslow realised that this is not really how things are. Moreover, he was not thinking about leadership when he launched his idea. The thorniest problem is that the hierarchy continues to circulate even though research has not succeeded in proving that Maslow's conceptual model is correct (Abrahamsson and Andersson 2000). And this is not because of any lack of researchers who are interested in motivation. The reason for this widespread interest is due, in its turn, to the many questions that research would dearly like to be able to answer. One of them is how human beings can best be motivated.

It is obviously impossible to find any unambiguous answer that will tell us how to motivate others, but one can try. Whoever formulates the ultimate concept will definitely become famous. Here we can see explicit differences between two camps in motivation research. The contest is between the group that claims that internal factors explain how people experience motivation and the other group that is looking for external explanations. This second group contains not least all the research that is referred to as organisational theory. Abraham Maslow belongs to the first group.

David McClelland (1985) is also usually cited in this context. He is behaviour oriented but maintains that needs, and with them motivation, can be learned and altered in the short term. If for no other reason, David McClelland is therefore a find for management consultants. Frederick Herzberg and others (1959/1999) also belongs to the behaviourist camp and is one of the founders of modern workplace research. He and his successors have claimed, for instance, that motivation is linked to satisfaction. If you are content in your work, you are also motivated, but unfortunately it cannot be taken for granted that contented workers are also efficient. Peter Drucker (1954/1986) claimed emphatically that satisfaction is not at all linked to efficiency. We ourselves have spent a long time searching through the literature on research and have not been able to find any links between contentment and efficiency either (Rombach 1991). It would be gratifying to be able to demonstrate that there is a connection between workplace satisfaction and being efficient. For almost fifty years now workplace researchers have been searching for a link without being able to find one. One day they may, but until then we will have to make do with the fact that the opposite has not been demonstrated credibly either.

Christina Björklund's thesis (2001) sheds some light on this problem. She argues that motivation is admittedly important for efficiency but that the error lies in evaluating it as contentment. The link between contentment in the form of 'job satisfaction' and motivation is missing. The reason why people have stuck (and still stick) to this approach is that contentment can easily be measured whereas motivation is much more difficult.

A fairly recent issue of *Leadership Quarterly* includes a discussion of motivation from a leadership perspective (Mumford et al. 2000). This discussion ends with the conclusion that the links between the actions of managers and the reactions of their staff is still manifestly unaccounted for. Another conclusion is that a great deal of research is needed in this area.

Power and motivation

In roughly the same way as Abraham Maslow once developed a conceptual model for motivation on the basis of the literature, John Barbuto (2000) has done the same thing based on somewhat more modern texts. John Barbuto's idea is that there are three types of motivators – he refers to them as 'triggers'. They can be linked to power, relationships or values.

Each single category of motivator contains a number of variants, totalling ten in all.

The motivators linked to power derive from the social authority that leaders possess and actually make use of. A motivator of this sort is linked to benefits. It is based on the leader linking reward to the results attained and in the reliance of the staff on this reward system. In the film Luther makes a dangerous tackle because it will give him an enormous bonus. The negative version of a benefit motivator can be called a manipulation motivator. Here some form of sanction is linked to staff behaviour. There is no lack of examples in this film. One interesting version is provided by Cap's wife Cindy, who in striking him is not only showing him that he must not stop playing because then things will happen. Even though we do not understand what is going on, Cap evidently does.

Power finds expression in the allocation of roles (Pfeffer and Salancik 1975, Bandura 1986). Sometimes we do as we are told, not because we want to but because it was the boss who said so. Willie runs out on to the field after spending a whole season on the bench reading magazines quite simply because he was ordered to. He has no reason to protest, as he prefers to take part in the game to reading magazines on the sidelines.

Power can also be based on expert knowledge. The expert's opinion can in itself provide motivation. Tony is good at pointing out that he has had the most wins, experienced most and is quite simply an expert at being a coach. One example of this can be found in the short talk he has with Willie during the time out. 'Believe me', the experienced coach says time and again.

Subordinates can also identify with a leader because of his or her charisma. The question of whether this can be acquired or is something innate can be discussed. In individual relationships attraction normally develops over a long period of time. While Tony is working with Willie he develops sufficient attraction for Willie to go with him to his new team after the end of the film.

Relationships and motivation

Another group of motivators are those based on relationships. Abraham Maslow considered that people wanted esteem – and it is difficult to deny this even though we want to be autonomous individuals. Sometimes we do things to gain the respect of those around us. This is called external attribution. Motivation in general, and in football in particular, is based to a large extent on this. The jubilation of the crowd, even if it is only a small one, together with the attention of the media provides the most important motivator in all the sports and for all the athletes where there is no money to be gained. The question here is whether this does not apply to the wealthier sports as well.

There is also an internal version of attribution. This is when employees seek recognition within their organisation. They want the esteem of their colleagues – not merely from the public. You cannot succeed in a team game if the other members of the team do not rely on your actions. In the film we see that even Julian, the prima donna, wants the esteem of the rest of the team and does not avoid getting hurt.

Values and motivation

The value-related motivators are based on an individual's personal values. When there is a link between an individual's own values and those of their managers, work more or less organises itself. This idea is based on the existence of shared values. To some extent this is an ideal situation for a manager (see Katz and Kahn 1978, Bass 1985). Professional players can take a lot of scorn, derision and pain, as both they and the coaches actually want to win. This is not based on calculations; there are also shared values that get the players to act as they do – especially when they do it well.

One kind of value-related motivator comes into play if there happens to be a link between the ambitions of the leaders and of their subordinates. One example of this can be found in the film in Willie's fervent desire to invent new game plans when the old ones no longer work. The results find favour with everyone.

Yet another motivator in this main category is linked to the credibility staff attributes to the goals of the organisation. They follow the directions of their managers because they believe this is the way to attain the organisation's objectives. John Barbuto refers to this as identifying with the goals and claims that it is an important motivator. So do many other researchers, see for example Gary Yukl (1998) or Bernard Bass (1985) who are both regarded as major writers in leadership literature. Japanese kamikaze pilots are often quoted as examples. Football players follow their leaders only if they believe that this will result in the attainment of organisational objectives that coincide with their own. This second qualification differentiates them from the kamikaze pilots.

John Barbuto's reasoning is theoretical and even hypothetical and he bases his arguments on texts. He could just as easily have used the film *Any Given Sunday* to illustrate what he means. Motivation is demonstrated in the film, which is not merely about football but about organisation in general. In other words, the cinemagoer gets a powerful dose of management theory while believing that the film deals first and foremost with football.

Winning is not a sometime thing

The season comes to an end. It looks as if the Miami Sharks did not win the final game. The last scene starts with a formal speech in which Christina declares that her team is definitely going to remain faithful to Miami and not leave the city. She thanks Tony with the words 'And Tony. Know this. Wherever you go, you will always be loved and greatly respected. Thanks for helping me understand again what I had forgotten.' These are the words you address to someone who is about to retire.

Tony's thank you speech is appropriate for someone about to conclude a successful career. He finishes it with an unexpected announcement.

TONY D'AMATO:

> In thinking about change. I don't know, I felt maybe it was time for me to make a change too. And it was Willie Beamen who taught me how to give it another shot. So starting today I'm taking over as head coach for that new expansion team in Albuquerque, New Mexico, the Aztecs. Why, do you say? Because they're giving me full management control. But hoping not to make a complete fool of myself out there I just signed Willie Beamen as my starting quarterback and franchise player for the Aztecs. So, Miss P, I look forward to seeing you next season across those sidelines. So long. Au revoir. See you when the clouds come home.

The film concludes therefore with Tony dealing with something that could have turned into a crisis without being struck by the inability to act. Studies of how managers in organisations and companies successfully cope with critical situations show that this requires experience (Lind Nilsson 2001). Experience provides the courage to seek support. We suspect that Tony has talked to Willie Beamen, who he is taking with him to the new team, and his good friend and assistant Montezuma Monroe, who is going to start coaching youngsters. The management cannot do anything about the age of their managers, except when they hire them. But it should be possible to organise the courage to seek support.

(Restitution – moving on)

> On any given Sunday you're gonna win or you're gonna lose. The point is – can you win or lose like a man? (Tony D'Amato)

...and what does that mean?

CHAPTER 3

Matrix – the manager's reality

How do you know you exist? One answer to this question is that you don't. What we nevertheless refer to as reality is an agreement between an individual and the environment. Although it is practical to assume that we share a relatively similar reality, it is not certain that this is the case. There are good examples of the old adage 'he lives in a world of his own'. In the most extreme cases such individuals require psychiatric treatment but the condition may be harmless and even beneficial. Who knows where you stand?

If it is true that for a long time there has been a genuine reality and a dream existence, the latter has attracted increasing attention in recent years. One example of this is the trilogy by William Gibson that began with *Neuromancer* (1984) and concluded with *Mona Lisa Overdrive* (1988). William Gibson advances the thesis that there is a genuine reality that includes cars, guns, slum housing and the like. There is also cyberspace, a sort of electronic labyrinth that constitutes another reality. William Gibson allows his actors to move between these realities by logging on to what he calls Setnet. This is a dangerous place. At any moment some malevolent individual may turn up to take over your hard disk as it were and erase it. And if your hard disk is erased in Setnet, you no longer exist there, nor in reality either. The film *Matrix* (1999) uses the same theme – but the other way round. In *Matrix* the world in which we live as ordinary human beings is the virtual one. Only the rebels – those who want to rescue us from the artificial – know the real state of affairs and live in the genuine reality.

The whole business of increasing interest in unreality has also affected the social sciences. It all got under way in the mid-1960s when Peter Berger and Thomas Luckman published their book *The Social Construction of Reality* (1966). Their thesis was that phenomena in the world around us acquire meaning through agreements between people. There was nothing really strange about this – but it aroused great indignation in many quarters. Today many of us can see no alternatives to these agreements. During the decades since their book appeared, masses of articles and books have been written about one thing or the other that has been socially constructed. In the long run it became hardly remarkable in any area. Anyway, how could it be when everything happens to be socially constructed? In 1999 Ian Hacking dug his heels in and wrote *The Social Construction of What?* What annoyed him was the expression 'it is only a social construction' used to mean less real. A typical example is child abuse. Why should we bother about it if it is 'only ...'? Read his book!

Characterising our post modern world, like the world in *Matrix*, as uncertain and difficult to understand is not a reasonable interpretation. Those who see increasing chaos and incomprehensibility have no viable arguments. Even so it is a widespread conception. It may be that publications like Zygmunt Bauman's *Postmodernity and its Discontents* (1997) have spread this message. In *Matrix* most things are crystal clear, at times almost over-explicit. Any child can understand the film.

All of sociology's institutional theory, which today provides the principal theoretical basis for organisational theory in business studies, apart from network theory, is a further development of the analyses of Peter Berger and Thomas Luckman (1966). We can no longer understand the world, organisations and their leaders without thinking in terms of social constructions. If you want to read more about this, we can recommend the books by Walter Powell and Paul DiMaggio (1991), Richard Scott (1995) as well as John Boli and George Thomas (1999). But Ian Hacking (1999) makes the point that the chair we are sitting on is not merely a social construct. We would not be able to fall to the floor simply by imagining that it no longer existed.

Follow instructions

In the first chapter of this book we discussed what we call the surface of a film, what you see and what you hear. There are no major problems in writing about what is said, there are subtitles on the screen that can be quoted. It is more difficult to deal with images that have to be translated into text. When we do so, it helps if the reader has seen the film or can envisage what the film shows without having seen it. Colleagues of ours who have read this work in manuscript have been able to deal with the other chapters without any major difficulty. On the other hand, those who have not seen *Matrix* found it considerably harder to follow our argument in this chapter. It is not odd that those who have not seen the film find it difficult to follow us as the film is, in fact, strange. The solution is to demand some prior knowledge of anybody reading this chapter. Anyone who has read the trilogy by William Gibson and enjoyed it qualifies directly. But those who have not read the work or did so without understanding it and have not seen *Matrix* either maybe should watch the film before they read any further.

Look out for the details in the film. And keep careful watch of Morpheus and Neo in particular – what follows deals mainly with them. Neo (played by the delightful Keanu Reeves) is the pseudonym of the skilful hacker Thomas Anderson. Neo of course is an anagram of 'one'. Neo is 'the chosen one'. You can turn Thomas into doubting Thomas if you want to put some kind of sermon together. Doubting Thomas was the disciple who refused to believe in the Resurrection because he could not see Jesus. This is how it is described in St. John's Gospel:

> Now Thomas (called Didymus), one of the Twelve, was not with the disciples when Jesus came. So the other disciples told him, 'We have seen the Lord!' But he said to them, 'Unless I see the nail marks in his hands and put my finger where the nails were, and put my hand into his side, I will not believe it.'
>
> A week later his disciples were in the house again, and Thomas was with them. Though the doors were locked, Jesus came and stood among them and said, 'Peace be with you!' Then he said to Thomas, 'Put your finger here; see my hands. Reach out your hand and put it into my side. Stop doubting and believe.' Thomas said to him, 'My Lord and my God!' Then Jesus told him, 'Because you have seen me, you have believed; blessed are those who have not seen and yet have believed.' (The New Testament, John 20:24–29).

This does not fit in with what happens in *Matrix*! In the film it is exactly the opposite. The problem facing the liberators is that the people in their slimy cocoons are logged on and they believe with all their hearts. They only become free when they use their eyes and stop believing. What conclusions a manager can draw from this is unclear. We consider, however, that managers should adopt the doubting role.

Neo leads a double life. During the daytime he works for a large software company and at night he races around the net. Neo is derived from

Greek *neos*, which means young and new. Neo is a prefix that means 'new', which turns out to be apt in the context. The details in the film are pretty important. Whether this applies to our reality is more doubtful. Names may prove an exception. Many people seem to believe that a child's future actions will be influenced by the name it is given (Solli 2005). Why otherwise pay so much heed to the whims of fashion or follow them so slavishly? Maybe names like trademarks and their value have attracted increasing attention in recent years. And among trademarks we find anyway the names of services and products – and the names of those employed in films, for example, or strip clubs.

According to the manuscript of the film (Internet reference 3) Neo is a man who knows more about what it is like to work with and in computers than about the life around him. Falling asleep in front of a computer screen is more natural than unnatural to him. One night a computer that interrupts his normal searches with the simple message 'Wake up, Neo' wakes Neo. He tries to regain control of the computer but someone else is in charge and Neo becomes more and more surprised by his lack of control. A new message that says, 'The Matrix has you ...' flashes on to the screen. Not even the Escape key helps. Instead there is another message that says, 'Follow the white rabbit' and finally another 'Knock, knock, Neo'.

At that moment there is a knock on the door of apartment 101. It is Choi, who wants to buy a copy of a computer programme from Neo. This is no problem even though he is two hours late. Neo has hidden the programme in a book called *Simulacra & Simulation*, written by Jean Baudrillard (1981). There is some symbolism in his destruction of one of the classics of postmodernism. He has cut out a substantial cavity that starts after the second page of the chapter entitled 'On Nihilism'. It provides room for a number of diskettes or the like.

In our version of the work, translated by Sheila Glaser in 1994 and printed in 2000, the chapter 'On Nihilism' begins on the right hand page (not the left like Neo's). And even if we sacrificed the first page of the chapter as well it would not make much of a hiding place. The entire chapter occupies three pages and then our book comes to an end. Perhaps the answer can be found on the last page of the book where it says: 'There is no more hope for meaning. And without a doubt this is a good thing: meaning is mortal' (Baudrillard 1981/2000, p. 164). Another answer may be found in Jean Baudrillard's fairly hackneyed arguments for terrorism as an eye-opener. In this modern age there are simpler courses of action.

> Against this hegemony of the system, one can exalt the ruses of desire, practice revolutionary micrology of the quotidian, exalt the molecu-

lar drift or even defend cooking. This does not resolve the imperious necessity of checking the system in broad daylight. This, only terrorism can do. (Baudrillard 1981/2000, p. 163)

Be that as it may – the deal with Choi concludes with the customers feeling that Neo should go with them on something that seems to be some form of drug-related activity. '... mescaline. It's the only way to fly.' All Neo really wants to do is go to bed. Working both day and night is tiring, but when one of the customers, Dujour, turns out to have a white rabbit tattooed on one shoulder he perks up. '... when suddenly a White Rabbit with pink eyes ran close by her. There was nothing so very remarkable in that', as it says at the beginning of *Alice's Adventures in Wonderland* by Lewis Carroll (1865). Just like Alice, Neo follows the white rabbit without finding anything remarkable about it. And sure enough he will soon find himself falling without knowing what really is reality.

Neo lacks any plan of action. He is groping his way forward unsystematically. He follows the white rabbit but could just as easily have failed to do so. Even so, he is the successful hero who wins the princess and his share of the kingdom. Later in the film he misses one opportunity (perhaps because he is afraid of heights) and then gets a second chance. In other words there is no shortage of opportunities. Here there is a message for all stressed-out managers. It is rarely a case of 'now or never' and there is no reason to be lured into acting under stress. Despite all the books about the need for speed (see for instance Virilio 1980, Handy 1990 and Gleick 1999) it is not reasonable to consider that time is something that our generation is short of.

Trinity in a jam

The film begins by introducing us to Trinity. She is a strikingly beautiful woman in rubber clothes (played by Carrie-Anne Moss) who quickly and efficiently kills a number of police officers that try to arrest her. She also eludes three artificial agents that look like FBI operatives. We see her disappear into empty space as she answers the phone. A brisk scene.

Neo and the gang go to some kind of club. When they are there, Trinity contacts Neo. She begins with 'Hello, Neo'. As his name is a pseudonym, Neo is surprised that she knows it. It turns out that Trinity is not just anybody but a very famous hacker who once 'cracked the IRS D-base'. This is how to become a hero for other hackers. Trinity tells Neo that what drives him is the same question that once drove her to work intensively for hours in front of the screen. The question is 'What is the Matrix?' and who is behind it. Trinity also tells him that a lot of people are watching him. Some people want to harm him. But there is an answer out there and Trinity says that it will find him – if he wants it to.

In the next scene Neo is woken as usual by his (Panasonic) alarm clock at 9.18 – too late in other words. He starts his day at Metacortex by being told off by his boss. He is close to being sacked. When Neo then gets to his workplace in the gloomy office landscape a parcel is delivered to him. It contains a telephone (Nokia) that rings immediately. The caller is Morpheus (played by Laurence Fishburne, who fits the role perfectly). Neo knows this. Morpheus explains calmly and reassuringly that there are agents after Neo. And right on cue, they step out of the lift just as Morpheus said they would. Morpheus guides Neo through the maze of cubicles so that he can elude the agents. He nearly succeeds. Neo has a chance of climbing across to scaffolding from what seems to be about the twenty-fifth floor he is in, but he lacks the courage. Instead the agents apprehend him.

In the film Morpheus appears as a caricature of a good manager. If he is measured against any of the models offered by popular management texts, he will get the maximum score. He lives up to them in every way! His concern for both production and his staff would already have given him a top score from Robert Blake and Jane Mouton in 1964. Morpheus is also the democratic and flexible leader that many management gurus have advocated over the years as the ideal.

There is nothing wrong in possessing the features that the management texts suggest are needed for success. However, we are sceptical about evaluating both physical and mental qualities as a method of identifying the best leaders. Time after time it has turned out that successful organisations are not led by the right kind of person. And the concepts involved can easily become reformulations of what someone in some situation considers desirable. They can only be defined in circular terms. Morpheus is a good leader because he is a good leader.

Unable to speak

The agents are vicious, especially Agent Smith (played by Hugo Weaving who will always be Agent Smith). For instance, he converts Neo's mouth into zero when he requests to be allowed to ring a lawyer. When Neo refuses to collaborate with the agents in their hunt for Morpheus and his associates, they operate a disgusting implant into his body. Then they know exactly where he is.

Next day Neo wakes up wondering if all this really happened or if it was just a dream. If the Morpheus that Neo spoke to was the son of Hypnos, the god of sleep, he is in the habit of sending people to the land of dreams. Morpheus rings again and explains to Neo that he is 'the One' that Morpheus has devoted his life to trying to find up until now. Neo finds this flattering, to say the least, and joins the resistance movement. Morpheus wants to meet him.

Morpheus arranges to meet Neo under a bridge on Adam Street. It is raining, rather like it often does in Göteborg and in films about the future! Trinity and Switch meet him. Trinity has a dreadful apparatus that can remove the agents' implant, but somewhat painfully. The agents are working to safeguard the Matrix and 'it is the world that has been pulled over your eyes to blind you from the truth' to cite Morpheus' own words in the subtitles. The outcome of this blindness is that anyone who does not revolt is enslaved.

To understand what the Matrix is, you must, according to Morpheus, see it for yourself – and he does not seem to be the kind of person who lies. To be able to see you have to choose the right pill. The blue pill means choosing not to have to see, in other words returning to life in the Matrix without knowing it. Choosing the red pill means choosing the difficult path, but one that will enable the traveller to know the truth. You stay in wonderland and find out how deep the rabbit hole is. Again a reference to Lewis Carroll. The film contains several that we intend to bore you with. In her world Alice drank from a bottle 'and tied round the neck of the bottle was a paper label, with the words DRINK ME beautifully printed on it in large letters' (Carroll 1865/1982, p. 21). Pills seem more modern than tincture in a bottle. Neo chooses the red pill. The classical choice – we opt for the truth irrespective of what it will make us feel like.

The pill and some patently old-fashioned equipment lead to Neo being reborn with slime, cables, mechanical spiders and much pain. He ends up in the water and is raised naked from it towards the light, like a soul reborn en route for paradise. When he gets there Morpheus welcomes him to reality. The finishing touches involve removal of the cables – but not the inlet socket in his head. Neo's muscles are strengthened by tons of acupuncture.

NEO: Why do my eyes hurt?

MORPHEUS: You've never used them before.

The boss has opened the new recruit's eyes. The modern organisational culture that the boss has designed forces employees to see reality as it really is. Even this newfound ability to see would seem old-fashioned if it were not a physical reality. When organisational cultures were on everybody's lips in the 1980s, many considered them to be a form of management tool. The job of the leaders was to create cultures that would make everybody think alike, work together and see the world around them with new eyes.

By 1992 Mats Alvesson and Per Olof Berg had been able to point out that cultural concepts were disappointing in actual practice. Organisational cultures exist and are not unimportant – but they are difficult to design and are definitely not subject to the direct control of managers.

Matrix also demonstrates the dangers of too rigid an organisational culture. Morpheus has made all his associates see the world in the same way. Some were born in the genuine reality and probably recruited by Morpheus because they saw the world as he does. The others have chosen the red pill. All but the traitor Cypher (there will be more about the betrayal later) have become cultural clones and the whole organisation sees things in exactly the same way as its leader. Cypher sees things he does not want to see and betrays the guerrilla movement in exchange for oblivion of the culture that has been forced on him by the truth pill. Only Neo succeeds in liberating himself and can take the next step. In the end he can see the construction of the construct itself and due to this he can save himself and the world of good.

After a time Neo wakes up. When he asks Morpheus what has happened to him and what kind of place he has come to, the answer is that it is a good deal more important to know when it is than what. This is not 1999 in reality but closer to 2199.

Training begins

Now Neo can begin his training in earnest. Morpheus shows him round his vessel (a hovercraft) named Nebuchadnezzar built in 2069 in the USA. The interior of the vessel has seen a great deal of wear and resembles an early submarine. Captain Nemo's Nautilus was a lot more up-to-date. Why not read *Twenty Thousand Leagues Under the Sea* (Verne 1870/1994) once again or see one of the film versions made in 1916 or 1954? Nebuchadnezzar may be named after the Babylonian king who razed Jerusalem to the ground and burnt the Temple in 588 (or perhaps 586) B.C. Or perhaps after a bottle of champagne (or of course Bordeaux as well) that contains twenty ordinary bottles, or perhaps after something else. We are never told why the name was chosen.

We see nothing outside the vessel until much later in the film. Nor do we see any of the other 'good' vessels that exist. In addition to Morpheus, the crew of the Nebuchadnezzar consists of the two women, Trinity and Switch, as well as Apoc, Cypher, Mouse, Tank and his elder brother Dozer.

Switch and Apoc are less important members of the gang, the kind that normally get shot before we get very far in an action movie. They go here and there, sit around for a while, assist and help to fill the screen. They add nothing to our analysis. Although they are not shot when the time comes but merely disconnected, they still die.

The only woman with a real role in *Matrix* is Trinity. It is doubtful if we can learn anything from her about 'man-agerial work' (Collinson and Hearn 1996, p. 1) except that it is mainly an occupation for men. And, moreover, it takes an effort to realise that there is anything strange about this. The construction of gender in the organisations we are familiar with, as in the ones in which we spend our time, limits our ability to see (cf. Eriksson-Zetterquist 2002). If our boss placed a book he has read (!) about leadership and gender (the two above for instance or something quite different) in some very visible position on his desk, we would be able to make progress. The way things are at the moment; we are standing still, both in the film and in our real reality.

Neo is connected to the Matrix through a plug inserted into the socket in his head, and hey presto he finds himself in an environment that looks like ours. In the Matrix he is wearing attractive clothes and has no socket in his head. Morpheus explains it as well as he can. 'Your appearance now is what we call 'residual self-image'. It is the mental projection of your digital self.'

The shift from reality to the Matrix enables Morpheus to show what the real world looks like somewhere round 2200. It has been bombed to bits. The world in which Neo lived his earlier life was (is) a construction of interactive nerve simulation, and that is what the Matrix is.

The dreadful state of the planet may be assumed to be the result of the creation by human beings at the beginning of the 21st century of 'AI', artificial intelligence. But something went wrong and clouds that made everything dark wiped out the planet. AI needs energy to survive and human bodies generate energy. Therefore they are bred in endless pastures. As is often the case, there are parallels to *The Hitch Hiker's Guide to the Galaxy* by Douglas Adams (1979–1984). There the mice needed Arthur's human brain so that they could cut it into cubes. He was to be given a new and somewhat simpler electronic brain programmes so that he would not notice the difference (Adams 2002, pp. 168–174).

The Matrix is nothing more than the method of control used by AI. Without it the people being bred would be discontented. They might even notice what they were being used for. The agents we met earlier in the film are sentient programmes that work in the software to correct the control when it does not work as intended.

Tidy-minded readers may ask themselves here why AI has to breed people. If we can believe that the method worked, then other mammals (why not even mice?) could generate energy. This would make things considerably easier. The chickens, pigs and cattle that humans beings breed to supply energy do not need advanced sentient programmes. Nor do any of them break out to foment revolution by informing other animals. Militant vegans and terrifying viruses are required instead. Not very good thinking on the part of AI.

Apart from the crews of Nebuchadnezzar and the other vessels, there are real people. They have taken refuge in Zion, a place near the centre of the globe where it is still warm. Tank and Dozer have no plugs in their necks. They were born in Zion, produced in the traditional way.

Our impression is that Zion far away – at least two films further. Just as elsewhere in the film, there are links to the Bible. In the Old Testament Zion was the hill in south-eastern Jerusalem. In the New Testament it sometimes symbolises the Church or the Realm of Heaven. Our first thoughts went to Bob Marley's *Zion Train* (1980) – perhaps that says something about the age we live in …

> Oh where there is a will
> there always is a way
> Where there is a way
> Where there is a will, there's always a way
>
> (Bob Marley 1980, *Zion Train*)

Neo's education is very rapid. The method is far superior to the teaching techniques used today. Imagine just putting a floppy disk into a computer that transfers the data to Neo through the socket in his neck. Neo is a model pupil and is given top grades by Tank.

TANK (to Morpheus): Ten hours straight. He's a machine.

It is a bit deceptive when an instructor's assessment can vary in this brave new world (Huxley 1932). But anyway, it is not enough to sit being stuffed with knowledge and skills. To get any benefit from the programmes, practice is needed as well. During these practice sessions Morpheus demonstrates to Neo that there is knowledge that you have to realise you have. This provides some consolation for those who spend their lives teaching and studying. The Matrix is a programme with rules that can be circumvented and sometimes broken. But to break them successfully you have to liberate your mind, realise for example that it is possible to jump 75 metres between two skyscrapers. The trick is knowing that you can do it; it is not enough merely to believe that you can.

Cypher turns out to be a traitor – he has already displayed decadent tendencies. He drinks spirits from a jerry can and is somewhat jealous. Suddenly 'Mr. Reagen' (Cypher) is talking to Agent Smith over a splendid dinner. In exchange for becoming as oblivious as all the others in the Matrix, although rich and important (like an actor?!), he promises to betray Morpheus.

One of the keys to Morpheus' leadership is that he can win the gang's support by offering this small group the chance of making the world better for the vast majority. All of this makes you think of the situation of guerrilla fighters. A shared enemy can admittedly spur on an army, but with nothing like the same force as the vision of the good society. The price that Morpheus' associates have to pay is a life full of sacrifice and the risk of dying. They can deal with the latter by regarding their starting point as non-life. Cypher is the only one who does not accept the image of reality described by Morpheus. He considers that living with unconscious fantasies in the slimy cocoons is preferable.

Cypher's treachery is a failure for Morpheus. He is so busy with his most recently recruited star, Neo, that he does not pay enough attention to the rest of the group. Cyber is the weakest and the first to succumb.

It is not obvious that what the leader sees is what really applies or that the leader sees what all the others see. Even those who lead construct their own reality. For instance in health care sometimes consensus conferences are arranged so that agreement can be reached about the most suitable treatments for certain diagnoses. In a way, conferences like this result in a decision about what reality looks like. The same thing goes on in other organisations. It leads to greater manoeuvrability – when the boss turns the steering wheel the car turns. Too much consensus is also a well-known organisational problem that leads to perceptual inertia – the inability to see problems. Signals that the car should start turning do not reach us and we drive happily over the edge of a cliff (see Hedberg and Ericson 1979).

In the next scene we see what the crew of the Nebuchadnezzar eat. It looks like diluted gruel and probably tastes like cornflakes. When it comes to food we would rather be Captain Nemo's guests. There all that was lacking was bread and wine (Verne 1870/1994, p. 57 in the Swedish edition from 1992). However unpleasant it may be, the potage served in Nebuchadnezzar's canteen consists of single-cell protein with synthetic amino acids, vitamins and minerals – which is all that the body needs according to the nutritional theory that applies in this film.

The old in the new is one of the film's recurrent themes. It is easy to see everything as new. One example from not so long ago is all the talk about the new economy. Closer study revealed that most of the old survived in the new. Attitudes to the labour market, working conditions and relationships between women and men were, for instance, patently old-fashioned (see for example Rombach and Svedberg Nilsson 2000). In the new world of the Matrix even sentient programmes (the agents) have to bug telephones, chase around and shoot at people.

Otherwise it is odd that the food in descriptions of the future is often so awful. When new technologies make so many things possible it would seem that a three-course dinner (with wine and bread) should be a relatively simple accomplishment. If anyone wonders what the actors 'really' ate in Matrix, it was rice and honey. 'And it tasted amazing, believe it or not!' is how Carrie-Anne Moss answers a question in a 'chat' published on the Internet (Internet reference 4).

Off to see the oracle

The next important phase in Neo's education is a meeting with the oracle. At the same time this is the first occasion when Neo returns to the Matrix for real. They have hardly had time to enter the Matrix before Cypher hides his operating Nokia in a dustbin to make it easier for the agents to track them down. Indeed there are a great many other mobile phones in this film. We see all the main characters using them, but when it comes to the crunch they are still not up to the mark. If you want to return to your chair on Nebuchadnezzar, you have to be phoned from a fixed phone – preferably an old-fashioned one.

The function of the oracle is not really to predict what is going to happen but rather to help others to find the right course. Her ability, because she is a woman who, according to the film manuscript, 'looks like someone's grandma' (Internet reference 3), is based on her knowledge of how things and people will develop. The oracle receives them in a very ordinary apartment.

Neo is ushered into the waiting room where there are quite a few people, who also show great promise as the chosen one or ones. In the waiting room a remarkable meeting takes place between Neo and a very skinny boy with a shaven head. The boy is holding a spoon that is swaying backwards and forwards as if it were made of grass. Neo gets the spoon, which suddenly looks and behaves like an ordinary spoon.

BOY: Do not try and bend the spoon. That's impossible. Instead, only try to realize the truth.

NEO: What truth?
BOY: There is no spoon.
NEO: There is no spoon?
BOY: Then you'll see that it is not the spoon that bends. It is only yourself.

With the boy's advice in mind, Neo bends the spoon as easily as Uri Geller and the boy did. Uri Who? 'Geller, Uri, born 1946, Israeli illusionist. G. arrived in the USA in 1972, where millions watched him bend keys and make clocks stop, for instance, without any visible contact. He was able to convince a number of scientists of his alleged parapsychological abilities but illusionists have demonstrated that he was a conjurer. A television programme with G. in 1974 gave rise to a Geller epidemic in Sweden. Today he lives in Great Britain.' This is the entry from the CD version of the Swedish National Encyclopaedia (2000). Why bother to store something in your own memory when it only takes seconds to retrieve it using the nearest computer?

The film's oracle is an ordinary person in many ways, but she says a great many confidence-inspiring things. She discloses a secret: 'Being the One is just like being in love. No one can tell you you're in love. You just know it through and through. Balls to bones.' Heavy stuff! The sequence with the oracle is definitely not the film's strongest scene.

After she has examined him in more or less the same way as a family doctor examining someone with a cold, the oracle declares that she does not see Neo as the chosen one. The following dialogue takes place.

ORACLE: Sorry, kid. You got the gift but it looks like you're waiting for something.
NEO: What?
ORACLE: Your next life, maybe. Who knows? That's the way these things go.

And as if that were not enough she adds: 'You're going to have to make a choice. In the one hand, you'll have Morpheus' life. And in the other hand, you'll have your own. One of you is going to die. Which one will be up to you.' An unrelenting message from someone who claims to know what she is talking about. Even she finds it unpleasant to have to utter these words.

Of course it is unreasonable to ask what the oracle really means. Oracles say what they say and usually do not know what they mean. The listener is obliged to interpret the assertions of the oracles just as they have to interpret other people. One partial interpretation in this case is that the oracle is emphasising that Morpheus is the leader of the group because he is the one who is prepared to sacrifice himself. '… the king or the chief is nothing without the promise of his sacrifice …' (Baudrillard 1981/2000, p. 25)

When you talk about leadership and bosses in films, the question of who really is the leader is justified. Is the oracle really the genuine leader? Or just another consultant? She leads with her mysterious predictions. It reminds you of Alan Greenspan (former Chairman of the Federal Reserve in the USA) who gazes into his crystal ball and makes inscrutable statements. The difference is that he can do something as concrete as lower the bank rate (and raise it again). All the oracle can do is bake nice cookies!

One left behind

On the way back from the oracle Cypher's treachery takes effect. Small changes in the Matrix programming close the exits. Soldiers kill Mouse. Cypher makes his way back to Nebuchadnezzar first and shoots the operator, Tank, and then Dozer, who both remained on board. He also pulls out Apoc's and Switch's contacts and they both die. The agents capture Morpheus. Just when Cypher is about to remove Neo's plug, Tank revives and kills Cypher. Neo and Trinity manage to get away and make their way back to the vessel.

Morpheus is taken to a building under military control and exposed to torture of the most vicious kind. He obviously has no chance of resisting the treatment meted out by the agents. It is only a matter of time before they get him to disclose the programme code for Zion. On Nebuchadnezzar, Tank considers pulling the plug on Morpheus. Admittedly this will mean the death of Morpheus but Zion will nevertheless survive. Just before Tank is about to remove the plug he says to him: 'Morpheus, you were more than a leader to us. You were a father.' Neo stops it all and decides to make an attempt to save Morpheus, despite the protests of the others. In the end he and Trinity set off on a rescue mission. Leaders are often envisaged as men and then the father metaphor readily comes to mind. But if you consider what they do in practice, the classical mother's role would be more appropriate.

Lobby shooting spree

What we are shown is a grandiose orgy of effects and surprises. The liberation begins with Neo walking straight in through the main entrance of the building. At the request of the security guards he calmly opens his coat to show that he is carrying six different weapons, and the trunk he sent through the X-ray scanner contains even more. Then the action explodes.

Later Neo sees a helicopter that some soldiers have placed on the roof of a building. It could make their mission easier.

NEO: (to Trinity):
Can you fly this thing?

TRINITY (Trinity rings Tank):
Not yet.

TRINITY (to Tank):
I need a pilot program for a B-212 helicopter. Hurry.

TRINITY (a few seconds later to Neo):
Let's go.

And then Trinity flies the helicopter like a trained pilot – which is of course what she is. The difference between learning today and in the future in this film is really enormous. There is not much need to acquire knowledge for different potential situations when you can learn to fly a helicopter in a few seconds. Where simpler skills are concerned, among which we must include flying, we have not got that far yet. Nobody reacts to the fact that it still takes as long to become a good cook or learn how to sew an attractive dress as it always has. But where traditional book learning is concerned, there is considerably more resentment.

Why learn what can be found in the reference books or that you think you will be able to find on the Internet when you need it? Once upon a time the answer given to young people was that you have to learn where to look, but for a long time now the search engines (one favourite is Internet reference 5) have outdone university courses in this respect. All that is left is the belief that what the educational system teaches is truer in some sense or makes it possible to evaluate what can be found on the Internet. That may be the case. We will not pursue this path any further as we have followed it some distance in an earlier work (Ohlsson and Rombach 1998).

What role does education play in an era when lexical knowledge is only useful for quizzes? The answer is that practical skills have to be taught. These are necessary and they take time to learn. One of the practical skills that we warmly advocate is the ability to think. The ability to argue for ideas in speech and writing also stands high on our list. This is not the only list. In an increasingly differentiated educational system we must realise clearly that there are several lists and that they look different. If advanced educational qualifications or degrees are not merely required by the employer's academic vanity (my employees have been to better colleges than yours), an employment interview should contain a few check questions.

After their helicopter trip Neo and Trinity succeed against all (!) odds in freeing Morpheus. At one stage during the flight Morpheus asks Trinity if she now thinks that Neo is the chosen one. She does not answer even though she has known the answer for some time. Neo explains to Morpheus that in fact he is not the chosen one and refers to the oracle. This argument has no effect on Morpheus. Instead he says: 'She told you what you needed to hear. That's all. Sooner or later you'll realize, just as I did, there's a difference between knowing the path and walking the path.' If this last statement lacked truth, management researchers would be running companies – indeed the entire world. But fortunately things are not like that.

Subway showdown

Morpheus, Trinity and Neo find a telephone that transfers them to Nebuchadnezzar. Morpheus is transferred first and just as Agent Smith turns up Trinity is transferred. Neo is left behind. After a violent struggle with Smith, Neo manages to escape. While Neo is trying to find a phone that can transfer him to the Nebuchadnezzar, the vessel has in its turn been discovered by the agents' surveillance robots or sentinels. Their mission is to find and kill. The squiddies as they are called, search for vessels, destroy them by cutting them to pieces and also kill the crews. The only weapon that has any effect against them is the EMP – an electromagnetic pulse that knocks out every electrical system nearby. To avoid the squiddies Morpheus has to switch off the electrics on the vessel, which means that Neo cannot return – talk about a decision situation! Back in the Matrix Neo continues to flee pursued by the three agents.

Just as Neo reaches the right telephone in room 303 at 'Wabash and Lake', Agent Smith shoots him. Neo dies – for real as it were. The only one who is not surprised is Trinity. She whispers into Neo's ears (still on the vessel): 'I'm not afraid anymore. The Oracle told me I'd fall in love, and that the man I loved would be the One. So you see you can't be dead. You can't be because I love you. You hear me? I love you.'

Incredible as it may seem, Neo comes back to life stronger, faster and convinced that he can even destroy the agents. He succeeds in this feat, at least where Agent Smith is concerned – the two others run away in terror.

Just before Morpheus discharges the electromagnetic pulse Neo has managed to get back to the vessel.

Viewers may ask themselves the disturbing question whether what has started is a religious revival or a global revolution. Up until the resurrection it seemed to be a global revolution with Morpheus as its leader and Neo his instrument. We also see the blind obedience that every revolutionary leader seems to demand. Then suddenly Morpheus is demoted to a prophet while Neo becomes a Jesus figure. Are we watching a modernised version of the Christ legend or can agents of change always assume this guise?

Anders Piltz offers the following interpretation in *Moderna tider*. '... human beings are trapped in an illusion, an impotence that they cannot redeem themselves from. A saviour who can grant them enlightenment therefore rescues them. The enlightened are then raised to a higher sphere from which they can judge everything from the correct perspective and save others' (Piltz 1999, pp. 44–45). But God knows. For most of the film this digitised Jesus seems to know nothing. Neo is more of an administrator who is good at learning by rote.

Perhaps our concern is misplaced. This film can be seen as a pure action movie. Made so that we can watch people being kicked in the head, with the usual murders and gun smoke that the audience can identify with. And this is nothing to sneer at. Matrix is a film that is not just a Jesus spectacular but also an action film. But perhaps most of all it is film about leadership, in spite of everything.

Final connections

The film ends with Neo ringing to AI, the opponent in other words, to make the following announcement.

NEO:

> I know you're out there. I can feel you now. I know that you're afraid. You're afraid of us. You're afraid of change. I don't know the future. I didn't come here to tell you how this is going to end. I came here to tell you how it's going to begin. I'll hang up this phone. And then I'll show these people what you don't want them to see. I'm going to show them a world without you. A world without rules and controls, without borders or boundaries. A world where anything is possible. Where we go from there is a choice I leave to you.

While Neo is making himself clear on the phone, in the background we can see the Matrix in the form of never-ending columns of figures on a monitor. A message also flashes up to say that someone is trying to trace the call, presumably AI. The trace fails, probably for the first time. Neo and his associates are obviously not as vulnerable as they once were.

The impact is enhanced when afterwards we see Neo put his shades on and fly (!) straight up into the air as only Superman can. And we hear Rage Against The Machine playing *Wake Up* (1992). No doubt about it, there was definitely room for a sequel. It is not surprising that leaders can create their own worlds – the rest of us can as well. The difficulty is persuading others to believe in them.

CHAPTER 4

Elizabeth – action and image

'Total power demands total loyalty' is what it says on the box that our copy came in. That does not seem to lack interest. The film *Elizabeth* (1998) is about leadership and about the importance of loyalty for a leader. Even though the picture of leadership offered by *Elizabeth* is broader than that, the film was not an obvious choice for us.

We were looking for a film that was not sexist, with a successful woman leader in the leading role. On the other hand, it would probably have been asking too much for the film not to reflect the gender system in the way it presented female leadership. In fact, Elizabeth is not a bad choice. We have to expect descriptions of women in leading positions in film, as in the rest of the community, to be offered more or less unconsciously on men's terms. Men are the norm (see for instance Hallberg 1992, Hirdman 2001 and Wahl et al. 2001). The chapter on *Elizabeth* will reflect to some extent the reproduction of the gender system that is constantly taking place. One reason is almost certainly that we are two middle-aged men watching and analysing the film. But, in our opinion, it is mainly due to the film itself.

We looked at quite a lot of films. Whoopi Goldberg's (her real name is Caryn Johnson, and she was born in 1949) films *The Associate* (1996) or the one in which she trains a basketball team (*Eddie*, 1996) are not quality products. And that can definitely also be said of a film with a promising title – *Lady Boss* (1992). The latest film about France's national saint Jeanne d'Arc directed by Luc Besson (1999) is far too long, pompous and unrealistic to stand up to any appraisal of its quality.

Carl Theodor Dreyer's (who can hardly be related to Egon) classic *La passion de Jeanne d'Arc* is definitely good enough. But a silent movie from

1928 would probably not attract any response from most people. There are several film treatments but they do not excel *Elizabeth* as historical dramas or *The Bridge on the River Kwai* as war films. As the space traveller Ripley in the *Alien* films (1979, 1986, 1992 and 1997), Sigourney Weaver does not really play the role of a leader and it can be difficult for those who are no longer teenagers to watch monsters. Helen Mirren (who was born as Ilyena Mironoff in 1945) is fantastic as DCI Jane Tennison, but that is a television series (*Prime Suspect*, 1991–1996). The long episode *Prime Suspect* has been released as a film but it has to be ordered. And one can go on and on like this ... Leaders in films, as in real life, are most often men. It's a man's world here like there – the film industry is still one of the most fiercely defended male reserves. So anyway, let's go, it's time for *Elizabeth*.

Mary I

England in 1554. Henry VIII (1491–1547) is dead. The representatives of his sickly son Edward VI, who died of tuberculosis in 1553 barely sixteen years old, govern the country. England is divided with Catholics contending against Protestants. Henry's eldest daughter (Edward's half-sister) Mary I (Mary Tudor, 1516–1558), a devoted Catholic, is queen. Between the two of them Lady Jane Grey (1537–1554) was queen for nine days. Mary I is childless. The Catholics are afraid the she will be succeeded by her Protestant half-sister, Elizabeth.

This is what we are told before the film begins and by the general works of reference. The action begins with three Protestant heretics being shorn of their hair and burnt at the stake. 'Let them burn for all eternity in the flames of hell!' chant the representatives of the Church. Just think how well the Church has condemned itself. Even so, there seems to be surprise about its failure to attract new audiences. Would anyone buy Windows if Bill Gates had everyone who went over to Macintosh burnt at the stake? And if many of those burnt had not made the switch?

The self-assured Norfolk (Thomas Howard, 1538–1572) and the Earl of Sussex (Thomas Radcliffe, 1525–1583) want Elizabeth (1533–1603, reasonably well captured by Cate Blanchett) convicted of conspiracy even though she has conspired with nobody. Apparently heedless of this threat, she dances around on the meadows of Hatfield and meets the young Lord Robert, who plays a major role in the film. 'Sing tirralo, sing tirralay, The Wuggly Ump lives far away', as Edward Gorey so aptly puts it in *The Wuggly Ump* (1963/1980). In it the trusting brother and sister are eaten up on the last page: 'Sing glogalimp, sing glugalump, from deep inside the Wuggly Ump.' For Elizabeth a different fate awaits. As we watch the film we know that Elizabeth will be queen (Elizabeth I), become popular with her subjects who will refer to her familiarly as 'Good Queen Bess'. A somewhat better label than her half-sister's – 'Bloody Mary'.

At the beginning of the film Elizabeth is captured by soldiers led by the Earl of Sussex and taken to the dreaded Tower. The accusation is that she has conspired together with Sir Thomas Wyatt (1521–1554) and others against the queen. 'You are … arrested for treason.' One night she is led before the queen. Her half-sister Mary, the daughter of Catherine of Aragon (who was also the aunt of Charles V, 1485–1536), lacks the courage to condemn her to death even though she had previously decided to do so. They both have the same father after all. Elizabeth's mother was Anne Boleyn (1507–1536), beheaded by Henry VIII for infidelity after a few years of marriage.

Sir William Cecil (later Lord Burghley, 1520–1598) warns Elizabeth. He then introduces the Spanish ambassador and through him the Spanish king as a suitor for her hand. If we consider suitors as potential partners in a merger, this openness is surprising. Major organisations (like England and Spain) should check the market before they make or allow themselves to receive a merger proposal. An open inquiry demands an open response. Perhaps that was what the King of Spain wanted to achieve. When it is impossible to say no, yes is all that is left. Anyone who has ever been on a committee knows that. Committee work in politics and societies provides knowledge about negotiation techniques and the importance of voting rules that no leader should be without.

There are indications that Queen Mary is pregnant. Philip II of Spain, who she married in 1555, cannot be the father of her child as he has shown little interest in his wife for a very long time. The indications of pregnancy turn out to be caused by cancer, which takes her life in 1558. The picture of Mary we are given by the film is far from flattering. Even so she presumably married for love and during her reign she is guided by her faith. The assiduous execution of opponents is a method that many men have adopted both before and since Mary. It is more difficult to learn from history than can be believed. It is normally designed to suit the current *zeitgeist* and the ruler. The Earl of Sussex hands the dead queen's ring to Elizabeth. The Queen is dead. Long live the Queen!

Coronation and male advice

Norfolk displays the crown to the various quarters of the compass and Sir William marches ahead of the future queen towards the throne. Elizabeth is crowned Queen of England, Ireland and France. 'God Save Your Majesty!'

This is a change of leader celebrated with stately ceremonies. Perhaps celebration is an undervalued element when other organisations undergo a shift of leadership. A great deal of energy is devoted to plans for the future and to emphasising the break with (the often less than successful) history. But in the audience we want bread and circuses. After all, the future is never what we were promised it would be.

The chances open to newly appointed leaders to fulfil the task entrusted to them are not affected only by their formal mandate. Officially Elizabeth had enormous power. Admittedly, like other leaders, on the first day after her accession she encountered a structure that was already in place (cf. Mintzberg 1983). There were also staff, expectations and routines but it was possible for Elizabeth to change all of this. The situation is given but susceptible to reinterpretation. In spite of her strong position, in ruling and in ruling well Elizabeth was obviously dependent on many others and on structures that she had not created herself. There are clear parallels with the situation of a newly appointed executive today. The scope for manoeuvre that Elizabeth was eventually to acquire was one that she had helped to form and also to delimit (cf. Crozier and Friedberg 1977).

All the time, others surround Elizabeth. Some are plotters and others offer good advice. Lord Robert loves her but later becomes both a counsellor and a plotter. Not even in her private life is she left alone. Moreover it is worth noting that we the viewers are often privy to it as well. This woman, who must reasonably have been strong, intelligent and enterprising, is portrayed in the film as if she spent most of her time in meetings with her lover, intrigues and other aspects of relationships. It is worth comparing for example the depictions of Superintendent Beck (in chapter five) or Richard Nixon (chapter six). Elizabeth's counsellors – all of them men – appear however to focus on circumstances and action. Vigilant viewers will observe how the usual conception of female leaders is reproduced here.

The newly crowned queen amuses herself, is admonished and given good advice. 'Your majesty should know that you have inherited a most powerless and degenerated state.' She is threatened by France and Spain and also by Mary Stuart (1542–1587) who is a claimant to her throne, and by Norfolk, 'who lusts after it'.

Sir Francis Walsingham (1532–1590) returns from exile and is entrusted with the task of ensuring the safety of the queen by Sir William. Norfolk's emissary did not have the courage to use his knife on him and instead had his own throat cut. The choice of Walsingham as security expert turns out to be a wise one. You will find him in the reference books if you look up espionage. This was not something he invented, but according to

Sweden's National Encyclopaedia (2000, one of Sweden's most reputable reference works) has been 'undertaken since the dawn of time', as shown by evidence in the form of written 'espionage reports' from 1370 B.C. Sir Francis Walsingham was, however, a pioneer when it came to developing an efficient, state-run system of espionage.

The general impression of the men surrounding Elizabeth is that everything will depend on whom she chooses to marry. The French ambassador, Monsieur de Foix, announces that King Henry III of France wants Elizabeth to consider the suit of his brother – the Duke of Anjou (Alençon). The King of Spain declares his interest via his ambassador, Monseigneur Alvaro de la Quadra. The ambassador points out that the marriage of a queen is the outcome of politics, not passion. And according to Dick Harrison, for instance, in Sweden's National Encyclopaedia (2000) Erik XIV of Sweden also joined the queue of suitors. And she could not simply send all the suitors or their representatives home without risking warfare. Diplomacy – which is what many executives are involved in today even though it is called something different.

Besieged by her suitors, Elizabeth requests a volta and dances it with Lord Robert. They are fond of each other and meet in secret at night. But it is difficult to keep secrets when you are observed. And in addition it is difficult to oppose control when you no longer own yourself. Sir William says: 'Your Majesty's body and person are no longer her own property. They belong to the state.' Here there are clear parallels to our own period. Senior executives driven to illness by stress no longer own their health either. Age and illness can bring them down, but so far they have not had to allow inspection of their bed sheets every morning.

Lured to action

Elizabeth is dragged out of bed just after Robert has managed to leave it. Norfolk and the council want action. Mary de Guise (who by the way is the Duke of Anjou's aunt) has reinforced the army in Scotland with 4,000 men. The council considers that there is a risk that the French will attack a weakened England and they should be subdued without delay. Only Sir Francis Walsingham advises against it. 'A prince should rather be slow to take action, and should watch that he does not come to be afraid of his own shadow.' Elizabeth herself dislikes wars as 'they have uncertain outcomes'. Analysis of both these opinions is interesting. Delay is an often underestimated requirement for success (cf. Nadolny 1983).

High-powered action-heroes are the kind of leaders that are highly rated today. One Wednesday in July 1999, Ericsson, the major Swedish multinational group, announced, relatively unexpectedly, that it was time to replace its chief executive once again. The current incumbent had not been energetic enough. This may or may not have been the complete explanation. What is interesting is that lack of energy could be offered as a reasonable argument for replacing a chief executive. There was quite a lot in the newspapers about the switch and some mention was made of imperfect personal chemistry and the classical need to find a scapegoat for a weak showing in the stock market. The impression made by the chief executive in the media was also referred to. But his successor was not much better in this respect. The joint trade union organisation at Ericsson supported the replacement, but considered that the restructuring had been too slow and focused on the wrong things. This is not an odd reaction when making Swedish staff redundant was one of the areas in which this energy should have been demonstrated.

In the public sector we can also see how the same focus has been placed on energetic action. The increasingly insignificant role of classical Official Government Reports is one sign. There have been testing times for enquiries in the past. Their findings have not always been used as the basis for political decisions and references to ongoing enquiries have unsettled political debate. But energetic action has never been as important a component in the assessment of political assemblies as today. What politician now has time to think before making a decision?

The public administration is emulating the eagerness to act shown by the commercial sector. It does not matter whether it concerns pension systems, care of the elderly, educational development or mobile phones. More urgent action is required everywhere. There should be more happening and new models have to be developed more and more rapidly. Thinking is a luxury that neither our straitened economies nor our late-modern value systems allow.

Here we need to stop to consider the concepts of energetic action. The word action can be used in its everyday meaning. This is something intentional that has physical effects on the environment outside the agent. The action hero will not be given a role in the next film if he persists in thinking and indulges in intensive reasoning. The audience want him to kick someone. Talk does not interfere as long as it consists of no more than 'one-liners'. The degree of energy is linked to both the strength or visibility and the frequency of the actions. These have to be numerous, frequent and not trivial.

Demonstrating energy does not always mean having to do very much oneself. No chief executive is expected to manufacture telephones and politicians are not required to look after the elderly. It is a question of getting things done. Or rather making it look as if one is the cause of the actions undertaken by others in the organisation. Making decisions is an accepted way of making it look, as one is the cause. But if nothing is done, masses of decisions will not serve as evidence of energetic action.

There are other ways of linking oneself to action. Often the link is embodied in a role, such as the chief executive or leader of the majority party in a local council. Another popular way is to take responsibility for a culture or a working climate that is assumed to increase the number of actions or speed them up.

Energetic action is not merely a description of what has happened. It is also a forecast and indicates potential. If the hero has kicked like a maniac and shown that he has mastered Asian hand movements of various kinds, baleful glances will suffice, at least until his injuries have healed. Anyway, he does not have to kick. Foolhardy actions of many different kinds will do. Energy can to some degree consist of an assumed capacity for action. However, little prominence was given the previous merits of Ericsson's chief executive. Action heroes cannot afford to take time out for any longer periods.

It can also be noted that action heroes are men. Ask in the toyshops and you will find out. Even so it can clearly be seen that *Barb Wire* (1996) is a woman. When *Nikita* (1990) was remade in a version to suit the USA market better (*Point of No Return*, 1993) admittedly they replaced the hard-bitten Anne Parillaud. The role went to Bridget Fonda, who is so feeble that the action is incomprehensible – but they are both women. There are a number of exceptions that do not disprove the rule. Energetic action is something that is ascribed to men and which they aspire to. With the exceptions of the exceptions, when a woman displays energetic action it is called something else. She is prodigal, foolhardy, manic and hardly an alpha type. If women want a leading role they must grit their teeth and become men. Or do what Elizabeth did: remain virgins, which is to say be like 'real men' and have no relationships with men. By the way, Carole Levin has written a good book about queens as men called *The Heart and Stomach of a King* (1994).

Maria Edström has studied how women in leading positions in business are described in the media (see Wahlberg 2002). Women are called 'cleaners' and 'capable' while men are referred to as 'business doctors' and are of course 'equal to their tasks'. These labels, like those used about energetic actions, play a not insignificant role in the reproduction of men as representatives of sound leadership.

When it comes to action heroes, it must be added that their actions are often inappropriate. Nothing is at risk if Jean Claude van Damme is on the wrong track until well into the film. Whatever happens we can guarantee that he will see the light and earn the name of hero. Not even when the hero is on the wrong track does he harm many women, children or bank clerks.

Despite the unwillingness of action heroes to acquire reliable information and reflect, everything turns out right in the end. In the world of film it is often a matter of not wanting to rather than being unable to. Action heroes are not stupid, but they despise thinking and are terrified by the idea of having to do anything of the kind themselves. Actions lead action heroes. There is not nearly enough trial to call it 'trial and error'. Admittedly there is no shortage of error, but action is self-correcting. It does not matter what the action hero does, later it will turn out on the whole to have been sensible. Films can be really unlike reality.

If we are amazed at the focus on action today and the way in which energetic action has become an ideal, there must be some alternative state. Our youngsters point to the drama section at the back of the video store as the opposite. We ourselves would perhaps rather suggest some early short films with artistic ambitions. But the question is whether these really are opposites.

Another conceivable opposite to energetic action is coma. This is a 'state of unconsciousness, characterized by loss of reaction to external stimuli and absence of spontaneous nervous activity, usually associated with injury to the cerebrum. Coma may accompany a number of metabolic disorders or physical injuries to the brain from disease or trauma. Different patterns of coma depend on the origin of the injury'. All according to the Internet edition of Encyclopaedia Britannica (Internet reference 6). In coma a protagonist only has gravity to rely on. Not much for a chief executive. It may be an opposite, but in no way is it an alternative.

Opposites are problematic. There is a scale that goes from more to less energetic action. The extremes, no energetic action and maximum energy of action, are not opposed to each other. Nor can we use lazy or patient as examples of the opposite. It is more as if these concepts explain less energetic action.

Energetic action can only be contrasted with a state where action is less energetic. This does not mean that some other value automatically rises when the degree of energy abates. Less focus on action admittedly leaves room for other things. Thinking would fit the bill.

Thought processes can precede action and in some way improve it, make it more considered. This need not, however, be the case. Many thought processes have no direct implications for action. One can easily imagine individuals who think slowly and deeply and those who think quickly and without depth. If we combine this with very energetic action and less energetic action we end up with a four-way matrix. The action hero ends up in the square with very energetic action and rapid, shallow thought. Thorough consideration can be combined with rapid energetic action or no action at all. Neither of these two combinations is obviously better than the other – it depends on whether the action is desirable. For the same reason shallow thinking that gives rise to no action is not always a bad alternative.

Our current focus on action has its effects. About that there can be no argument. In the public sector energetic action mainly finds expression in constant structural changes. As if all changes were for the better. If you rush into energetic action without working out in advance what it will lead to, you should be pleased if you end up with more or less the right outcome in twenty-five per cent of cases. Often it ends up wrong, and frequently you find yourself somewhere you have already been earlier. Unfortunate when rapid reforms are a drain on staff and cost a lot of money.

And what about all the chief executives who drive themselves to death and do neither themselves nor their families any good. It is not energy we should be looking for. Short-term stock price focus, fixation on the next quarterly report, expansion right now and continual change is not obviously healthy, for either the company or the community. What about the long-term view, thinking even further ahead, continuity and well considered solutions? Neither the commercial nor the public sector would suffer.

It can be pointed out that many leaders have been informed about the risks of one-sided focus on action. This has often taken place in seminars and simulation involving presentation of what is called the 'eastern' way of thinking. Here rapid action is contrasted with introspection. We would like to contrast action immediately with action preceded by analysis. We do not believe that executives will find answers of general interest by contemplating their navels.

Elizabeth cannot resist the demand for rapid action, but follows the advice and goes to war. The uncertainty of the outcome is not a viable argument. And the question is whether it was uncertain – England could expect to be soundly defeated. The bishops made sure that England sent children as reinforcements and after the defeat demand Elizabeth's abdication. She does not abdicate – but rushes around, suffers and weeps. No wonder that going to the cinema often makes feminists angry (see Bang 2000, p. 5). Women cannot even manage to send children to their inevitable death in a war without becoming hysterical …

Managing a meeting

The bishops pose a problem for Elizabeth. They are against her and not afraid of her. Moreover they play an active political role and do not expect her to survive. The question is how she will be able to deal with the one thing that takes precedence to royalty – religion.

The solution is a law on conformism. Elizabeth wants to retain Protestantism as the state religion but still show some tolerance towards Catholics. She summons a meeting and manages it superbly. Spontaneous but at the same time fantastically well prepared. Leaders often find themselves at meetings that must be managed. Here the group is a large one and the issue of unusual gravity, but successful leaders can confront a group.

The queen begins the meeting by pointing out: 'If there is no uniformity of religious belief here, then there can only be fragmentation, dispute and quarrel. Surely my Lords it is better to have one Church of England. A single Church of England – with a common prayer book and a common purpose. I ask you to pass this act of uniformity, not, not for myself, but for my people, who are my only care.'

MAN IN THE CONGREGATION:

Madam, by this act you force us to relinquish our allegiance to the Holy Father.

ELIZABETH:

How can I force you, My Grace? I am a woman. I have no desire to make windows into men's souls. I simply ask, can any man, in truth, serve two masters and be faithful to both?

MAN IN THE CONGREGATION:

This is heresy!

ELIZABETH:

No your grace … this is common sense. Which is a most English virtue.

MAN IN THE CONGREGATION:

Your Majesty would improve all these matters, if you would agree to marry.

MAN IN THE CONGREGATION:

Yes, marry.

ELIZABETH:

... but, marry whom Your Grace? Would you give me some suggestion? For some say France and others Spain, and some cannot abide foreigners at all. So I am not sure how best to please you unless I married one of each.

MAN IN THE CONGREGATION:

Now Your Majesty does make fun out of the sanctity of marriage.

ELIZABETH:

I do not think you should lecture me on that Milord, since you yourself have been twice divorced and are now upon your third wife. Each of you must vote according to your own conscience. But remember this: In your hands, upon this moment, lies the future happiness of my people, and the peace of this realm. Let that be upon your conscience also.

SIR WILLIAM CECIL:

My lords, the house will divide.

The queen's proposal is carried by five votes. One reason for this outcome is that Sir Francis Walsingham has had Stephen Gardiner (1482–1555) and a group of bishops locked into the cellar. Here Elizabeth exploits not only the process but also the structure. A successful leader creates an organisation (with fewer bishops) that is then managed well. The most energetic opponents are manoeuvred out before the meeting. A cellar that can be locked could serve as a useful metaphor for today's leaders.

This meeting is a clear example of how the gender order is reflected in the way in which female leadership is depicted in this film. Elizabeth uses her femininity. She does not comply with the norms for male leadership. She declares at the meeting, for instance, that she cannot force the bishops to renounce their faith. After all she is a woman! She appeals to common sense, to the English virtue and to their consciences. These arguments are feminine and emotional rather than masculine and factual. She cannot threaten the men and the impression she makes is almost that of a tender mother (cf. Moss Kanter 1977).

When, after she has killed her opponents, it is no longer possible for Elizabeth to be the tender mother, she becomes maiden instead the iron. Dangerous admittedly, but without threatening the men who survive, as she is a virgin who is there for England alone. You can see how the film reproduces our social conceptions that women are more emotional than men. As a woman she is good at dealing with relationships, as with the bishops. On the other hand the men she works with need not view her as a threat. Rosabeth Moss Kanter (1977) refers to this as the contrast effect.

Recurring suitors

Elizabeth is bothered by persistent marriage proposals. These could be seen as metaphors for merger proposals. If she fails to marry and conceive an heir, Elizabeth can never rest secure. And the heir is ... or could be seen as a metaphor for something else. Work it out for yourself! And try to see the metaphors in your own surroundings.

A lot has been written about metaphors. Jacques Jimenez and Timothy Johnson (1998) identify six main metaphors in (north American) business circles. In a male-dominated commercial sector they find these male metaphors: the gambler, the warrior, the athlete, the farmer, the craftsman and the engineer. You have to imagine that the degree of masculinity varies between these categories. This work, *Metaphors at Work* (1998) by Jacques Jimenez and Timothy Johnson, makes a sexist, inane and shallow impression. This may be due to the way in which the authors reflect a reality in which most of the frequently used metaphors in the workplace are just that – sexist, inane and shallow. It would not, in that case, have been inappropriate to point this out. Anyway, they succeed in showing that metaphors are not necessarily an elevated form of expression (cf. Ohlsson and Rombach 2000).

During a festive trip in a number of small boats, Lord Robert jokingly proposes.

ELIZABETH:
On a night such as this, could any woman say no?

LORD ROBERT:
On a night such as this, could a queen say no?

ELIZABETH:
Does not a queen sit under the same stars as any other woman?

Later Elizabeth discovers her French suitor dressed as a woman, which means that he can be eliminated from the list. And anyway he was not particularly high on it after his entry. Anjou was a little too facetious, and when he arrived he immediately kissed the queen on the mouth. He then told her that he had dreamed about the moment when they lay together naked in bed '... then I will be able to caress your hips and perhaps also your ...'. This seems un-English. 'Your Grace, although my affection for you is undiminished I have, after an agonising struggle, determined to sacrifice my own happiness for the welfare of my people', Elizabeth tells him. She does not want any explanation of the women's clothes.

In kissing Elizabeth on the lips as soon as he arrives and then making indecent proposals in front of everyone else, Anjou is harassing her sexually. It is interesting that not even a queen can avoid this and that the perpetrator is not punished. What Anjou does is of course related to power and to the gender system that prevails (see Wahl et. al. 2001).

As the Queen of England, Ireland and France Elizabeth should have the upper hand over Anjou, especially as in the film he is depicted as stupid with his flute and his women's clothes. Even so he takes control at their first meeting. The image this communicates is that a woman, however senior, is subordinate to men. But it is also a demonstration, if you like, that when it comes to the crunch men are unable to control their behaviour. Anjou has an entire kingdom in his grasp and then makes a fool of himself with his harassment and his cross-dressing. The second fits in well with the belief that men's sexuality cannot be controlled (cf. Wahl et. al. 2001).

After this, the Spanish ambassador succeeds in persuading Sir Robert that he can help Elizabeth by joining in the plot. As a result Robert talks to the queen and tells her that the King of Spain is a friend and that she should form an alliance by marrying him. The marriage would not stop Elizabeth from continuing to meet him. However, this proposal fails to take root and Sir Robert has played his last card.

But first there is time to dance a volta with Robert. The volta gives Elizabeth a chance to talk to him privately. A bit like a trip to the pub with the blokes. Her body language is different from the previous volta. 'I am no man's Elizabeth, and if you think to rule, you are mistaken. ... I will have one mistress hear ... and no master!' You can hardly put it more clearly than that.

Sir William Cecil, with his unceasing marriage suggestions, has also exhausted his usefulness. After the following exchange he is pensioned off as Lord Burghley.

ELIZABETH:

Your policies would make England nothing but either part of France or Spain. From this moment I am going to follow my own opinion, and see if I do any better.

SIR WILLIAM CECIL:

Forgive me madam, but you are only a woman.

ELIZABETH:

I may be a woman ... but if I choose I have the heart of a man!

Abruption

The dictionaries should contain the noun abruption, but it does not exist. If it did exist the definition would be 'rapid, involuntary loss of office'. This has happened to many both in films and in reality. The chief executives of local authorities are more likely to retire for this reason than because of age. And if the readers have failed to realise it, the title of lord was Sir William's golden handshake. A brusque form of abruption is to bump someone off, an effective way of terminating his or her employment – but socially acceptable methods can also be pretty brusque.

We take a companionable boat trip that preceded Elizabeth's rupture with Robert. Suddenly an arrow is shot from a crossbow. One of the guards on Elizabeth's boat collapses. Another arrow strikes not far from her. An attempted assassination. There is not much a leader can do while it is taking place. Could it be Norfolk? Or the Vatican (Pius V, 1504–1572)? An English priest was received there who seems to be prepared to kill the queen. Or is it the Spanish ambassador attempting to recruit Lord Robert? Whatever it is, it interrupts Lord Robert's proposal. Later Sir William is able to report that Lord Robert is already married.

The historical Robert referred to here turns out towards the end of the film to be Lord Robert Dudley, Earl of Leicester. Reality, according to the Swedish National Encyclopaedia (2000) for instance, seems to have differed from the film in a number of respects. According to the reference works Robert did not propose until he had probably poisoned his wife. Her mysterious death also seems to have ruined his reputation (Thomas 1998, p. x). There is also a scheming Robert Devereux, Earl of Essex (1566–1601) in the history books. He was Elizabeth's favourite in the latter half of her reign. Here as elsewhere in this work, our interest is in the fiction.

And in the Vatican his Holiness has issued a bull: 'It deprives Elizabeth, the pretended Queen of England, servant of wickedness of her throne – and declares that henceforth her subjects are absolved of their religions too. His Holiness also decrees that any man, who should undertake her assassination, will be welcomed by angels into the kingdom of heaven.'

The English priest is given the bull and a bundle of letters to the conspirators. When he reaches the coast of England, Norfolk is one of those waiting to greet him. In some way the priest has discovered that one of

Norfolk's companions, Thomas Elyot, is not a member of the group but Walsingham's spy. The priest uses a rock to kill the young man brutally some distance out to sea.

And immediately afterwards a new attempt to assassinate the queen is revealed. Isabel tries the queen's gowns on and greets her lover wearing one of them. 'I am the queen, am I not?' She dies alone, screaming on the floor after Lord Robert has made his escape. Here, as in the meeting before the Scottish fiasco, he turns out to be a real wimp. The fabric of the gown had been poisoned. French silk ...

Sir Francis Walsingham meets Mary de Guise, sister of the King of France. Her nephew, Anjou, takes to his bed with a cold. In a heart-to-heart conversation Walsingham offers to change sides. No illusions. He can consider going to bed with Spain or France. Tonight it is France. Next morning the woman is found murdered in his bed.

After the attempted assassination that cost Isabel her life, Sir Francis Walsingham advises Elizabeth to look for the priest. He is discovered at the home of Lord Arundel (Henry Fitzalann, 1512–1580) who is later beheaded for this reason. After intensive torture Walsingham extorts a confession from the priest. As a result Elizabeth is obliged to have the Earl of Sussex, Stephen Gardiner (1482–1555) and Monseigneur Alvaro de la Quadra (the Spanish ambassador) put to death. The first meets his end in his toilet with a whip in his hand, while indulging in religious (?) self-flagellation, the second in his armchair.

Norfolk signs his own death warrant, unaware that the woman he has had and hounded is one of Walsingham's network of spies. All the queen's enemies, except Lord Robert Dudley, Earl of Leicester, are executed or end up in the Tower. Robert is allowed to live but will never meet Elizabeth alone again. His task is to form part of the organisational memory – Robert serves as living evidence of how even the most intimate can be traitors.

This film shows us many versions of abruption: retirement with a proper golden handshake in the form of a Lord's title; another form is assassination; being sent to Coventry as a warning example could be a third: there are others. Even if abruption is frequent and takes many different forms, things remain remarkably quiet once the storm has waned. There should be just as much discussion of abruption as there is of recruitment.

Successfulness

During a discussion with Walsingham, Elizabeth realises that she has to assume divinity here on earth. Total loyalty to England is required of her. She makes sure that her hair is cut short and that her hands and face are chalk-white – 'I have become a virgin' – before making a very effective entrance. In reality her appearance and dress – at least on ceremonious occasions – was probably more or less what we see in the many portraits that have survived (see for instance Hibbert 1991). Her maidenly pallor required 'lotion of white of egg, alum, borax, poppy seeds and powdered eggshell' (Hibbert 1991, p. 101).

Wed to England, Elizabeth went on to reign for another forty years. Walsingham remained her most trusted and loyal adviser. When she died, England was the richest and most powerful country in Europe. Her reign has been referred to as a golden age.

It can be noted here that Jeanne d'Arc (1412–1431) who more than a century earlier had been the Maid of Orleans is said to have been obliged to prove her virginity. There was some concern that her revelations were the outcome of intercourse with the devil. It may possibly have been more appropriate to question a virgin of humbler birth. Yvonne Hirdman (2001) refers in another context to the difficulty of accomplishing what Elizabeth achieved.

> Individual women struggled in different ways with the existential problem area of similar-distinct. As they wanted to do something that lay outside the normal feminine sphere there must be something wrong with them. The 'unfeminine' desires they entertained had to emanate from a female body. Like later imitators of England's Elizabeth I, but without her obvious kingly self-assurance and divine right, they regarded themselves as hybrids, as 'men-women', as non-women, as men 'in fact'. (Hirdman 2001, pp. 118–119)

However, we claim that Yvonne Hirdman underestimates the problem. It was not easy for Elizabeth to assert her virginity either. And that it nevertheless was possible may perhaps have been because she worked a lot harder than others at maintaining her image.

> Elizabeth's image as Virgin Queen was powerful but it was countered with the rumors and gossip throughout her reign about her supposed sexual relationships with her favorites and the illegitimate children she bore – and sometimes supposedly destroyed. (Levin 1994, pp. 3–4)

One interesting question is how important images are for leaders. A good many successful leaders have made themselves or been made by others into easily recognisable trademarks. The question here is one of the chicken and the egg. Have they acquired their profiles later or did their image contribute to their success? Perhaps the role of the image is to enable them to retain their positions? Elizabeth did not willingly devote time to posing for portraits, but she still took great care to ensure that the paintings were not too dissimilar. 'For the depiction of her clothes as well as her features patterns were issued, and in representation of these the portraits were more reliable' (Hibbert 1991, p. 103). Several well-known portraits are reproduced in *Behind the Mask* by Jane Resh Thomas (1998). Whether the care devoted to those depictions was prompted by the significance of the image or mere vanity is difficult to judge. Modern companies and their executives can also be quite vain – it may be necessary, maybe not. There may be differences between various sectors in this respect. It could be wise to choose an image that suits the sector one is operating in.

But why did Elizabeth choose to be a virgin exactly? A lot of attempts have been made to explain this. The conversion may have been because the country needed a maiden.

> In turning from Roman Catholicism to Anglican Protestantism, one of the aspects of worship that was being cast substantially in the background was the Virgin Mary. Catholics of Elizabeth's day were devoted to the Virgin, even as they are today. In Protestant practice, the Virgin was still venerated but was no longer so intense a focus of worship. In a stroke of insightful genius, Elizabeth realized that her own virginity could fill the void that the absence of the Virgin Mary had created in the people's hearts. Certainly, Elizabeth did not set herself before her subjects as a god or goddess, but she did present herself as a new virgin, a virgin for a Protestant realm. (Axelrod 2000, pp. 48–49)

It may have been the truth – Elizabeth may actually have been a virgin. With a father like Henry VIII it would not be an unlikely decision. This is not the case in the film. It may have been the elevated position afforded to virgins at the time that was appealing. Or perhaps she was just not keen on sharing power with a man. In terms of *realpolitik* it was not easy either to choose a husband. It meant at the same time choosing an ally and that ally's given enemies.

Yet another explanation may perhaps be found in the difficulty of being accepted on the same terms as a male leader. Female bosses must be twice as good as their male colleagues and totally dedicated to their tasks to avoid being considered disloyal (Moss Kanter 1977). Devotion is referred to in terms like 'married to the job'. That is exactly what Elizabeth did when she became the virgin. Her choice excluded family and children, and in the film, lovers as well.

Elizabeth as CEO – Semper Eadem

Because of her historical role there are a great many books about Elizabeth I. Most of them deal with her leadership. It would be odd if they did not. In the context of our analysis we have settled for a few titles that seemed to relate to the issues that interest us here. We have already referred to works like *The Virgin Queen: Elizabeth I, Genius of the Golden Age* by Christopher Hibbert (1991), *The Heart and Stomach of a King: Elizabeth I and the Politics of Sex and Power* by Carole Levin (1994) and *Behind the Mask: The Life of Queen Elizabeth I* by Jane Resh Thomas (1998). Here we should like to pay particular interest to yet another title.

While we were finishing our analysis of the film about Elizabeth, we noticed a review of a book called *Elizabeth I CEO* in one of the major Swedish dailies (*Svenska Dagbladet*; Lorin, March 18th, 2001). And if we had missed it, the e-mails sent straight after breakfast by those of our friends who read the papers would have put us straight ... The author of the book, Alan Axelrod was, according to the reviewer Peter Lorin, lyrical about Elizabeth as an individual while he himself was somewhat tepid about the book. The fact that it had been published in a Swedish translation (by Svenska Förlaget) shows the potential circulation the work is considered to have. Allan Axelrod has also written a book about what we can learn from General George Patton's (1885–1945) leadership style. We have not read it, as we have not included any Patton films in this book. *Patton: A Salute to a Rebel* from 1970 with George Scott playing the lead is, with its seven Oscars, definitely not a bad film. It was eliminated because two of our nine films could not be old (albeit intelligent and well made) war films.

We are not citing *Elizabeth I CEO* because of its general literary virtues – quite the opposite! On the whole it is a pretty dreadful work. Superficial and unreflecting in a way that could well be used to mock the genre. Or what can be said about the following gems of thought piled one on top of the other?

> Elizabeth did not deceive herself into believing that she could remain a girl forever, but she worked hard to forestall decay of mind and body. Moreover, she understood that the effective leader must be willing to demonstrate – not defiantly, but always gracefully – the health and vigor associated with young strength and the inspiring strength of ever-youthful hope, ambition, and pride. (Axelrod 2000, p. 61)

> Elizabeth was a great walker who habitually took her exercise in the form of a brisk walk around the grounds of Hampton Court. It was soon noticed, however, that she walked 'briskly when alone', but that when she was conscious of being watched, 'she, who was the very image of majesty and magnificence, went slowly and marched with leisure'. A leader is a leader in everything she does. (Axelrod 2000, p. 63)
> Elizabeth never allowed herself to become so rapt in the loftiness of her station that she forgot to be human. Like all effective leaders, she remained connected to a root reality that gave an unwavering perspective on whatever changing circumstances and challenges confronted her. (Axelrod 2000, p. 69)

Alan Axelrod sees the simple points he wants to see. 'Most of all, the career of Elizabeth I is an example of vision, of creating vision, of communicating vision, and of realizing vision' (Axelrod 2000, p. xiii). But despite these shortcomings the book has something to offer, otherwise we would not have taken the trouble to complain about it with such energy. Alan Axelrod (2000, pp. x–xi) points to ten areas of leadership where he believes Elizabeth can teach us something.

1. A leader's first lesson: survival
2. Creating a leadership image
3. Combining the common touch with the air of leadership
4. Creating common cause without tyranny
5. Building a loyal staff – and a loyal opposition
6. Growing the enterprise and crushing the competition
7. Turning crisis into triumph
8. Holding on to the power
9. Doing business without excuse
10. Winning – and what it means

Survival (1) is something we have already dealt with. There is something in it. In the past you were assassinated or poisoned – today you are bought out. If Elizabeth had not hung on to her life and her throne she would admittedly not have been able to lead. It may be that her adaptability combined with the stability she displayed to others was the most important explanation for this. The queen's motto was 'Semper Eadem' (Always the same). She adhered to it, but fortunately did not follow it. Power (8), which is only partly the result of her position and survival, is a requirement if she is to be able to lead. The same applies to business executives. Avoid abruption! And endeavour to acquire the power base needed to lead.

Elizabeth herself was convinced of the importance of her image (2). We have spent enough time discussing virginity. Image is always important. Before printed media became accessible for the general population, public opinion was created in other ways (cf. Tarde 1900). That does not mean that it was less important then, than it is now. Anyway, it looks as if subscription of newspapers among a great majority of people is in the process of disappearing. Instead we have a wider range of news channels that we select depending on what kind of information we are looking for. And the availability of texts on the Internet, be they news articles, gossip or sheer lies, is rapidly increasing as well.

Irrespective of the medium, creating an image is one thing, maintaining, safeguarding and developing it another. Maintenance requires continual investment. The question is whether Alan Axelrod (2000) gets it right when he emphasises the common touch (3). Does this really apply to leaders in Europe? And is it true for Elizabeth?

If we want to attain shared goals, we have to strive for a common cause (4). And there is nothing wrong in pointing out how difficult it can be to create these shared goals. Much of the discussion is about how objectives can be used to manage, and not about how objectives or goals can be devised on which agreement can be reached (cf. Rombach 1991). The process that leads to the establishment of objectives can easily tear an organisation to pieces before the management has even started. Peace and religion were the keys for Elizabeth. Alan Axelrod's (2000, chapter four) primitive ideas about management by objectives can otherwise well be skipped.

Dependence on staff will be dealt with in more detail in the chapter about the Nixon film (chapter six in this book). In Alan Axelrod (2000, chapter five) it is supplemented by dependence on a loyal opposition (5). Leadership that permits criticism and involves listening to others is better. No room is devoted to this issue in the film. If it had been, we would have referred to studies of the public sector that show that functioning opposition leads to better considered decisions (for example Brunsson 1981).

It was under Elizabeth's leadership that England became a great power (6 & 9). This is an interesting fact, but it gives us more of a reason for taking an interest in her leadership than something we can learn from today. Even if the methods Elizabeth used are almost certainly still applied to some extent in the private sector, since then there has been a substantial shift in where we draw the line in deciding if methods of enriching an organisation are legitimate or not. Alan Axelrod admits grudgingly: 'It would be irresponsible to attempt to write a prescription for action based on Elizabeth's example (here).' (2000, p. 161)

Alan Axelrod (2000, pp. 145–148) points to the removal of harmful monopolies as turning a crisis into a triumph (7). Awarding monopolies was an important aspect of Elizabeth's system of rewards. This is another problem area that is not dealt with in the film. Even so point 7 is brilliant! It is obvious that crises have to be turned into triumphs. If defeats can be converted to victories the level of risk can be raised. It was this belief that enabled the standard-bearers of the new economy to flourish for a time (cf. Rombach and Svedberg Nilsson 2000).

Finally one can ask whether winning really is what it is all about (10). We have always believed that the idea was to have fun. And to have fun without ruining things for others or being ashamed when it comes to an end. That the only thing you owe life is to live it. But whatever it is, these are questions we will not have time to resolve before the end of this chapter.

CHAPTER 5

Beck – in the land of middle management

To begin with we believed a murder was taking place in the shower cabinet. The man could have been Anthony Perkins (in Alfred Hitchcock's *Psycho* from 1960), or perhaps not. Moreover, there are two people grunting away under the shower.

Peter Haber, Mikael Persbrandt, Figge Norling, Stina Rautelin and others start a no-longer-altogether-new Beck rolling. The film *Beck – Decoy Boy* was made in 1997 and is considerably more recent than the latest detective novel by Maj Sjöwall and Per Wahlöö. They produced ten books between 1965 and 1975. In the Beck films, which include the *Man with the Icons*, Rolf Börjlind devises the plots. Martin Beck and Gunvald Larsson are the names of characters taken from the originals but they are to some extent different.

'I love you', says Rosa Andrén, minister with special responsibility for development aid for the Baltic countries, including their military development. She says it to Jurij Gulkov, head of security at the Russian Embassy, who at that moment is worried about the hair he has in his nostrils. Later in the film he will have other things to worry about. Before we get there, Acke (the dog!) will find a loose foot and other body parts in black plastic bags out in a lake. Dogs that take walks in films often find body parts. Sometimes they rescue children.

Beck and the lads

MARTIN BECK:

Murdered woman. Shot three times in the back. One bullet missing. Head found some distance away.

GUNVALD LARSSON:

No marks on the body or tattoos?

MARTIN BECK:

No. X-ray identification of the skull tells us nothing. Must have been in her 60s. No fingerprints found. Results of hair analysis – doubtful. The woman had no clothes. Two back teeth missing as well. We're looking at dental records.

GUNVALD LARSSON:

The plastic bags, then?

BENNY SKACKE:

Ordinary grey plastic waste disposal bags. Four altogether.

GUNVALD LARSSON:

Four.

MARTIN BECK:

And we would never have found the sacks if dredging hadn't begun. They'd been sunk using heavy nets for reinforcing concrete.

GUNVALD LARSSON:

Professionals?

MARTIN BECK:

Yes. Unfortunately.

BENNY SKACKE:

Yes – there are two missing persons that might fit. One is Nadja Vassiljev, sixty-two, married to a building contractor and lives in the centre of the city. And a Svea Hörnberg from Kiruna, fifty-nine, single, disappeared while on a trip through Stockholm.

GUNVALD LARSSON:

And who the hell would want to cut either of them to pieces?

MARTIN BECK:

OK Skacke. You take the Hörnberg woman and we will try our luck with Vassiljev.

So far, so good. This is a small team of professionals with their boss. There can be no doubt that Martin Beck is in charge. Gunvald Larsson and Benny Skacke are the boss's men. Gunvald self-assured, on the ball. He seems to be good at his job and knows it. Benny is less relaxed although we do not know why. Even so, we are sure he does what he is told to do. Perhaps Benny is still there to learn. With different hair colour, Figge Norling, who plays the role of Benny, would look better as a stock trader.

Martin Beck leads the investigation and allocates the work. One could well ask whether someone else in the group could have done it just as well. Managing the team follows a set pattern. Both the team and the cinema audience know where they are. But it would have been just as easy if the pattern had been different. We get used to things. The most extraordinary and inappropriate routines can become institutions. Just look at schools, one of the favourite examples in institutional theory (for instance in Scott and Meyer 1994). We recognise what schools are doing wherever we come across them in the world. Schools are the same. This can be seen as well by those who have studied institutional theory with a sociological focus. Gunilla Granath's highly readable diary *Gäst hos overkligheten* (Visiting the Unreal, 1996), written while she was playing the role of a 48-year-old seventh grader, should convince sceptics. Despite their normality and stability, the way schools are designed makes them unsuitable for anyone who wants to learn anything (at least from the age of ten and upwards) anyone who wants to teach or anyone who wants a generally pleasant environment.

Social Darwinism, which should not be confused with today's normal Darwinism (cf. Dunbar 1996), has spread to the organisational world. The idea of 'survival of the fittest' does not, however, match reality when the form of organisations and organisational routines are concerned. And, moreover, the theory offers no satisfactory explanation of the course of biological development either (cf. Ohlsson and Rombach 1998, pp 59–61). The extensive organisational theory in this area (population ecology) thrives on the difficulty of defining what is 'fittest'. If that which survives is defined as best, then the best is what survives. For anyone who wants to read a classic in the field of population ecology we would suggest *Organizations and Environments* by Howard Aldrich (1979).

A great deal has been written about the dissemination of institutions and how they are translated (interpreted and perhaps adapted) when they encounter organisations. If two frequently cited works are to be selected from this plethora, again we can take *The New Institutionalism in Organizational Analysis* edited by Walter Powell and Paul DiMaggio (1991) and *Institutions and Organizations* by Richard Scott (1995). In these and other works we will find the observation that similar structures and routines are encountered in many quarters. And these can rarely be explained satisfactorily in terms of the needs of the individual organisations or their historical development. Individual experience is allowed to play a very small role, whereas the image of the experiences of others is given great weight.

Memories hide their heads
Memories conceal their faces
The headless lead each other

(Sumari 2000, p. 44)

A little about names

Up until now Gösta Ekman, Keve Hjelm, Carl-Gustav Lindstedt and Walter Matthau have acted the role of Martin Beck. Peter Haber is best! What is interesting is that in the films he is never (rarely ... then) called Martin or Martin Beck but people always use his surname. Here, as in the other chapters, we will use his entire name unless it gets too long-winded or contradicts what is actually said in the films. This is a matter of respect, even though the individual in this case happens to be fictional. Drawing the line between who is real and who is fictional can, by the way, be pretty difficult.

Casting Mikael Persbrandt as Gunvald Larsson was a stroke of genius. The men from the security service address him as Gunvald. There is no love lost between them and they needle each other. Using his first name is one aspect of their patronising approach. Martin Beck is also careful to use his subordinates' first names when he is annoyed and is giving orders.

Benny Skacke is addressed alternately by both his first name and surname. He is the child in this detective family and we could perhaps expect people to call him Benny. The explanation is that his surname, Skacke, is used more as a nickname than a surname. Martin Beck and Gunvald Larsson are the two fathers – do they have some kind of relationship? Or is that taking our interpretation too far? Lena Klingström (well acted by Stina Rautelin), who is introduced below, is a little too distant (and too competent?) to fill the role of mother adequately. So with no alternatives ...

Martin Beck and the other men call Lena Klingström Lena. This is probably to reduce her status, even if it need not be a deliberate strategy. She is obviously competent and the only woman in the team. Otherwise there are few important women in the film apart from Lena Klingström. Martin Beck's daughter can be seen, Rosa Andrén, the minister, is important, even though her role is minimal, and a prosecutor flashes by. Beck's ex-wife is merely referred to and the victim has been murdered.

Perhaps the men see Lena Klingström as a threat or else they merely reduce her status as a routine male precaution. A safety measure in the interaction between confused men and potentially strong women. If men are to retain power it is important not to breach the pattern that enables the construction of gender (Eriksson-Zetterquist 2002). Films offer one method of consolidating the given order.

The boss's boss

Martin Beck's boss, Joakim Wersén, turns up with the group's new information analyst – Lena Klingström. Beck takes Joakim Wersén outside and closes the door on his subordinates, Benny Skacke, Gunvald Larsson and Lena Klingström.

MARTIN BECK:
Who the hell do you think you are?

JOAKIM WERSÉN:
Your boss.

This is a wittier response than we thought Joakim Wersén capable of. One possibility is therefore that it has been thought out well in advance and then filed as a response to this particular question. This is not a bad technique for people who think ponderously as Sten Nadolny shows in his novel about the enormously slow but nevertheless successful Sir John Franklin (1983).

MARTIN BECK:
Yes ... which gives you the right to put whomever you like into my group. Without asking me. Without even talking to me. Just walk into my room and tell me whom I am going to be working with for years to come. Because you are my boss.

JOAKIM WERSÉN:
Do you have problems with women?

MARTIN BECK:

I've got a problem with you. How can you be so bloody unprofessional (Gunvald Larsson opens the door. Brilliant timing ... Typically masculine!) that you don't ask me what I want? What I need. Who I can consider working with. You've got no idea of what we are dealing with.

JOAKIM WERSÉN:

Lena Klingström is acting detective inspector and as from today she is a member of your group. If you have any official objection, I suggest you take it to the National Police Board. Lena Klingström is a good police officer.

MARTIN BECK:

And she talks.

There they separate, the boss and his boss. Martin Beck has really been put in his place. He has been given a colleague he does not want. Joakim Wersén has used his official position to get his own way. 'If you have any official objection, I suggest you take it to the National Police Board.' Pulling rank in such an explicit way is unusual. Especially when your subordinate's subordinates are present. In films this happens quite frequently in military contexts. In normal organisations it rarely has to go as far as this before the boss gets what he intended. There are tons of decision theories but a shortage of formal decisions, both in films and real-life reality.

The problematic position of the middle manager is made clear in this sequence. Joakim Wersén appears to be inexperienced, attentive to the inclinations of his superiors and also younger than Martin Beck. Not entirely without justification, the respect he is shown by Martin Beck is moderate. Either Joakim Wersén is far too clumsy to be able to lead without creating bad feeling or he wants to assert his rank in front of Martin Beck and the others. The latter seems most credible – after all Wersén is no longer that young.

It is more than possible (but perhaps not so credible) that Joakim Wersén has thought carefully about the allocation of roles between him and Martin Beck. He may have found this unsatisfactory and after making various attempts to remedy the state of affairs adopted this drastic method to show who is leading whom. Joakim Wersén is, after all, also a middle manager under pressure from both directions. Not even in this scenario is the issue he has chosen (choosing the staff without consulting the head of the team) the best possible. If you follow the advice given in the cookery books in the field of leadership (e.g. Berggren et. al. 1998), teams have to be built with greater tact. Here it seems evident that the head of the team should have a great deal of influence when new members are to be added to a group.

Joakim Wersén and Martin Beck meet again when Beck has been to see Olgi Vassiljev (who is the man with icons referred to in the Swedish title) to attempt to get some information out of him.

JOAKIM WERSÉN:
What did he say?

MARTIN BECK:
Nothing. He's lying.

JOAKIM WERSÉN:
Bring him in then!

MARTIN BECK:
I'll bring him when I think the time is right, and don't go running off to the prosecutor and getting her all worked up. We need time. We have no weapon, no fingerprints, and no circumstantial evidence to link him with the murder. And above all we don't have a motive.

JOAKIM WERSÉN:
Find one then.

GUNVALD LARSSON (who has been standing next to them):
We can't.

JOAKIM WERSÉN:
Why not?

MARTIN BECK:
Because he neither murdered his wife nor dismembered her.

We see this through Martin Beck's eyes. Joakim Wersén seems churlish and crass, but that need not mean he is wrong. And his words could be well-meant suggestions. As the superior officer, it is not unreasonable for Joakim Wersén to want information and to give good advice. This sequence, like the one in which the female officer is posted to the group, illustrates the importance of perspective. Here we see things from the point of view of the subordinate manager. Things often seem different seen from below or above, which is worth bearing in mind if you are a manager.

The security police are also Martin Beck's superiors in some way. They can close down the investigation he is working on. Or rather, they can get the prosecutor to close it down. The security police say that the Russians are involved, but Martin Beck is not certain that this is the case. The dismembered woman's missing teeth are the key.

MARTIN BECK:
Why would Russian intelligence extract the teeth from a sixty-two-year-old corpse?

Even so the prosecutor closes the investigation for security reasons. Actually she just announces the decision of the regional prosecutor, which she obviously accepts. Martin Beck and Gunvald Larsson are dismayed. In a way it is Beck that has failed. He should have been able to explain the significance of the missing teeth. Joakim Wersén corrects Martin Beck when he claims to have forgotten Arne Enberg's name.

JOAKIM WERSÉN:
Martin (first name) for God's sake!

MARTIN BECK:
Whose side are you on?

JOAKIM WERSÉN:
The book of rules (Good answer! Again . . .). From now on neither you nor your group are to spend any time on the Vassiljev case. It's been officially closed down. And that's an order! There is another case with an old lady burnt to death in her flat in Hägersten. Solve that instead.

The security police quickly come to the conclusion that Jurij Gulkov (the one who wants to marry the minister) should be deported for coercing a Swedish citizen, Olgi Vassiljev, to undertake espionage activities against Sweden. The Minister of Justice, the Foreign Minister and Rosa Andrén have only a short time to evaluate the material. When a meeting takes place the following day to discuss the deportation it turns out that the security police are lying. Martin Beck was right!!

Problems with women

Perhaps it is an exaggeration to say that Martin Beck has problems with women subordinates. In the film there is only one woman in this position. This is Lena Klingström, who works without any support from her boss. He believes that she was the source of the leak about the Decoy operation to Wersén, but then Benny Skacke confesses, somewhat queasily, in front of the autopsy table and the dismembered Nadja Vassiljev, that he is the guilty one.

BENNY SKACKE:
Why are you so negative about her (Lena Klingström)?

MARTIN BECK:
Am I?

BENNY SKACKE:
That's what it looks like.

MARTIN BECK:
Yes.

BENNY SKACKE:
I like her.

MARTIN BECK:
She leaked the Decoy operation and after that well …

BENNY SKACKE:
That wasn't Lena. It was me. Wersén dragged me into his office and wondered what the hell we were doing. He wasn't getting any information from you. At least he thought so. And I thought myself the whole operation was wrong. That it was illegal and that our boss should know what we were doing. We can't do that kind of thing …

MARTIN BECK:
Look. I'll decide what we can or can't do. Wersén is my boss. I'm yours!

BENNY SKACKE:
I'm sorry …

As if an apology would help! Of course Martin Beck getting things wrong about Lena Klingström has not improved the relationship between them. It also looks more equal when the conflict shifts so that he is dealing with another man, but despite this clarification the team still has the same problem. They will have to cope with Beck's mistrust of Benny.

By taking the way Benny Skacke by-passed him and went straight to Joakim Wersén so seriously, Martin Beck also shows us how weak he feels his middle-management position to be. He dare not just shrug his shoulders at what has happened.

MARTIN BECK:

That was incredibly stupid and disloyal. I thought I could trust you. This goes no further than you and me.

Martin Beck has a short fuse and can easily lose his temper. Here he restrains himself to stop the pathologist from being drawn into the internal conflicts in the team. It could also be a matter of saving face. Martin Beck is anxious to maintain a professional relationship to the pathologist and in his opinion; this almost certainly means that his team should present a united front.

And the cyber cop (Martin Beck's daughter's term) Lena Klingström is busy at the keyboard. She finds out when the lake froze over. Suddenly Martin Beck and his team know how long the dismembered woman has been lying in the water – and it was much longer than they thought. Given this, they soon identify a car that was scrapped after the murder rather than before. Luck or skill?

One of the myths cultivated in police films is that the truth will out in the end, in one way or another. If they had not found out about the date of the freeze, something else would have come up that they could use. In other words it does not pay to hide the truth. What should one believe – would such enormous numbers of people lie if it really did not pay? It must after all be easier to stick to one and the same version of a sequence of events. In order to lie a different version has to be constructed and then remembered so that the lie is not disclosed next time the sequence of events is discussed. As management researchers we are somewhat sceptical about the argument that lying is unproductive. Here we would like to advocate another thesis – lying often pays off. That does not mean one should lie. It is not uncommon to have to refrain from doing something that is profitable in economic terms. This is exactly the point dwelt on in the extensive literature on ethics in the business worlds. *Om företag, moral och handling* (On companies, morality and action) by Claes Gustafsson

(1988) is one of the few books worth reading in this area that we have come across.

MARTIN BECK:
Good work (to Lena Klingström). And quick. This information is important for us. (Martin Beck closes the door). I'd like to apologise. I was wrong. The leak did not come from you. I made a mistake.

LENA KLINGSTRÖM:
Do you know why?

MARTIN BECK:
No.

LENA KLINGSTRÖM:
Think about it.

Anyway – the film is over before Martin Beck can work out the answer. Problems with women is one suggestion. Does anyone have a better one? Martin Beck does not grope or hassle the woman in his group. But he also fails to give her a chance to be anything but, for him, a typical woman. And the way in which a senior position was filled in the media world in Sweden recently reminded us once again that groping need not be a barrier to a successful career. The description of the new executive we received included the information (which we were assumed to know) that he was a 'groper'. Widespread publication of one statement antagonistic to women would have put a stop to his advancement, but nobody seems to bother about what he does with his hands.

Martin Beck is more open where men are concerned. Although – what is a man? Neither his superior, Joakim Wersén, nor Benny Skacke are typical men. However, Martin Beck and Gunvald Larsson fit their individual male roles.

When Lena Klingström discovers that Arne Enberg scrapped Olgi Vassiljev's car before the lake froze over, the investigation takes a new direction. Not until now has there been a villain. Now the whole team is ready to listen. They are no longer deaf. Just a bit hard of hearing when the useful input comes from a woman. Lena Klingström provides the opening but it is Martin Beck that puts the puzzle together.

The boss knows best

Gunvald Larsson closes the door and in the next scene he and Martin Beck are driving in the rain. At Olgi Vassiljev's home the walls are full of icons.

MARTIN BECK:
A pretty expensive hobby – isn't it?

Martin Beck spots a bullet hole through one icon and nods to Gunvald Larsson. He looks and feels. The boss leads and allocates the work. It was Martin Beck that found the hole and gave Gunvald the job of inspecting it more closely.

MARTIN BECK:
How many have you got?

OLGI VASSILJEV:
I don't know.

Martin Beck accepts a plate of soup (borscht) on Gunvald's behalf and Olgi Vassiljev takes him out to the fridge. While they are fixing the soup, Martin Beck twists the icons round to find where the bullet went through the wall. He finds the entry hole behind the Holy Paraskeva. Gunvald Larsson had the chance to look for the bullet hole when he saw that it was not behind the damaged icon, but the fact remains – he failed to do so. On the other hand it was Gunvald who knew that the icon depicted the Holy Paraskeva. This may be a coincidence, but it is common knowledge that Paraskeva was dismembered and beheaded by the Roman Emperor Diocletian in 300 A.D.

The boss provides the thinking. And the emotions. Martin Beck consoles Vassiljev when he learns that the dismembered woman is his wife. Gunvald Larsson blunders along. He is incapable of comforting anyone.

Gunvald Larsson is interesting. He does the heavy work. When he and Martin Beck get to an apartment, Beck rings the bell and tries the doorknob. Gunvald breaks the door down. He is forceful and his speech is full of prejudice. It is surprising when Gunvald identifies the motif of the icon with the bullet hole and when he translates Russian to Swedish without difficulty. Gunvald Larsson obviously does not want to be a boss. Attitude is more important. A typical Stockholmer* (Waldersten 2002).

* People living in Stockholm have a reputation of having an attitude and are not always considered to be nice.

The boss's private life

Martin Beck has only a little free time and not much of a private life. He is first and foremost a policeman and his wife, Kerstin, left him because he was always working. At least so his neighbour says. Even so Martin Beck does not seem unhappy. Insofar as one can be certain in this respect. In *The Profit*, his excellent anthology of wise aphorisms, Kehlog Albran hits the nail on the head like this.

> If someone should find a wallet containing a boiled potato, a tooth, and a laundry ticket, should he be considered lucky? (Albran 1974, p. 89)

Martin Beck spends what free time he has renovating old pocket watches and tidying his apartment. He does not seem dissatisfied while he is doing it. He also takes the odd Calvados, which, in our experience, raises the level of contentment.

Martin Beck has a daughter (Inger), just beginning life as an adult, who sometimes comes to see him. She wants him to go with her to look at an apartment (on Krukmakargatan in Stockholm), and he actually finds the time to do so. When they smile and exchange glances we can see that Martin Beck has a good relationship with his daughter.

Things are different with his son, Micke Sjögren. Martin Beck and his mother divorced when Micke was two. Martin Beck moved to Stockholm leaving the two of them in Malmö. Martin Beck has no contact with his son and Inger does not even know she has a half-brother. We learn in passing that his son is involved in an amphetamine case that has connections with Poland and, unless our memory fails us, we learn more about this in a later film.

Martin Beck also spends a little time with his neighbour, somewhat reluctantly. This is the sort of neighbour that a lot of people would find difficult. His reluctance is not surprising, in other words, but in this case it is not due to the neighbour's behaviour. Instead we get the impression that Martin Beck does not want to mix with any neighbours at all. He wants to work, meet his daughter occasionally and spend what little time is left on his own.

Policemen in films and television series are not infrequently divorced, have problems with their children and are self-willed, as can be seen from the following introduction of the main character in the detective series about Tanner.

> Tanner is an extremely self-willed policeman who solves his cases in his own special way: he often passes the time inline skating at high speeds

on the streets and pavements of London: he drinks hard, chain-smokes and is a workaholic. He has – obviously – been divorced for a few years and he realises that he is not the world's best father for his son, even though he tries. (*Dagens Nyheter*, TV-guide August 1–7, 2001, p. 3)

The boss's actions

Martin Beck considers that he is excellent and praises himself. 'I said the man with the icons was interesting.' If you only have two choices, you should be right at times ... But others praise him as well.

Martin Beck makes decisions in the group. When, after it has turned out that the man with the icons is lying about the time of his wife's disappearance, Gunvald Larsson asks: 'Who's going?' Martin Beck's answers: 'Nobody. Yet. He won't run away. Have him trailed and find out if he made that report ...' He also gives orders. With all his weight behind them '... about harassment three years ago. Now, Gunvald.' Here Martin Beck resembles his own boss. 'NOW! Gunvald' – it did not have to be put that clearly.

When Gunvald Larsson interrogates a bit too energetically, Martin Beck merely raises a finger. That shuts Gunvald up. A gesture is enough. On the whole Beck and Gunvald Larsson understand each other well. They take turns in asking questions and each knows what the other is getting at. They help each other.

But Martin Beck can lie as well, or use the truth economically. Otherwise how can one understand his reaction when Benny (the leak) Skacke is offered a special assignment (via Joakim Wersén) with fewer murders and more entertainment? Martin Beck tells Benny that he should seize the chance to see more of Europe. He says that Benny is good at surveillance and his unit will always be there for him, Beck at least. Martin Beck also takes on the task of telling everyone else about Benny's new assignment.

Informal boss

Benny Skacke is really hesitant about continuing the investigation when it has been closed down. This is a serious breach of discipline, persecution, gross abuse of power and can lead to two years in prison. He is right! What would happen if every detective took the law into his own hands?

Images of heroism like this always have two sides to them. A lot of people support civil disobedience and protest against majority decisions. But when youths who have first shaved their heads and then put on boots that are far too solid for city streets start protesting, we do not appreciate their disobedience. We want the frank opinions of our staff and their commitment to their work. But we stop enjoying it when they start getting in touch with the media and necessary processes of change encounter internal opposition. Martin Beck gains our sympathy despite the pressure placed on an ordinary citizen. The explanation is that he solves the case. But what if he was unable to …?

Here you can ask if things are that simple. Does success always lead to forgiveness and should we, if that is the case, expect to be successful every time? The scandals in the public sector that attract the headlines and those that are concealed in the private sector are rarely linked to the success of the undertaking (cf. Johansson 2002). Visits are not made to strip clubs to improve a local authority's finances or credit cards misused to reduce unemployment. It is more a matter of idiocy than seizing opportunities. On the other hand, paying wages black, speculating beyond the set limits and disregarding procurement regulations is probably resorted to in much the same way as Martin Beck bends the rules here. There are many examples to show that success does not provide absolution. And if it did, the absolution would merely be temporary. The criteria of success change and old corpses are then exhumed.

Martin Beck intends to go on with the case but he renounces his official position as the boss. The group goes behind Joakim Wersén's back and continues its work, even though the investigation has been closed.

Somebody rips the teeth out of a corpse and Arne Enberg strides across cemeteries at night. Gunvald Larsson keeps his eyes open. Lena Klingström finds some gold fillings under a candelabra in the chapel. We begin to understand how the film will end.

When things hot up Martin Beck throws his weight about. Gunvald Larsson points out: 'For someone who's not in charge you sound very commanding.' This tells us something about informality and also how difficult it is to change leadership style. But a specific leadership style should not be regarded as an innate handicap. It is possible to develop. Although this takes more than the mere announcement of a change.

A middle manager among middle managers

Just as Olgi Vassiljev and his colleague at the crematorium are about to incinerate the murderer and butcher Arne Enberg, Martin Beck and Gunvald Larsson arrive to save him. Both Vassiljev and Enberg are talkative and everything becomes crystal clear. And while he is about, Martin Beck discloses the security service plot against Juri Gulkov to the minister. Embarrassing for the security branch.

That evening Martin Beck is standing on his balcony. His peculiar neighbour comes out on to his balcony and asks him: 'Done anything useful then?' Again, all Beck's only response is to gaze into space. Nevertheless there is nothing odd about the question – do middle managers do anything useful?

For some time middle managers have been under threat – threat of extinction. Lean production as it is called is what everyone is looking for. The number of employees and staff directly on the payroll must be reduced to an absolute minimum. Everything unrelated to the core (which is where production is assumed to take place) is questioned. A short throughput time for products is a key concept. A much discussed industrial application can be found for instance in ABB's T50 programme.

When organisations are being slimmed to fit in with current fashion, focus is not placed on the top or the bottom but rather in the middle. That's where you find the millstones, petty tyrants, bureaucrats and the unwanted fat. The book *Res pyramiderna* (Re-raise the pyramids, Ohlsson and Rombach 1998) problematises this image of the unnecessary middle managers. Before eliminating them we should find out what use they have. Martin Beck does not answer his neighbour. Perhaps it is because he does not want to be offered one of his neighbour's rough-and-ready drinks, or because Martin Beck should have no doubts about his own usefulness.

In Beck we learn that middle managers are competent, informed and considerate. He knows what to do and how to do it, gets on with things and protects his subordinates. Middle managers work a lot and do not mind boundaries being crossed. On the other hand they do not have much of a private life.

What strikes us is that the image of Martin Beck is fairly typical of a male film and television detective. Helen Mirren's Superintendent Tennison would fit in, even if she is a woman. In Sweden this is not surprising as Sjöwall-Wahlöö's Beck character has largely shaped the image of the detective and policeman, but we recognise the same kind of characters in the foreign detective series we have watched through the years. And many readers have undoubtedly come across the same kind of character in numerous detective novels. All the time we are being fed with this image of the middle manager and at the same time we believe that middle managers are unnecessary. Not Martin Beck and the other detectives – but middle managers in general.

In the public sector this reduction of the middle management level can be explained by the desire to create legitimacy. In a medium-sized local authority in central Sweden that we studied (Rombach 1997), as was the case elsewhere, cuts were required in various areas during the 1990s. There it was argued no cuts could be made in education or child care, for instance, if it could not be demonstrated at the same time that 'all the money was being spent on running costs'. No resources were being devoted to unnecessary analytical staff or 'other surplus fat': this would have been unacceptable to the taxpayers. The argument is an interesting one, as it hardly suggests that the main justification for levelling out organisations can be found in the savings to be made by eliminating the middle levels. Instead it is implies that getting rid of them helps to legitimise cuts in operational expenditure as well.

One explanation for the reduction in the number of middle managers is that they get in the way of the centralisation that is taking place. Under cover of the levelling-out theory, a shift of power upwards is taking place. Fewer levels in the hierarchy is the method. Then there is nothing to obstruct the signals on their way from the top to the bottom of the pyramid. At the same time levelling out also means that signals from the bottom do not reach the top as easily. If you have a large enough number of employees it seems pathetic to even try to bother about what each and every one of them has to offer.

If you are looking for another explanation for the threat to the position of the middle managers, it seems easy to heap the blame on them as well. They have been remarkably bad at explaining how they benefit their organisations. Parallels can be drawn with the personnel departments, which historically have also found it difficult to define their contribution to an organisation. Now that human capital is in focus, for the moment they need not bother about this.

Where the threat to middle managers is concerned, there is a parallel in the classic *Power, Innovation, and Problem-Solving in Personnel Management* (1978), in which Karen Legge deals with the reasons for the weak position of the personnel departments. The basic problem, in her view, is the link between personnel administrative measures and fulfilment of a company's goals. Karen Legge identifies three reasons behind the deficiencies in this link.

1. Personnel departments deal with human resources that are part of the input to processes and not the company's output.

2. Input from the personnel departments contributes to the output of units. These units take the credit for any successes.

3. All managers are involved in personnel administration. In other words, the personnel department is not alone in taking personnel administrative measures.

Karen Legge's scenario means that personnel departments can choose between two strategies to achieve success. They can strive to change the company's objectives so that good personnel maintenance, in its widest sense, becomes a goal, which is exactly what has happened since she wrote her book. The more difficult alternative is to make the links between personnel administrative measures and fulfilment of goals more explicit. Our point here is that middle managers should, as a group under threat, make the same analysis and take inspiration from its conclusions.

But hot-headed valour and our eulogies of middle managers should not lead us to forget that Joakim Wersén is a middle manager as well. His position places him at a slightly higher managerial level than Beck and somewhat closer to the organisation's waist. The investigation would have made much more progress and been more enjoyable on the whole if Joakim Wersén had not been on the payroll. Once again reality casts its shadow over what is otherwise relatively pleasant and pretty neat theorising. And keep in mind that every manager is a middle manager – even the Pope.

Allocating tasks

Martin Beck makes sure that things get done. The villain ends up behind bars in film after film. Managers are often judged in terms of what they succeed in achieving. Visions and strategies are all very well – but were any cars produced? The film may not give any instructions about how to manage but does give a great deal of food for thought.

Luck matters

It was up to Martin Beck to allocate the tasks to the team. How he did so, often did not matter very much. For the sake of the plot, initially the best thing was for him to take on Vassiljev himself. This is an exception. Normally the throw of a dice would have been able to decide. But those who have read *The Dice Man* by Luke Rhinehart (1971) know that this method has major disadvantages in the long run.

Be that as it may, luck plays a remarkably large role in Martin Beck's successes. If the water level had not sunk there would have been no case that could be solved successfully. And if the golden fillings had not been such a temptation, the security police could have been right. There are other examples. Luck appears to be an important characteristic for a manager. Now, it is in fact the case that there is no such thing as luck. Luck is rather what is left when everything is explained in terms of cause and effect, however hard you try. Even so, luck is an important quality for managers. There is no harm in other members of the team attributing what happens to the boss's luck, as it means they are giving her or him the credit for things turning out well.

A lot has been written about the limited extent of the real influence that bosses have. One classic about the relationship between the politicians we expect to run things and public officials with more power than we would like to believe is *Beslut och handling* (Decisions and Actions) by Nils Brunsson and Sten Jönsson from 1979. You find more or less the same ideas in Brunsson's *The Organization of Hypocrisy* (1989). The limited influence of managers does not obviously mean that their success is a matter of luck. From the boss's perspective success is good luck and setbacks bad luck. What sustains their own self-image is usually that they take credit for controlling the process or (when this is too incredible) the cultural and environmental influences that explain the success.

Throwing your weight about

Martin Beck gives a lot of orders – he clearly throws his weight about. The question is whether this is typical of middle managers and if it is positive. It is difficult to explain successes with this leadership style. The question is also if it is what it seems to be. Studies of police procedures (for instance Ekman 1999 and Ivarsson Westerberg 2004) show that policemen use a lot of jargon. Outsiders may perhaps interpret it more literally than subordinates do. And there is little scope in the film for the chat that is so important in management if it is not to lose pace.

We and others who have studied powerful professional groups in the health service (Rombach 1990) and in financial departments (Solli 1999), for instance, have found that there is only a limited need of management. When everyone in the group is good at their job, when they all know what should be done and how much is repetitive, albeit with some variation, no management is asked for. This does not eliminate the possibility of rational action by those who manage. What may appear to be one stage of a management and decision-making chain can instead be seen as an attempt to attain some joint action (Brunsson 1981). When Martin Beck gives an order it is a signal that it is time to get going and make progress – everyone already knows how and with what.

Discussion is taking place about whether the kind of management appreciated by subordinates varies from country to country and therefore between cultures. Martin Beck's leadership style could be typically Swedish. Although we have made no systematic comparisons, we can note that his leadership style differs from those we have seen in several English and German detective series on television through the years. In her PhD thesis *The License to Lead* Lena Zander (1997) demonstrates that preferences differ from country to country (cf. Jönsson 2004). This supports us therefore. The credibility of the analysis declines considerably however when she also believes that she can show that there are no differences where preferences in the different countries are concerned. We all know (nearly all of us!) that the differences exist, but she cannot see them with the help of her crude analytical tools. To provide an example of the wealth of support for the thesis on differences that can be found in the literature we can again refer to Jönsson (2004).

Do not obey the decisions of superiors, regulations or the law

In view of the many explicit orders that Martin Beck gives, it is surprising that he himself will not accept the same kind of management. It is normal for bosses to manage in the way in which they are managed. The explanation is that this reduces their risk of failure. It also sets a good example and enables measures to be explained simply to subordinates. In our study of management by objectives, managers admittedly abandoned this pattern with apparent success (see Rombach 1991). There they did what the executive management wanted – they managed by objectives without being managed by objectives themselves. In Martin Beck's case things are different. He clearly disobeys orders and even adopts unlawful methods. The question is what managers can learn from this.

The management situation may explain why Martin Beck seems to dislike being managed in the way he manages others. Throwing his weight about appears to be a good way of leading the group in this context. In this management situation direction is accepted and functional. Managing the group requires military straightforwardness. When a boss is dealing with subordinates individually, the situation is different. Then another, more egalitarian, form of management is needed.

Working all the time

Martin Beck has 'worked away his family' as seasoned hardened colleagues in the consultancy business would put it. They are not at all unheeding or unaware of the problem but there is little they can do about it. The voluntary singles are not particularly sagacious but they do have more time for their work.

The question is whether being a manager has to mean working all the time. We have no ready answer. Many years in our business has taught us that spending a lot of time at work does not necessarily correlate with major success; 'luckily' you might say.

CHAPTER 6

Nixon – sacrificing the man in charge

There are not many people who want to be like Richard Milhous Nixon. At least not just after seeing Oliver Stone's film *Nixon* from 1995 with Anthony Hopkins in the leading role. Even so Nixon is not portrayed as stupid, wicked or a failure but rather as unhappy with no chance of being happy. The story presented on the surface of the film is highly suitable for an analysis of leaders in films. *Nixon* demonstrates more aspects of leadership than most other films we know. The film about Richard Nixon shows us a remarkable leader.

The end first

According to its preface the film is a dramatic interpretation of events and characters. This interpretation is based on publicly available material with added material from sources that are not as reliable. The events have also been compressed and sheer hypotheses inserted. The milestones in Nixon's life are based on reality, between them a drama is enacted.

The story begins with what every television viewer and cinemagoer knows led to Nixon's fall, the Watergate break-in. It takes place and the perpetrators are caught. The next scene shifts us eighteen months forward, to 1973.

We hear thunder and it is raining. General Haig arrives at the White House, while we hear a radio announcer saying that the Watergate burglars have been sentenced to up to forty years in prison and that the White House is still denying any involvement. One radio voice succeeds another and it is implied more and more that the White House is involved, in spite of everything. In the middle of it all, the Vice President, Spiro Agnew, resigns after accusations of tax fraud.

Alexander Haig turns out to be on the way to a meeting with Nixon. At that meeting Haig hands over the tape that was missing at the trial. Nixon knows that his career will soon end. Before Haig leaves he says: 'Hey Al, men in your profession give'm a pistol and then leave the room. I don't have a pistol.'

Nixon, who is not particularly technical, finally gets the tape recorder to start and listens on his own to the recording from the Oval Room. As the tape is playing the viewers are shifted back in time to the Oval Room. The recording is about Nixon learning at an early stage what the break-in was really about. He was not really very interested and wanted instead to go to a meeting with Henry Kissinger, but as he realised his staff had something unpleasant to tell him he stayed.

It turns out that the burglar, Howard Hunt, was on the White House payroll. Hunt has been taking part for a long time in quite a lot of doubtful activities, to say the least, in Nixon's periphery. Nixon says: 'You open up that scab you will uncover a lot of pus', and wants Hunt's silence to be bought. Nixon gives a series of orders about how to make the payments and how the FBI and the CIA are to be misled. Back to Nixon listening to the tape alone. He does not feel well and is unable to open a package of pills. It ends with the jar emptying itself – on the floor.

The victor loses

The next scene shows the first television debate before a presidential election in the USA. It takes place between an elegant John Fitzgerald Kennedy and a sweating, pasty Nixon. Nixon wins the debate. But he does not win the confidence of the voters. Nixon lost the 1960 election by a handful of votes. He won more than 34 million votes, only a few hundred thousand less than Kennedy. There is a lot to suggest that Kennedy's side rigged the election.

Be that as it may, Nixon loses the election. His staff has masses of explanations of why he did not win. Nixon's explanation is that Kennedy was served everything on a silver plate by his father while everyone has always mocked Nixon. Wrong clothes, wrong schools, and wrong family. At this moment of defeat Nixon identifies with his father – a failure who died without a cent in the bank because he was honest.

Nixon grew up with his mother and father and four brothers and sisters. They owned a shop in which the entire family worked more or less. Richard regarded his mother as a saint. His father struggled all his life without being defeated by it in any way. Oliver Stone returns frequently to Nixon's childhood experiences.

When Nixon lost against Kennedy he made an agreement with his wife to give up politics. This agreement did not stop him, however, from running for governor in California two years later. He lost that election as well. Pat Nixon (played by Joan Allen who really looks like the original) is fed up with her husband's political career by this stage. She thinks that his work is not doing the children any good: 'The girls ... They only know you from television anyway', even a father can be known by fiction! Not only is his career harming his relationship with Pat but also it is directly destructive for Nixon himself. Pat wants a divorce. Then Nixon shows us what a brilliant rhetorician he is. He makes a fantastic speech of atonement and promises to renounce politics. He announces this at a press conference.

As someone in the media world believed that this marked Nixon's exit, a political obituary is published in the form of a television documentary. Nixon was a small-town lawyer who was elected to the House of Representatives at the age of thirty-three. At thirty-five he became a senator. He was presented as a war veteran. He took his war experiences with him into politics – he did not have opponents, only enemies.

Vice-president

Nixon became a leading figure in the House Unamerican Activity Committee, cross-examining, for instance, trade unionists and Hollywood celebrities. It was the Alger Hiss affair that really established Nixon's name. Alger Hiss – who was one of President Franklin Delano Roosevelt's intimates – was a diplomat accused of espionage by the media. Nixon was able to ensure Hiss's conviction, not for espionage but for perjury. According to the documentary, some thought Nixon was a hero, others that he was merely interested in his own reputation. He was definitely not sympathetic.

Nixon began to attack both previous and contemporary Democratic presidents, not least for their foreign policy. In 1952 he became Dwight D. Eisenhower's running mate as candidate for the vice-presidency. In what became known as the Checkers Crisis, Nixon was accused of concealing a secret slush fund. His response was the unusual manoeuvre of going on television to account for all his earnings. This list included the family's house, car, Pat's coat and something that was to become historic – a gift from a businessman in Texas. This turned out to be a cocker spaniel puppy, which was given the name of Checkers.

In the documentary the voice-over says that Nixon's television appearance in connection with the Checkers Crisis was brazen, manipulative but enormously successful. Now, more than fifty years later, the speech appears instead to be pathetic. Rhetoric is good if it is effective, which makes it dependent on time and context. In other words it does not have to endure. In theory we find it difficult to support the idea of a distinction between classical rhetoric and 'new rhetoric' (see for instance Perelman 1990). This artificial differentiation merely means that simple things become complicated. All of the methods used by Nixon to convince can be found in the arsenal of devices provided by classical rhetoric (see for instance Burke 1950).

Nixon was vice-president during both of Eisenhower's terms of office. The report concludes with the statement that Nixon lost against Kennedy in the Presidential election in 1960 and against Pat Brown for the election to governor in 1962.

A second attempt

It is not long before Nixon is hankering after politics again. He says that he misses making entrances, the actual spectacle. Things look hopeless. Who can beat Kennedy? Nixon believes it is impossible. But then Kennedy's life comes to an end.

Nixon was unmistakeably annoyed at not being invited to Kennedy's funeral and his explanation was that both Bobby and Teddy Kennedy hated him. Losing a brother was something that Nixon was familiar with. Nixon remembers when his younger brother died of a painful illness and the scene is enacted before us in the film.

The Vietnam war escalates under the presidency of Lyndon B. Johnson. Nixon is genuinely surprised when Johnson announces that he is not running for re-election. This makes it possible for Nixon to become a candidate himself, successfully. In the film he finds it easier to be nominated and elected as candidate than to convince Pat that running for the presidency is good for both of them. One of his staff values her participation as worth between five to six million votes. In the end Nixon manages to convince Pat that her backing would make him happy and she promises to support him.

The head of the FBI J. Edgar Hoover (who would definitely not have approved of being portrayed by Bob Hoskins) plays an increasingly important role and is asked to comment on a television debate in which Nixon participates. What Hoover has to say about Nixon is definitely not friendly. Finally Hoover gets fed up and says that the television has to be switched off. He wants to meet Nixon, as he is supposed to have said that Hoover had too much power.

Faced with a choice of Bobby Kennedy or Richard Nixon, Hoover chooses Nixon as the lesser of the two evils. The meeting with Nixon is to enable Hoover to remind him that he needs the FBI more than the FBI needs him. The meeting takes place at the Santa Anita racetrack. Hoover has obviously backed the right horse even though, very unusually, the favourite stumbles in the final straight.

Hoover takes Johnny Rosselli with him, a dubious character who can normally be found in Havana. Nixon had met him many years earlier at a club that is definitely not appropriate for a presidential candidate. Hoover has the tact to send Rosselli away before Nixon walks up to him. He then tells Nixon that it is because he does not want to discredit him. Nixon denies ever meeting Rosselli but they both know that he has.

Nixon chats to Hoover as if he was a close friend and wants all kinds of information about his opponent Bobby Kennedy. To add interest to the film it is said in passing that someone should 'shoot the son of a bitch'. In this context it does not seem likely that Nixon really would have backed this up to the hilt. The conversation finishes with Nixon and Hoover agreeing to support each other. Nixon also realises that the reason for the meeting was that Hoover wanted to warn him: the FBI is not something to play with – or rather against.

Dubious actions

The film continues to shift in time and place. Suddenly the scenario moves to Nixon's final days as president. In one scene he tells one of his closest associates that Johnny Rosselli arranged the contacts between the White House and the Mafia in the attempted assassination of Fidel Castro. Nixon dealt with the entire thing as vice-president, in other words at one time they had been close to each other. Others were also involved, among them the Watergate burglars. Quite a scandal! As Nixon says this in the Oval Room, it is all recorded on tape.

When John Kennedy got to hear about the plan to kill Castro after the attempt failed, he gave Nixon a real dressing down. The two never spoke to each other again. When Nixon reflects over everything he realises that death has paved the way for him. John Kennedy, Bobby Kennedy, the Vietnam war and even the death of Nixon's elder brother are the explanation of his success.

Nixon's elder brother Harold was to have gone on to study, but not Richard. The family only had enough money to pay for one son to go to university. As his brother died just before he was to start studying, Nixon got his place at university. If he had not studied law, it would have been difficult for him to reach the White House. A bad conscience can come from less.

One major problem for Nixon was the enormous number of leaks to the press from his administration. On one occasion a whole sheaf of secret documents were published that showed that the President had lied on a number of points about the Vietnam war. The most enraged was Kissinger, who claimed that it was impossible to conduct foreign policy with leaks like that. The whole thing ended with Nixon approving the establishment of an intelligence service in the White House whose task would be to plug the leaks. He realised this was unlawful, but knew that many presidents had adopted the same approach. Kissinger and Nixon advocated powerful measures to stop the leaks.

Good at rhetoric

Back to Nixon's nomination at the Republican Convention in 1968. The mood was highly jubilant and Nixon gave a rabble-rousing speech when he accepted the Republican nomination for President. The extract below shows his mastery of rhetoric.

RICHARD NIXON:

> When the strongest nation in the world can be tied down for four years in a war in Vietnam with no end in sight, when the richest nation in the world can't manage its own economy, when the nation with the greatest tradition of the rule of law is plagued by unprecedented lawlessness, when a nation that has been known for a century for equality of opportunity is torn by unprecedented racial violence, and when the president of the United States cannot travel abroad or to any major city at home without fear of a hostile demonstration – then it is time for new leadership for the United States of America.
>
> As we look at America, we see cities enveloped in smoke and flame. Millions of Americans cry out in anguish: Did we come all the way for this? Did American boys die in Normandy and in Valley Forge for this?
>
> I pledge to you that the current way of violence will not be the way of the future.
>
> Let us begin by committing ourselves to the truth, to find the truth, to speak the truth and to live the truth.
>
> A new voice has been heard across America today. It is not the voice of the protest groups or the shouters. It is the quiet voice of the majority of Americans, who have been forgotten, the non-shouters,

> the non-demonstrators. They're good people; they work hard and they save and they pay their taxes.
>
> And who are they? Let me tell you who they are. They are in this audience by the thousands. They are the white Americans, and black Americans, Mexican Americans and Italian Americans; they're the great silent majority.
>
> And they have become angry, finally. Angry not with hate, but angry, my Friends, because they love America. And they don't like what happened with America these last four years.

The speech was popular and it made an impact. There was great deal of elation at the convention. Otherwise we can see that the speech in the film is shorter and more impressive than the one that Nixon really gave in August 1968.

Contact with reality

As the war in Southeast Asia escalated the protests became more frequent and more widespread. The student revolts which ended with a number of casualties were discomfiting, to say the least, for Nixon. He tried to shrug them off as unimportant but was noticeably depressed when he did not need to show how decisive he could be. At times he tried to explain the criticism by saying that there were communist interests behind the revolts. But he could also see the tragedy when so many young men were dying in the war. One member of his staff suggested that he should express his sympathy to their next-of-kin. Nixon's response was: 'I'd love to. But Nixon can't.' He often refers to himself in the third person.

Nixon was one of the first to realise that the USA could not win the Vietnam war. Even so he believed that the war could be exploited to drive a wedge between various communist interests. Together with Kissinger he began to probe the possibilities of a rapprochement with China. The strategy was to negotiate with the Soviet Union and China separately – triangle diplomacy as it was called. Nixon claimed that he could approach China as he had demonstrated in both word and deed his opposition to communists.

The film continues and Nixon begins to talk to 'ordinary folk' more and more to find out what is going on. Manolo, who works in the White House kitchen, has to explain one night why everyone wept when Kennedy died.

On another night Nixon visits the Colosseum, wanting to talk to Abe Lincoln. When Nixon's limousine slowly glides up to the monument he sees a horde of sleeping young people around it. Instead of a 'chat' with Abe, a group of young people come up to Nixon. He introduces himself as

Dick Nixon and begins to talk about football with one of the young men. They are interrupted by a woman saying that they were not there to talk about football. Nixon can understand.

Nixon puts it to them: 'Probably most of you think I am a real asshole … I know that. I understand how you feel. I want peace too, but peace with honor.' The woman wonders what that is and Nixon answers: 'You can't have peace without a price. Sometimes you have to be willing to fight for peace – sometimes to die.' When his security men arrive the woman continues to ask why Nixon has not put an end to the war.

RICHARD NIXON:

Change always comes slowly. I pulled out more than half the troops, I tried to cut the military budget for the first time in 30 years, and I want a volunteer army. It's also a question of American credibility. Our position in the world.

WOMAN (who will not back down but wants an answer, finally answers herself):

You can't stop it, can you? Even if you wanted too. Because it's not you, it is the system. The system won't let you stop it … you are powerless!

RICHARD NIXON (who does not want to agree with her):

No, no I'm not powerless … I believe I can control the system. Maybe not totally, but tame it enough to make it do some good.

The woman thinks it sounds as if he was talking about a wild animal, and a reflective Nixon agrees with her. Finally he leaves the Colosseum with his bodyguards. Nixon is impressed by the young woman who is only nineteen but understands what it has taken him twenty-five years to work out – that it is a question of wild animals in the form of the 'CIA, the mafia, those Wall Street bastards'.

Successes and problems

Nixon accomplished the impossible when he started diplomatic cooperation with China and later also visited the country. He says to Mao Zedong (Tse-tung): 'You look very good Mr. Chairman.' Mao's answer is: 'Looks can be deceptive.' Nixon goes on to say: 'We know what a risk you are taking inviting us here.' Mao shrugs it all off by saying: 'I am too old to be afraid of what anyone thinks.' Mao and Nixon reach agreement that they are friends as they both see the Russians and the North Vietnamese as enemies. Mao analyses Nixon's role: 'You are as evil as I am. We are the new emperors. We are both from poor families. Others pay to feed the hunger in us. In my case, millions of reactionaries. In your case, millions of Vietnamese.'

On the flight back from China the journalists (who are flying with the president in his plane) ask him to join them. Nixon is prepared for swingeing criticism but receives standing ovations instead. This seems to be one of Nixon's few moments of happiness as a leader.

When Nixon is under great pressure from the oil magnates, whom we can assume provided much of the funding for his campaigns, he resists them easily. He does so knowing that they do not have much of a choice, all the alternatives to Nixon are much worse for them.

The 1972 election was a walkover for Nixon. His victory is the second largest in America's history. This although the Watergate scandal is already under way. At the same time the scandal is attracting more and more attention and is only eclipsed by the peace in Vietnam. The war comes to an end but in the film the press only show increasing interest in Watergate. Nixon has to pay larger and larger sums to John Mitchell to buy his silence. Finally he tries a different strategy and makes as much as possible public, at the same time getting rid of most of his staff. The change means that Nixon is increasingly isolated. Even Pat no longer endorses his actions. This is at a time when a great deal is happening. Trials, hearings, a state visit by Leonid Brezhnev with discussion of the SALT agreement, and more. Nixon has a lot to keep track of.

At one trial it is disclosed that everything said in the Oval Room was recorded on tape. And everything means everything, even conversations between members of his family.

Resignation

The tempo of the film changes and most of what we have already seen is repeated in fragments and finishes with Nixon ending up in hospital. He has pneumonia, caused by a virus. We did say he was burnt out until we heard the Swedish stress doctor Thomas Danielsson. He advocates the reasonable thesis that it is all a question of degrees of exhaustion. Burnout is very unusual. Thomas Danielsson would certainly claim that the job of president of the United States is the kind that makes you a little more susceptible to viruses. Not much to make a fuss about. And sure enough, Nixon soon recovers.

Back at work, Nixon meets a prosecutor who demands access to nine of the recorded tapes. Nixon refuses. He claims that the tapes are his private property. At the same time Congress is on the warpath and demanding impeachment on four counts. These are abuse of his powers, obstructing justice, refusing to abide by the decisions of Congress and bombing Cambodia. Nixon's response is to sack the prosecutor and a whole bunch of people. Things merely become more confused and desperate around Nixon. When on television he solemnly declares that he knew nothing about the blackout, Kissinger's comment is: 'I think I am going to throw up. Can you imagine what this man would have been, had he ever been loved? It's a tragedy because he had greatness in his grasp …'

However much Nixon tries to turn both himself and his surroundings upside down and inside out, his resignation becomes inevitable. The last conversation he has before he signs the resignation documents on August 9, 1974, is with Kissinger, who consoles him by saying: 'History will treat you far more kindly than your contemporaries.' They pray together before Kissinger leaves.

On his way to submit his resignation with Al (General Haig) and Kissinger, Nixon says that all leaders have to be sacrificed in the end: 'They needed someone to sacrifice something … I am that sacrifice.' His wife meets him in the corridor. It is night and she is wearing a dressing gown. She listens and consoles him.

RICHARD NIXON:

I'm so afraid. It is darkness out there. I would always see where I was going. But it's dark out there. I have always been afraid of the dark.

And then it is time for the solemn speech of resignation.

RICHARD NIXON:

There are many fine careers. This country needs good farmers, good businessmen, good plumbers, good carpenters. I remember my old man. I think they would call him sort of a little man, a common man. He didn't consider himself that way. You know what he was? He was a streetcar motorman at first. Then he was a farmer. Then he had a lemon ranch. It was the poorest lemon ranch in California, I can assure you. He sold it before they found oil. Then he was a grocer. But he was a great man because he did his job. And every job counts up to the hill regardless of what happens.

Nobody will ever write a book, probably, about my mother. Well, I guess all of you would say this about your mother. My mother was a saint. When, I think of her, two boys dying of tuberculosis, and seeing each of them die. And when they die … Yes, she will have no books written about her, but she was a saint.

Now, however, we look to the future. I remember something

Theodore Roosevelt wrote when his first wife died in his twenties. And he thought that all light had gone from his life forever, but he went on. He not only became president, but as an ex-president he served his country always on the arena; impassionate, strong, sometimes right, and sometimes wrong, but he was a man. As I leave as an example I think all of us should remember.

We think sometimes when things happen that they don't go the right way. We think that when someone dear to us dies, when we lose an election or when we suffer a defeat, that all is ended. Not true. It is only the beginning, always, because the greatness comes not when things go always good for you. But greatness comes when you are really tested. When you take some knocks, some disappointments, when sadness comes. Because only if you have been in the deepest valley will you even know how magnificent it is to be on the highest mountain. So, I say to you on this occasion: we leave proud of the people who have stood by us, worked for us, and served this government and this country. We want you to continue to serve the government if that is what you wish. Remember: always give your best. Never get discouraged. Never be petty, and always remember others may hate you. But those who hate you don't win unless you hate them. And then you destroy yourself. So we leave with high hopes, good spirits, and deep humility. And I say to each and every one of you: not only will we always remember you, but you will always be in our hearts, you will be in our prayers. And only then you will find what we Quakers call 'peace at the center'.

Richard Nixon was buried and honoured by the presence of five presidents on April 26, 1994. A form of redress, although much too late for those who do not believe in a sequel that will take over where episode one finished – *Nixon II*. Opinions are divided on whether it was right or not to make amends to Nixon. The film is relatively positive. The opposite opinion can be found, for instance, in a book called *The Arrogance of Power* by Anthony Summers (2000). This is unduly long and hopelessly gossipy, but still not a totally unreadable book that presents the bad sides that Nixon could be considered to have had.

The film about Nixon focuses on many different aspects of what leadership involves. In the eyes of many, Nixon is primarily an example of a failed leader. Paradoxically enough he succeeded in everything he aimed for. From that paradox – failing and succeeding at the same time – the theme of responsibility materialises as well as a theme that touches on the question of why people become leaders even though they do not enjoy it. Both themes in their turn have a number of closely related sub-themes.

Nixon was forced to take his responsibility

Responsibility is an area that frequently receives attention in classical administrative theory. Searching a library database using the terms 'responsibility' and 'responsible' will yield a large number of hits. In our field we find good old familiar titles like Henri Fayol's *General and Industrial Management* from 1916. His concept of responsibility is moralistic. Responsible individuals must behave honourably, but responsibility is also linked to power. In 1938, in his book *The Functions of the Executive* Chester Barnard suggests that responsibility involves agreement between moral principles and actions. And in *Administrative Behavior* from 1947 Herbert Simon writes as follows:

> Responsibility. Writers on the political and legal aspects of authority have emphasized that a primary function of organization is to enforce the conformity of the individual to norms laid down by the group, or by its authority-wielding members. (Simon 1947/1997, p. 9)

So we have named the same classical titles as Nils Brunsson (1990), whose own observations on responsibility are interesting. Where developments after the Second World War are concerned, Ulla Johansson asserts in her PhD thesis (1998, p. 61) that the concept of responsibility was rarely dealt with during the period. Rational decision making left no room for the moralising that had been the ideal, but of course this approach was not unvarying. Well-known writers like Philip Selznick (1957) and Peter Drucker (1968) continued to moralise. Amitai Etzioni's *The Moral Dimension* aroused a great deal of discussion on its publication in 1988. By and large Ulla Johansson is certainly correct. But she herself points out that the quantity of research is really less interesting as conceptions of responsibility survive like flies in amber.

And indeed many aspects of responsibility are timeless and worth discussing. The responsibility of the individual versus the system is problematised in a case study by Herbert Kelman and Lee Lawrence 1972, that is still relevant today. How large was Nixon's share of the responsibility? Was there any point in him taking the responsibility? Was that really the best alternative available if we take the broad perspective? It was probably impossible to draw a clearer borderline between the system's responsibility and Nixon's. If we want to believe that the office of President carries with it absolute power, we have to ascribe complete responsibility to its incumbent. The same applies to the leaders of organisations.

Patrick Maclagan's discussion in 1983 of formal responsibility to an organisation versus subjectively experienced and personal responsibility still has validity as well. Responsibility can be allocated but also assumed. It is more than possible to assume greater responsibility than one has been assigned both in victory (where responsibility is called honour) and defeat (when it is called blame). Those who claim too much honour are boastful, and those who take too little blame are accused of trying to wriggle out of things. Our impression is that national and organisational cultures vary in their sensitivity to boastfulness and trying to wriggle out of things. Nixon's unwillingness to both boast and extricate himself seems un-American to Europeans like us – a label he would really have hated.

Driving the goat into the forest

What we thought we could go into more detail here is the idea of the scapegoat that is obliged to take responsibility and then sacrificed so that the rest of us can get on with our lives. To begin with (if there ever was a beginning outside films) a scapegoat was in fact a goat. A priest heaped the sins of the people on the goat's back and then it was driven out into the forest. It was expected to die there, and with it the sins. The disappearance of the goat can be explained biologically, the dissipation of the sins is less clear.

Nixon is a clear example of a scapegoat, but there are references to the same phenomenon in two of the other films analysed in this book. In *Any Given Sunday* (chapter two) Anthony D'Amato claims that being a leader means sacrificing oneself. However, he does not claim that one should turn oneself into a scapegoat. Towards the end he is the one sacrificed, even if the setting conceals what is happening. One way of understanding what the oracle really means in *Matrix* (chapter three) is that in predicting that Morpheus will sacrifice himself she is constructing his role as leader. All leaders have to be sacrificed in the end – our knowing that is what makes them leaders. Even so, Morpheus is not a scapegoat while Nixon is.

Even though the subject of scapegoats is a narrowly defined one, more has been written about it than there can reasonably be a readership for. One well-known classic is *The Scapegoat* by René Girard from 1982. But after the violent hammering it received in Johan Asplund's *Rivaler och syndabockar* (Rivals and scapegoats, 1989), it provides us with nothing to build on. In his book Johan Asplund dismembers Girard's arguments in a manner rarely seen in the social sciences. Definitely exhilarating even for those who have never read René Girard.

Neither Nixon nor other leaders are really the kind of scapegoat that René Girard (1982 and 1985) and others are writing about in this genre. 'If the scapegoat mechanism is really going to work according to Girard a number of conditions have to be fulfilled. To begin with the selection of the scapegoat must be arbitrary ... Secondly the killing of the scapegoat has to be communal ... In reality the scapegoat is innocent, but the collective must be unhesitatingly convinced that it constitutes the root of all evil' (Asplund 1989, p. 32). Leaders who are sacrificed have not been chosen arbitrarily. They are rarely 'killed' by communal lynching, even though there is often a large majority in favour of this expedient. It is often doubtful whether they are even in reality, 'innocent'. Moreover 'innocent' is a concept that is more complex than Johan Asplund would like to pretend.

The symbolic goat does not even have to be an individual. In Eva Haldén's PhD thesis from 1997, the scapegoat was Sweden's National Board of Education. The agency was made to take the blame for the failures of the educational system and closed down. This was a genuine sacrifice that required genuine guilt. In its place a new agency was established, the National Agency for Education. This was organised as something different so that previous shortcomings could not return from the recently sacrificed scapegoat and infect its successor.

The actual scapegoat mechanism itself means that the ritual sacrifice leads to peace. The scapegoat alone was the cause of war and through its solitary death brings peace. Here we see another disparity. '... immediately after the slaughter of the scapegoat the (collective) switches to worshipping its corpse' (Asplund 1989, p. 33). This is not what happens to the corpses of leaders! Quite the opposite, no little energy is devoted for quite a long time to maintaining the conviction that it was correct to get rid of the leader. Nixon had to wait until a few days before his death before any serious attempt was made to restore his reputation.

One obvious reflection is that there may be different kinds of scapegoats. In an article Giuseppe Bonazzi (1983) differentiates two types. 'Expressive scapegoats' have caused some catastrophe and become the victims of widespread, spontaneous aggression. The other group consists of 'instrumental scapegoats' who have not been the cause of anything in particular but have been apportioned blame by those in power and then sacrificed. This sheds light on the fact that scapegoats are not in any way uniform, even though the two categories are not satisfactory. Nixon fits in neither pigeonhole.

Little scope for action

Leaders have powers and responsibilities. Henri Fayol (1916) was already arguing that these should be linked to each other. This would seem fair and functional. Perhaps this is why powers and responsibilities have been brought closer to each other in many places. According to job descriptions, powers often almost match responsibility. Generally, however, the responsibility is greater. Even so the difference is not large enough to explain why managers have now been discussing this relationship with each other for a century or more.

The explanation for their dissatisfaction with this relationship between responsibility and powers is, in our opinion, that powers have nothing to do with this conceptual system. Senior executives, like presidents, have enormous power. They do not need more to match their responsibility. Instead it is their scope for practical action that is too restricted in relation to their responsibility. Leaders only want to be held accountable for what they can actually influence and not for what they could have done something about if circumstances had been different.

Nixon feels that he has been treated unjustly. Several of the circumstances that compel him to resign were outside his control. The environment or the staff of an organisation can, for example, never be controlled precisely, however much power one has. At times, however, chief executives have to resign because the share price is too low. To what extent is this due to factors that he could have predicted and affected? And what about all the coaches who get sacked because 'sporting victories did not materialise'? How far do these losses depend on them in fact? A team that has a chance of winning as soon as they get a new coach can hardly be dreadfully organised or trained.

One can ask how the risk of becoming a scapegoat (or perhaps we should call them sacrificial lambs) affects the work of senior executives. If there is a tradition that they will be sacrificed unexpectedly and unjustly, some effect can be guaranteed. In the films we used to watch at childhood matinees, no good gunfighter sat with his back to the saloon door. In their world friendliness to strangers and trust were things that only children and simpletons could afford.

Justice in imbalance

There are other things that niggle Nixon when he is on the way down. Nothing is done to offset his only failure with all his positive achievements. He wants to see justice in the form of 'fairness'. Perhaps he has been influenced by all the discussion aroused in the early 1970s by the American philosopher John Rawls (1971). However, his theories dealt only with distributive justice, in other words how resources are acquired and allocated.

If Nixon had taken his theory of retribution from the Old Testament instead, he would have realised that, irrespective of previous good deeds, what applied was an eye for an eye and a tooth for a tooth (The Bible, Exodus 21:24). This retributive principle does not permit the loss of all your teeth if you have only caused your opponent the temporary inconvenience of a black eye. How serious was Nixon's crime?

In Nixon's case the good never had to be balanced against the evil. The focus was totally and completely placed on one problem. In a process like this somebody has to take responsibility and this can never be offset by other merits, however great. Otherwise the responsibility would still be unresolved – and someone must assume it.

Dying by the sword

Nixon would not be Nixon if he complained in public. When young people play computer games on the Internet a rapidly written pidgin develops. They write while they are playing and have no time to waste. What they have learnt about writing at school does not matter. Anyway, if a player wants to earn respect it is important for him (him!) to be able to 'take a loss'. They must be able to lose without blaming circumstances or whingeing about their teammates or opponents, however justifiable it may be.

There are also rules about how leaders should be able to 'take a loss'. Nixon was sure that Kennedy was mixed up in rigging the election but did not appeal against the result. This may have been wise considering the rest of his career. What is more important is that an appeal would have been a breach of the unspoken rules that applied to leadership at the time. For the same reason, towards the end Nixon never referred to his inability to influence the course of events. He simply accepted his own responsibility.

Missing sacrifices?

Not all of those responsible are sacrificed. We remember an event during a previous study (reported in Rombach 1986). A local council was discussing the way in which the social services had grossly exceeded their budget. The chairman of the social welfare board was under pressure and gave an account of what he considered to be the real reasons – the administrators had not adopted the correct measures and had failed to act quickly enough. He was sure of his ground, still walking tall. But his explanations were not good enough! The pressure mounted and we scented blood in the air. Was he quite simply going to be forced to resign? But then he went back up to the rostrum and apologised to his staff (even though none of them were there and were presumably largely to blame). He then took up on himself the blame for the whole thing. In saying so he assumed the entire responsibility. There were shouts of acclamation and, if we remember correctly, even applause in the chamber.

In this case the chairman of the social welfare board had admitted his responsibility and therefore the case was closed. One may wonder what really happened. Nobody resigned. Why was there no ritual sacrifice? Is the correct interpretation that nobody was held accountable? We do not think so. It is obviously possible to sacrifice different things. Senior executives can sacrifice junior managers. In this case the chairman got down off his high horse and became another more or less successful manager. He sacrificed his own standing and the standing of the social welfare board. This was big enough to be acceptable.

Nixon tried sacrificing a few of his close associates but this was obviously too late. It is likely that earlier in the process he would have been able to sacrifice something instead of himself. Right at the beginning, a real purge of his staff would perhaps have been enough. If he had seen what course things would take, he might have chosen this approach. Later he could have sacrificed his reputation as president and the reputation of the office itself by showing that his actions were quite normal. For a long time different forms of chicanery had been part of the job as president. We do not know if this would have been a satisfactory sacrifice. In the film it is implied that Nixon considered it excessive.

One conclusion that can be drawn is that leaders should carefully consider how responsibility is accounted for and how it is assumed in their own organisations. Now that parachutes have become old-fashioned, it is not much fun to be thrown off the plane.

Central staffs

We have already discussed the limited scope open to Nixon for action. This theme merits deeper analysis. If a classic needs to be cited, it must be *Actors and Systems* by Michel Crozier and Erhard Friedberg from 1977. And here things can be made really complicated. In fact, in previous publications we have done our bit to muddy the waters (for instance in Rombach 1986 or Solli 1988). What is an action? A simple question like that ...But if we go cautiously, managers do a lot of talking, they make some decisions, but they do not do much actual work. The actions we are thinking of in the concept of scope for action are intentions that are visualised in discussions or more formal decisions that lead to their implementation in the organisation.

In our own field of research – local government finance, organisation and management – ever since Nils Brunsson and Sten Jönsson wrote their book *Beslut och handling* (Decisions and Action) in 1979, researchers have been aware that most power is in the hands of officials. This is a major sector of the community where those with the ultimate power (the politicians) are in a weak position. Despite their restricted scope for action, they are regarded by the media and by their own administrative systems as the ones who are in charge and can be called to account.

In the film about Nixon we can see how dependent he is on his immediate staff. If they are on his side and support him, he has considerable room for manoeuvre. If they want to pursue a different course, he does not have a chance. His scope for action is determined by the attitude of his staff. We believe that this is typical for those in leading positions.

If a leader wants to increase or maintain some scope for action the important thing therefore is to control his staff. We can already see that senior executives do not switch just their own jobs. They are inclined to take some member or members of their immediate staff with them. This should be taken into account in recruiting. In other words companies should not be advertising for senior executives alone but along with some members of their staff that are really equipped to lead the organisation.

One reasonable question is how far the staff is responsible for ensuring that dependence on their functions is not a drawback. Here the organisations run by politicians differ to some extent from others. If the central staff starts running a company, the outcome may be bad or good. It is only a drawback if the senior management is better equipped than the staff to make the company grow and yield a profit. In politically controlled organisations most of us would consider that democracy should come first. Irrespective of whether officials (army officers for instance) can manage a country better than the politicians available, we want those we elect to continue to govern.

Democracy is the paramount value in politically controlled organisations. The form of government is the primary goal, which is why any talk of opposing effectiveness to political influence is nonsense. Effectiveness obviously diminishes if political influence is also reduced. Lennart Lundquist has written a valuable book (1998) on how the staff (public officials) can be made to act as the guardians of democracy so we do not need to go into this in any more depth.

The attractions of leadership

One can wonder why Nixon ran for president. He could have earned more money as a lawyer. The office of president does not even appear to be particularly glamorous. And Nixon was not the kind of person who sought glamour. Quite the opposite, we remember him as a pallid, sweaty, unshaven and uneasy figure in the limelight. He definitely did not come across well on television. He may have been the last head of state that managed to be elected even though he did not live up to the demands of the media community. There is something in Neil Postman's misgivings (1985) about what will happen when politics, religion, news, education, journalism and commerce become entertainment. In the last resort humanity opts for amusing entertainment programmes rather than the kind of thing that will lead to long-term survival.

Nixon was a good speaker, as his handling of the Checkers Crisis proved. But he did not do so well debating against Kennedy. Perhaps Watergate gave the media a chance to spell out the demands they would make of future presidents and to assert the primacy of media scrutiny of how they exercised their powers – above the opposition and the electorate. Here we can see a change. It took eighteen months from the first media suspicions in the Watergate affair before it became newsworthy. During the intervening period attempts were being made to verify and clarify what was going on. When President Bill Clinton made his mistake it took eighteen hours rather than eighteen months before the journalists got the story to press. Media demands apply to all those in leading position. We cannot understand why managerial training programmes do not devote more attention to this.

Why does Nixon want so much to be a leader when it is so unpleasant? He claims himself that the motive is being able to make entrances. He says that this is what he likes. In other words it is being on stage that attracts him. This explanation applies not only to presidents and politicians. Executives who leave the stage describe the silence. Now nobody wants anything any more, when previously people wanted something all the time. Their diaries are empty and the phone never rings. Maybe those who dislike silence become leaders.

In descriptions of what it is like to be an executive, for decades now it has been surprising to what extent the daily routines of executives are fragmented and beyond their control. Below are a few quotations from Sune Carlson's pioneering study *Executive Behaviour* (1951) that throw some light on to what executives do.

> Alone intervals of 5 or 10 minutes are, of course, not only of little value for working purposes, but are also unsatisfactory as rest intervals. (Carlson 1991, p. 60)
>
> ... The vast majority of written communications used by the chief executives were of the incoming kind. It was relatively seldom that they used written communication media when they themselves had to convey anything to their subordinates. (Carlson 1991, p. 74)
>
> The median figure for the time the chief executives spent in receiving visitors in their offices during what I called a 'normal working day' ... was nearly 3 1/2 hours ... Conferences and private talks with

visitors in the office were also the most time-consuming of the various occupations recorded ... and most of these visitors were subordinates. (Carlson 1991, p. 79)

Kind of action	Decentralized organisation
	Per cent
Getting information	39.6
Advising and explaining	14.6
Taking decisions	6.3
Giving orders	6.8

(Carlson 1991, p. 88)

Forty years later *Executive Behaviour* was published again in the series 'Acta Universitatis Upsaliensis' (Studia Oeconomiae Negotiorum 32). Henry Mintzberg and Rosemary Stewart conclude the reissue with their own extensive comments (altogether fifty pages).

In his observations Henry Mintzberg claims that not much additional knowledge has come to light since Sune Carlson wrote the book. Carlson showed that POSDCORB (planning, organizing, staffing, directing, coordinating, reporting, budgeting) is not what leaders devote their time to. Even so these beliefs survive in the world of textbooks. Henry Mintzberg's explanation of why '... we failed to come to grips with the essential nature of managerial work' (Carlson 1991, p. 100) are less interesting than his point of departure. Sune Carlson's study is still front-line research (p. 97). To some extent this conclusion is certainly influenced by jubilee fever and perhaps some disappointment on the part of Henry Mintzberg can be read into it. The field that interests him (for example in Mintzberg 1973) should have attracted more researchers. Henry Mintzberg has immersed himself in the literature without finding much to please him.

> What I found was most discouraging: almost no theory, instead a great many lists, the vast majority repetitions of earlier ones (often still the classical functions of planning, organizing, coordinating, and controlling, etc.), or else sloppy combinations in which to the proverbial apples and oranges have been added elephants and laughter. (Henry Mintzberg in Carlson 1991, p. 102)

Rosemary Stewart agrees without carping so much. In spite of everything, others have confirmed many of Sune Carlson's conclusions.

> Many of his findings have been taken up and confirmed in later studies, particularly the fragmentation of executive work and the small amount of time that his managing directors spent alone and uninterrupted. (Rosemary Stewart in Carlson 1991, p. 120)

When we probe somewhat superficially into the literature on leadership a few years later (Källström and Solli 1997, Jacobsson and Rombach 1999, Rombach and Solli 1999) we can see that Sune Carlson's book stands up well. What we have read adds nothing really to the area in which he laid the foundation. What is striking instead is the strength of myths and popular beliefs in the field of leadership. Books about leadership often contain things that are not correct. Even though in several books the point is made that things are not the way the reader believes, under and around this statement there is a great deal that the authors definitely should not believe themselves.

We discovered one thing in the more recent leadership literature that is worth comment. The spotlight has been focused on new dimensions. Today's leadership literature contains discussion of gender issues, for instance, and also what makes leaders successful or less successful. If you shift focus, you discover new things. People can choose to become managers because they like what they imagine being a manager is like or because they actually enjoy what it means in practice. In Nixon's case the latter may well have been true.

Another important motive for Nixon wanting the job of supreme leader was, according to him, revenge. He came from the wrong family. They lived humbly and were short of money. Kennedy had everything! Nixon wanted to show his capabilities. On the formal level he definitely succeeded. Nobody can have any doubts that Nixon became president. The revenge should also have included being respected and popular – others have to acknowledge the revenge for it to be complete.

It is doubtful whether Nixon himself had any real answer to the question 'why?' His lack of self-confidence meant perhaps that he was unable to say that he became a leader in order to put the world to rights, reduce injustice and encourage development a little and also to do the best he could. Or perhaps he had an answer that could not be articulated, for example a thirst for power.

We believe that the reason for becoming a leader has an important impact on how one functions and enjoys the work. Revenge may not provide a firm foundation to stand on. Once attained where is there to go? The question then is whether it was enough and whether the revenge has been acknowledged or new opponents have to be sought. If being president is not good enough, perhaps you can take on Bill Gates. Awareness is important in itself even if the answer is merely 'I am a leader so that I can bask in the splendour of my office'.

CHAPTER 7

The Mozart Brothers – the art of discipline

The film called *The Mozart Brothers* (1986) begins with some kind of singing practice at the Opera. The director (Walter) played by Etienne Glaser sings – or rather shouts – 'I am Don Giovanni'. He is producing Mozart's *Don Giovanni* from 1787. It would not be far-fetched to assume that the way in which Walter directs incorporates aspects of Suzanne Osten's techniques as she herself is a celebrated and innovative feminist theatrical producer (cf. Svens 2002). At the same time Walter is a Don Juan – who lets his children down and attracts women who should know better.

Walter begins by appealing to the cast's previous experience. 'Some of you have perhaps done it before. So we assume we're on solid ground.' Lena T. Hansson (who is brilliant!) says: 'I've been studying Donna Anna for a year now.' Loa Falkman – or Eskil – who is to take the part of Don Juan has 'read the literature in depth'. 'You can never be prepared enough', Walter comments. This is just how things are. Here comes the boss with something new and we are well prepared. We know exactly how to play our roles so that anything new will be exactly like what has gone before.

F ... sit down

The director also says that we have 'other building material ... ourselves'. This will be something that reading cannot give. But that does not sound as promising. How can individual introspection 'give life to the petrified and the conventional', as promised in Leonard Maltin's *Movie and Video Guide* (Maltin and Blomkvist 1999, p. 73). Surely all we can find inside ourselves will be rigid conventions? Where else are they likely to be preserved?

Come what may, long sections of *The Mozart Brothers* consist of talk. It is film version of a theatrical production. Admittedly there are quite a few amusing scenes but it would be impossible to watch with the sound turned off and most youngsters would rather watch any other film than this. It has to be listened to. And the singers, Elisabeth Eriksson (Elvira), Iwa Sörenson (Anna), Gösta Zachrisson (Ottavio) and Rune Zetterström (the Commander) sing well. The same is true of some of the actors we see in the film as well. As a grown-up one can well agree that Suzanne Osten's film was worth the Golden Beetle she was awarded for best direction (1986) by the Swedish Film Institute (an annual award since 1964). *The Mozart Brothers* is probably best known, however, as the film that Prime Minister Olof Palme went to see on the night he was murdered February 28, 1986.

Ein Mensch

Walter talks and talks. Not all of it is easy to understand, however good it sounds. 'In opera, we like silence in music. Silence. That is everything that falls into death. Music is life. ... But beautiful singing is not an end itself. ... For me, most opera singing is about as appealing as two bound Chinese feet. ... I hate opera and theatre that doesn't utilize silence.' And the director seems to have his own clear conception of what he is trying to achieve. 'I can see it before my eyes.' What he is trying to attain is, he says, 'pure eroticism' and a little 'real terror'.

The reactions of the soloists are relatively positive as the director begins to work on the production. The musicians are neutral but this soon turns into discontent. Some members of both groups have heard rumours of his earlier work. 'I believe he had sections of the chorus in Malmö sing in the nude and 'he had the orchestra play in the nude in Oslo'. In the same way, every new boss is surrounded by rumours about his history. How true they are is uninteresting.

In the film we follow the director's attempts to get the soloists and the musicians to dare to dismantle their old preconceptions about this opera and about opera in general. Convention has to be broken – it spells death. The musicians are made to walk around, demonstrate the significance of their instrument without playing it and improvise with toy instruments.

The soloists are made to dress in the wrong clothes and go through different exercises. In pairs they are to probe the erotic in practice. This is difficult. The soloists attempt to do so, even though they, like us in the audience, are easily embarrassed. On another occasion they have to write down an erotic memory and handle an object erotically. On their own. This in fact works better with saucepans, rags and bellows than with another member of the cast. What does that tell us about human beings?

One can wonder if this is the way to destroy old preconceptions and conventions. Can you adopt Walter's technique in a bank or a library? We will return to Walter's strategies later. But we should add that at the individual level we know no more than you do. If you want an answer, organisation theory is the wrong area to start looking.

At the organisational level reforms are often regarded as a way of coming to terms with the past. The management is considered to be able to achieve this by reorganising structures. As *The Mozart Brothers* is not a film about organisational reforms, we are not going to bore you with a lot of text on this subject. We can summarise the current state of knowledge by saying that apparently dramatic, revolutionary reforms often lead to very little. And the references that should be cited here in support would not fit into a parenthesis. If we are going to limit ourselves to one title, it will have to be *The Reforming Organization* by Nils Brunsson and Johan Olsen (1993). That is not a bad place to start from.

It's a bit overdone

The soloists and the musicians react negatively to the director's exercises and ideas. Georg, the Commander, protests on behalf of Wolfgang Amadeus Mozart. 'This will kill the opera. Everything I've lived for. ... I think the public knows what it wants.' Invoking the public makes no impression on Walter. At first he does not react at all. It is as if he has heard nothing. The leader is so preoccupied with his vision that he hears no objections. Insight inertia (Hedberg and Ericson 1979) is what this could be referred to in organisation theory, if he is wrong. Here it is not easy to know what is correct. You cannot use a public fiasco as your criterion, if what you want to do is make the audience think differently. This is a problem if your starting point is that the customer cannot be wrong.

Quality movements, evaluation trends and certification systems all assume that the customer is never wrong. Some sectors and some categories of customers have to be excluded – pushing drugs and young people for instance. But these customers are not wrong either. They just do not know what is good for them. The question is whether it only applies to artistic productions that one indication of high quality is that the customer is wrong. Ideas about how deviant such undertakings are obviously differ among the researchers who have studied them. Emma Stenström (2000) argues in her PhD thesis that they do vary, while in his Rickard Wahlberg (2001) shows that the differences discussed by others are not particularly large in practice.

Even the cloakroom attendants take the audience's side at a tempestuous mass meeting. A rumour has spread that the opera is to be performed without an interval. They protest vigorously. 'The audience want their coffee.'

Nevertheless the opposition of the soloists is a problem for the director. If they fail to act it will merely be a choral recital. Walter tries to bring the commander and the others round with the help of flattery. He spreads it on thick. 'The Commendatore is the counterpoise ... In the end the Commendatore wins. ... the opera's epicentre. ... foundation of the work.' When flattery fails he can scold. Ia (Donna Anna) is told that she is 'lazy'. That hurts. She puts so much effort into her work that she almost bursts and asserts that 'he's tone-deaf'. What could be worse? 'We'll show him the power of song, as opposed to his damned vitality!', Ottilia, the singing coach says. She is definitely against the director's new ideas. Referring to Walter, Anna responds: 'There are people who cannot experience beauty without destroying it!' Here there are different ideas about what they are aiming for. Beauty is not Walter's goal.

Ottilia is interesting as the extreme defender of hidebound conventions. 'He [Mozart] didn't root in the dirt like a truffle pig!' Twice she attacks Walter physically. She strikes him with an umbrella and hits him hard just before he gives a press conference, which by the way provides all the heading for this chapter. Nicely put even though they are not all in English!

Defending what already exists with Ottilia's energy is ridiculous. Even so, most of us have come across her in the process of organisational change. If we tone down her role a little, we also realise that she is vital for the organisation. Why should all changes be for the better? And could it be even better in that case if discussed thoroughly in advance? Criticism is in short supply, as are millstones. When full speed ahead irrespective of the direction is the approach endorsed by most people, there is need for an Ottilia. The literature about organisational change is unreasonably preoccupied with inertia and implementation problems. One clear finding from our own studies of the public sector is that a great deal would be gained if there was time to think before acting (see for instance Rombach 1997).

In the canteen Walter summons up all his charm and attempts to disarm Ottilia's animosity with the help of flattery. He sits at the table at which she is sitting with Ia. 'You look like a painting by Picasso.' Aha – which? 'It's obvious Ia has been trained to use all her resources.' Walter says that he would like to take singing lessons himself and is about to succeed. Then Ia starts to cry – jealous tears?

The director is steering towards his own image of what it will look like in the end. He provides the others with no explanations. Walter even seems to be unwilling to seek their support for his own vision. This means that some of the employees actively oppose him. Rehearsals result in incredible resentment. Anna feels 'insulted and defiled'. Even if this may be the outcome of anxiety about what has to happen, it is hardly successful leadership in a process of change.

All is well and the rest is sad

But it should be pointed out that the director sees the anxiety. 'That's the unique gift, anguish.' As a leader Walter also makes some very concrete concessions. For instance, none of the actors is required to be bald. Nor does he present everything at once, but tries to move the soloists forward step by step. If we use Kurt Lewin's three-stage model of change 'unfreezing – moving – freezing, (1959, p. 210) then more time should perhaps have been given to unfreezing. Here we are not going to go into how this could or should have been accomplished. It can be added that it is not unusual for dissatisfaction with the current situation to provide the unfreezing. Waning confidence is then followed by change and greater trust (cf. Jönsson 1988, p. 79). But this kind of process is not possible as it would demand more time than Walter has at his disposal.

There are many models that enable processes of change to be divided into phases (see for instance Blomquist and Packendorff 1998). The process is often presented by a curve in which we see initial resistance progressively shifting to acceptance and then change. This is an apt description of what happens during the production of *Don Giovanni*. Much of Walter's work consists of eliminating the initial resistance. According to Kurt Lewin, Walter is acting correctly in trying to change groups of individuals rather than individuals separately. 'It is usually easier to change individuals formed into a group than to change any of them separately' (Lewin 1959, p. 210).

But anxiety is not primarily a group phenomenon. Walter displays great sympathy for each individual's protests and bizarre routines. He himself describes how Eddy Merckx (born in 1945) continually measured the height of his saddle stem. If the height of the saddle was not perfect, he felt he could not cycle fast enough. So he measured it time after time. However true this cycling anecdote may have been, one of the stagehands falls for it hook, line and sinker.

Admittedly Walter is an old-fashioned leader. He goes at it like a bull at a gate and uses simple expedients. He believes in flattery. He relies on his charm and his charisma as a leader. This approach has certainly been his guiding principle in previous processes of change – or productions. This time it does not always work. This may be because his ex-wife Marianne (who sings the part of Donna Elvira) knows the trick too well. 'He expects, no, demands! Then, when it comes right down to it, he walks away.' And he gives little of himself in return. If there is any more to give. After all, Marianne's opinion of Walter is that '... his emotions are as clear cut as ground beef'. In the opera Don Juan loves Donna Elvira for three days, and then abandons her. She vows revenge.

> In questa forma dunque
> mi tradì il scellerato, è questo il premio
> che quel barbaro rende all'amor mio?
> Ah vendicar vogl'io
> l'ingannato mio cor: pria ch'ei mi fugga ...
> si riccorra ... si vada ... io sento in petto
> sol vendetta parlar, rabbia e dispetto.
>
> (Mozart 1792/1974, p. 9)

> This is the way that scoundrel betrayed me!
> Is this the way that barbarian returns my affection?
> Ah! I want revenge for my deceived heart!
> Before he escapes me. I'll have recourse.
> I feel only revenge in my heart, rage and malice!
>
> (Internet reference 7)

Only in a few individual scenes do we see more of what we might consider traditional direction. Don Ottavio (Olof) is at the receiving end. Here the director displays openness for the ideas of others. 'Anybody has a better idea about how to do this?' Yes, Donna Anna, i.e. Lena T., has an idea that gives Ottavio the key to his interpretation. Don Juan gets help to understand how to sing his role. The most important things happen on the fly. It is as if all the major conflicts and sweeping gestures only take place while waiting for these brief moments. Only then can something really be communicated or rather arise.

The protests against the director's behaviour also include demands for more direction or leadership. We easily forget that there are not only individuals who want to lead, there are also those that want to be led. When management techniques are evaluated it is often taken for granted that the manager's perspective is the correct one. Even so management by objectives, for instance, is a well-known technique that cannot be used to direct people but which in certain situations meets the need they feel for management (cf. Rombach 1991). At the beginning the repetiteur says: 'I just want to know, what we're supposed to do. If I know, I'll do it.' Later Marian has a similar line. 'If you just tell me what to do, I'll do it. That's the least I can ask, right?' When she is then given concrete direction, she says: 'I don't want you to tell me how I should do it.' Directing is not easy.

Don Juan's children are looking for their father. Walter's own children are searching for him. In vain. It is too explicit and spoils it all. After all, we are all looking for our parents. Or is it leaders we are looking for?

Pull yourself together

Initially the director treats the musicians in the same way as the soloists. He tries to defrost them stage by stage using flattery like 'the orchestra has the leading role', and exercises. Working with the exercises is pretty awkward. 'We can't walk and play at the same time', 'I'm a musician' and 'what you are doing is just crap', send explicit signals. The musicians are recalcitrant. They do not want to 'feel naked'. To some extent the explanation is that musicians are not the same kind of people as soloists. Musicians are shy. The work of singers and artists is to 'make fools of yourselves'. But not of musicians. But after a time Walter persuades the musicians to give way to their playfulness. Even the trade union is won over.

To get the musicians to work, the director works at getting the informal leaders to give up their resistance. Where the double-bass leads, others follow. But the double bass will not succumb. The soloists do not have the same kind of informal leaders. Here there is a point that is often overlooked in change processes. Different groups of staff have different informal structures. The soloists are individuals with names. The musicians are a group. They do not have names of their own, but are known merely by their instruments. If that really is merely …

But in terms of formal structures the musicians are a different group. They form a unit, an orchestra. The trade union may not be powerful. Even so the orchestra's trade union representative (Henric Holmberg) speaks on behalf of the collective. 'From the union's point …' And something happens when their conductor (Okko Kamu) arrives. Only he can conduct the orchestra.

The repetiteur's attempts to conduct the orchestra fail ignominiously. The soloists are admittedly opposed to most of the director's antics but in some way they still accept him. On the other hand the musicians accept neither the director nor the repetiteur. They want a conductor. For instance, the repetiteur is told to make notes on the cover of the score instead of in it. While rehearsals are taking place the musicians ask: 'Anybody know when the rehearsal starts?' and someone shouts: 'Shall we give him a fly-swatter? Mozart grabs his hair.

After just over 50 minutes (on the video) Walter meets the trade-union representative in the canteen. 'You must be aware of the forces you're releasing. It's all right with me. But you can't speak to them as people.' No, that is just it – the orchestra does not consist of individuals.

It is worth noting that the repetiteur (Flemming) is also a failure in areas outside his professional role. He has bad breath. When the stage manager falls in the mud, Flemming stretches out a helping hand but falls into the mud himself. Instead of being thanked, he ends up covered in mud while the stage manager gets up himself and shakes the mud off. Only Flemming spills coffee all over himself. People like that cannot lead professionals!

Once the musicians have got their conductor they are placid as lambs. They play their hind legs off and smile when in a Finnish accent he pronounces the magic word 'Fine!'. In his presence they also enjoy 'fooling about'. They raise empty glasses to each other's health, play with their instruments, parade around in fancy dress, laugh and make a lot of noise. They are all involved and the trade union fawns on them. The explanation may be that the musicians see themselves as professionals. Their opposition to the director and the repetiteur is based on principle.

The chorus are also a group. They even experience collective pleasure when they are given Massetto's text to sing. Massetto, the individual, is not so happy. Even the children taking part in the production are directed as a group and act as a collective.

Art for art's sake

It is somewhat remarkable. The film shows us a leader who does not seem to like the people working for him. This may be due to his inability to get anything in return. Walter comes to life when he meets the cleaning staff, played by Saara Salminen, M A (what names – if any – are concealed behind these initials we do not know) Numminen and Pedro Hietanen. He gets something from their singing. And anyway the cleaners are very keen on what Walter is doing. Saara says that she is not there for the cleaning. 'I'm here for the singing.' As she dusts the candelabra she weeps silently at '... feel it beating, put your hand here'. It is beautiful.

At times the singers also reveal approval of what they hear. They like the result but protest on the other hand at the approach chosen by the director. Is the chosen approach really the only one? And what is the director contributing exactly? 'Of all my ex-husbands, he's the one who talked the most and did the least', says Walter's ex-wife.

Susan, who (together with Håkan who wordlessly carries the camera around) is making a video of the work on the production, has taken a shine to Walter, and he to her. A lot of what Walter does seems to be addressed to Susan; as if it is her film that he is actually directing. The opera production is really only to give the others something to do. With nothing to occupy them they may all go back to their own homes. Susan is in the same situation as Suzanne Osten. The coincidence of the names cannot reasonably be an accident. The audience demand some kind of plot. Therefore Suzanne Osten and her co-writers Etienne Glaser and Niklas Rådström present their 'totto'. (What on earth is a totto? – see Osten 1986, p. 147)

Not only Susan has or wants a close relationship with Walter. She (Susan) seduces him. What we expected in other words – the peasant girl Zerlina really seduces Don Juan. His ex-wife is still charmed by him. Malla, the receptionist, says that she wants to 'drink [herself] into a stupor, be abused, whipped and screwed' by Walter. Only by Walter, and it seems to be an acute need. A woman musician he meets in a corridor expresses her approbation noisily. Usually Walter is evasive. When necessary, he can really hurt to get away. Ia who is not fazed by anything – 'nothing shocks me', his ex-wife who more than understands what she is doing and the musician who screams 'Idiot!' are dealt with in this way. He runs away from Malla. He himself is interested in Susan, and the cleaning lady also gets what she wants – a pat on the cheek.

I believe in you

The boss's (director's) boss (the theatre manager) believes in him. 'Manager and manager, Walter. I'm a man.' Walter is consoled when he complains. 'It's totally discouraging to work with people who won't do anything.' It is important. 'But dad ...' 'Ah, it'll be fine when the maestro gets here.' At a mass meeting without Walter the theatre manager tries to calm the tempestuous emotions. He only partly succeeds. On the other hand Flemming, wearing Walter's shirt and sent there by him, succeeds well. Perhaps because he understands what he has been asked to do and been given Walter's shirt.

Even Mozart is positive. He appears now and again during the film. He is particularly delighted by the way the cleaners enjoy singing. Happy and moved is how we would put it. When, towards the end, Walter is feeling depressed in front of a model of the stage, Mozart walks through the room. Walter gets a hug. One may wonder why it is the repetiteur, Flemming, who plays Mozart. It cannot merely be because Philip Zandén acts him well.

When the repetiteur is about to give up because of '... never being able to give an opinion', Walter resorts to his usual flattery. 'I appreciate your support enormously.' Perhaps that is how it really is. Wolfgang Amadeus Mozart gives Walter his support. And a kiss. Two kisses. When he has stained his shirt with coffee, he gets Walter's in a pretty intense scene.

As the goal draws near, the director seems to have lost sight of his vision. Instructions about the set become especially hazy. Should there be leaves or snow? What about the marble statue? And does everything really have to come off the stage?

All through the film the scenographer Fritz (acted excellently by Henry Bronett) is bullied by Walter. Even so Fritz does exactly what he is told to. He even uses a chainsaw to open a grave in the floor of the stage, although the stage manager has threatened to kill him if he does. And perhaps he is pushed around because he is so obedient. Walter needs opposition to be able to work. But there is more to it than that. The scenographer is told off for his own initiatives as well. Perhaps Walter has adopted a less successful way of maintaining the hierarchy. The hierarchical relationship of different professional groups is often unclear. The director's behaviour makes it clear that the scenographer is well below him on the ladder.

Let bygones be bygones

Let bygones be bygones. When the audience comes tramping in, Walter is really nervous. He stands outside the auditorium listening. We see the audience's reactions reflected in the repetiteur's face. The production is an enormous success. Walter smiles when he hears the thunderous applause.

When they leave the performance, talking animatedly, the audience is moved. Walter leaves alone. The soloists and the musicians are allowed to take the glory. Or perhaps they stole it. 'Actually we haven't had much direction. Walter has worked more as an organizer. He's largely let us use our own ideas.'

Could Walter really have taken the glory? Even the manager of the theatre says when the journalists are entering that Walter is 'a subordinate'. And what would Walter do with the glory if he got it? The scenographer stretches out in the water-filled moat. 'It's beautiful, it's wonderful, it's absolutely beautiful ... we've done it!' But 'the dream is ... an escapee' and after all we cannot 'deprive him [Mozart] of his responsibility'.

Successful leadership

We have to make our minds up. Is Walter a successful leader or is he a victim of circumstances? Walter is successful in the sense that at the end things are more or less what he envisaged at the beginning. That is what direction is about – getting where you want. Perhaps this also includes working out where you really want to get. Walter is successful according to the people working with him and the customers, a term used in the film otherwise for those who buy tickets. Everyone there actually likes the final product. The only reason why the success is not overwhelming is that Walter is not really overwhelmed by success.

If we now decide that Walter is successful, we can ask what he does and how generally applicable this is. We have identified a handful of strategies that Walter resorts to. These are not the flashy, attractive kind but unpleasantly realistic ones instead. We have to learn powerful but not socially correct management strategies, in other words, how to get others to do what we want them to.

Vague plans

Walter adopts a vague plan. In being vague it can be adapted to prevailing circumstances. On more than one occasion Walter orders an about turn. This is permissible when it happens in the context of a indeterminate plan.

If Walter had complied with the accepted ideas in the recipe books in this area, he would have gone on planning until he knew exactly what to do. Plans of this kind are useful if circumstances are stable or changes predictable. If normal circumstances prevail, exact plans are unusable. In addition, plans like that obstruct your own learning.

Detailed instructions

In the midst of all this vagueness, Walter uses purely Tayloristic (Taylor 1911) instruction about details. We recognise this as something that leaders should avoid. The current view is that management should stick to overall objectives and leave the details to those familiar with the work. But at the micro-level the grey area between overall and detail is enormous.

As we see it, Walter's success is due to his control of the things he wants to control. It is not such a silly idea to make decisions about details if this works. Totally excluding detailed instructions from the arsenal of management tools does not seem wise.

Criticism

Leaders normally praise often and criticise seldom. Even so when they are interviewed in the trade journals they often say that they should be better at giving praise and that they ought to do so more often. This is based on anxiety about being too critical. Walter does what leaders worry about doing. He criticises a lot and rarely praises, but when he does he makes sure that it can be seen and heard.

Ignoring

Ignoring seems to be an effective management strategy. There are a number of examples of directing by ignoring individuals in *The Mozart Brothers*. The stage manager does not want holes sawn into his stage and repeatedly receives the answer 'Okay, we'll discuss it later' when he protests. Later, sure enough a hole is sawn into the stage. When the staff hold a protest meeting Walter ignores it and goes off for a drink instead. The downside of ignoring things is that it makes the leader look undemocratic or unenterprising. It seems appropriate therefore to use it sparingly.

Not infrequently a situation can arise that is called in business studies a high degree of uncertainty. Ignoring it makes it possible to endure this kind of chaos. However, dealing with uncertainty by ignoring it is a risky management method. Because not all situations sort themselves out best on their own. Admittedly the staff can do what they feel like doing, but it is not certain that this will resolve any problems that may arise.

Anna Cregård claims in her PhD thesis (2000) that ignoring things belongs to the management category that she labels special. If management by ignorance is to be used at all, it should be applied to individuals rather than collectives or situations that involve collectives. Normal chaos is one example of this latter group.

Making an example

Making an example of someone is one way of getting things done. For instance, if you have a problem with an opponent or general grumbler, you can do what Walter did. He removes them from the security of the group, puts them where everyone can see them and then dresses them down. Mean? Of course, but very effective. It is just as mean to tell someone they look like a painting by Picasso, and just as effective if you want to annihilate them.

But making an example of someone can also have a positive effect. Walter annoys one of the singers by telling her she cannot sing. The insult makes her practise more than ever.

Redefining

Walter's arsenal of management devices is bigger than this. We have used the term redefining for one group. This is a variation of the vague planning strategy but is worth attention in its own right. When the soloists complain about something they cannot manage, something that according to them is almost impossible, Walter redefines the situation. He does it by saying that the individual concerned is the only one capable of this difficult task and that there is nothing he wants more than for her or him to do it. Some people would call this flattery – and so what?

One way that makes it possible to redefine is to display patience and to nag. It is difficult to resist nagging forever. Parents have been using this method since time began. With varying success, we should add, on the basis of our own experience.

Fragmentation

There is one form of ignoring that we call fragmentation. Walter has the soloists practising isolated sections of the opera without letting them see how they relate to anything else. If his entire conception could be seen straight away, it would be difficult to get everyone to prepare properly before the premiere. Fragmentation is a method of eliminating some of the conflicts at least.

Fragmentation can result in failure if the wrong focus is chosen. The repetiteur attempts to keep musical techniques and emotion separate. He is then unable to keep the orchestra in order as he opts to concentrate on technique. The maestro solves this problem by focusing exclusively on the emotion in the music. The musicians know the technique – it is merely a matter of enabling them to use it.

Another problem with fragmentation is that the technique does not give the entire collective a chance to contribute profitably. How can you develop your role to the benefit of the production as a whole if you do not even know the overall extent of your own role?

Manipulation

On the whole we see Walter as an effective leader. His fundamental concept of management is that it involves manipulating his staff in various ways. However, we usually do not want to be manipulated at work. In the cinema, on the other hand, it is not so stupid – is it? But manipulation can also be used in the work place. In the film it goes so far that the soloists assert that it was because of their ideas that everything turned out so well in the end. But we know better. Just as in his directing, the film in the film, Walter defies conventions. As we see it, he mainly flouts the conventions about what leadership is and how it should be exercised.

In terms of the outcome, Walter is definitely a successful leader. That is why it is difficult to explain why he is not given the praise for what he has achieved. Instead, all the others involved take their share. In normal cases we (like the leaders themselves) sing the praises of the leaders, even if they have no idea why things turned out as they did.

The path of discipline

It is impressive that a sole director can get a large group of stars to do exactly what he has envisaged. In this film it seems to be particularly difficult as all the members of the group have their own ideas about what should be done. It is not so surprising when a director like Ingmar Bergman gets his stars to listen, as he has authority to back his words. Walter has to earn his authority during the relatively short rehearsal period.

In modern organisations, we imagine that what matters is getting the staff to think in the right terms so that we can achieve a good result. In the theatre things seem a little different at first glance. There using the body correctly seems to be what matters. Thinking does not have to be involved. The point is that it should look like something, not be it. When a murder is to be committed or lips kissed, obviously it is an advantage if both parties are in the right place at the right time. John Ransom captures this situation in the quotation below. And in traditional theatre everything has to be repeated, performance after performance. It is not odd that good actors are attracted by experimental theatre!

> Get a firm grip on the body and its forces, bend them to your will, and the mind will follow. (Ransom 1997, p. 33)

We should not, in other words, underestimate the importance of disciplining the body. This works directly through phenomena that can be observed rather than by means of a set of rules that have to be remembered. Walter does not require Don Juan to be a Don Juan, he merely has to act like one.

Discipline is a word that immediately recalls not only the army and its drill but also life in prison. In an attempt to reform prisons, Jeremy Bentham (1748–1832) constructed the prototypical disciplinary technology. He called his creation the panopticon – from the Greek prefix 'pan' that means all and 'opticon', which relates to vision. 'Total vision' took the form of a circle with a tower at the centre. The tower was equipped with large windows overlooking the interior of the circle. The circular building was divided into cells, each provided with two openings. One faced the tower, the other faced outwards to admit light. The warden in the tower could then see silhouettes of what was happening in the cells. The cages were individualised. The individuals were visible all the time but never knew when they themselves were being observed.

Supervision presumes individualisation. Accountants call this the demarcation of units of accounting. This also requires visibility, i.e. accounting for what has been done and sometimes not been done. Individualisation can be considered as a form of separation, which Michel Foucault (1974/1998, pp. 159–266) claims is a significant component in what is called management. Separation includes both ranking and categorisation.

Michel Foucault's idea is that subordinates are separated from each other in the way they are presented in terms of discipline. The subordinates are ordered (sic!) in categories such as 'good at following the score' and 'sings off tune'. Places are awarded on merit, or in other words how disciplined one appears to be and the extent to which one lives up to expectations. This is one explanation of the great importance given to various forms of measurement and evaluations from different standpoints in organisations. The actors strive for the best possible judgements as this gives them the best positions. Mike Savage (1998, p. 67) claims that it is this careerism that provides cohesion in large and complex organisations.

Nowadays repressive methods are not enough to maintain discipline. They probably never have been. Magnus Hörnqvist (1996) points out the multifaceted character of discipline.

> The series of rewards and punishments is extensive and offers scope for variation: it runs from repression, from prison and physical coercion as the most extreme forms of punishment, to ostracism, personal humiliation, material loss and verbal assault, shifts into tolerance or no reaction at all, and then branches out into a multitude of rewards – acceptance, momentary acknowledgements, extra benefits or enduring earned privileges. (Hörnqvist 1996, pp. 203–204)

In the film Walter uses almost the entire battery listed by Magnus Hörnqvist. He ignores, humiliates, admonishes, flatters, charms, praises and asks for advice.

Discipline is not therefore a question of punishment and behavioural norms. Anna Cregård (2000) claims that discipline is characterised by a calculating relationship intended to normalise. Frequently both punishment and rewards can take subtle or noticeable forms. There are many techniques! Mats Alvesson writes as follows.

> In companies not only carrots, whips and directives are used to get people to act correctly, but values, concepts, information about the company's situation, feelings, identification, group membership etc are mobilised as the objects and instruments of company management. (Alvesson 1998, p. 112)

On closer reflection, *The Mozart Brothers* is an excellent example of how many organisations, probably most, function. They move from chaos to order by imposing discipline. Car factories are designed round assembly lines where everybody knows precisely what has to be done. If a fitter starts removing sparking plugs instead of fitting shock absorbers, his foreman will react straight away. And if he is dexterous enough to be able to fit a sparking plug and a shock absorber at the same time, he may get a rise or perhaps promotion to foreman.

Hospitals consist of routines and positions with books of rules that say exactly what applies. If a doctor operates on the wrong leg, she will be referred to – exactly – the disciplinary committee. If she is better at operating than others and does not make a fuss about resources, she will be promoted to become Senior Medical Officer. The people making decisions on aeroplanes have checklists that have to be ticked off, even if they have done so only recently. If they forget to go through the checklist and the plane crashes, they will be in trouble. A pilot who flies according to the rules will soon be given a bigger plane. In the academic world it is tongues and keyboards that count. The motto is 'say what I say' and 'write what I write'. In other words quote what is up-to-date at the moment and you can be promoted, otherwise not.

It is not difficult to see what is physical about the theatre. And once you have done so, it is easy to see that other organisations are not so unlike theatres.

CHAPTER 8

Life of Brian – the search for a model

Life of Brian, or *Monty Python's Life of Brian* is brilliant, at least in its own genre. Graham Chapman, John Cleese, Terry Gilliam, Eric Idle, Terry Jones and Michael Palin succeed in doing what all Monty Python fans thought they were capable of. It does not make the film less interesting to learn that it was totally forbidden in Norway when it was issued in 1979. The whole point of using satire is to make someone really furious.

Satire derives from Latin's 'satura', which in this context stands for mixture. The understatements and exaggerations of satire, in conjunction with alternative interpretations of otherwise familiar texts, offer new perspectives. Satire is not therefore something that we are merely supposed to laugh at, although that is involved as well. It is often a way of depicting something that has just as much to tell us as drama or 'real-life narratives' for that matter. We remember with admiration Charlie Chaplin's *The Dictator* from 1940, which was marvellously funny and also expressed vital social criticism.

From choirs of angels to crucifixion

The Life of Brian begins with the sound of choirs of angels and we see three wise men riding on richly decorated camels. They are carrying gold, frankincense and myrrh to the new-born Brian Cohen, or rather his peevish mother Mandy Cohen. They quickly return to retrieve their gifts. They were intended for Jesus in the crib a little further away. Then we see the credits. And singing. Perhaps there is too much singing in this chapter. We include it because it offers such a good illustration of human desire to attribute significance to anything whatsoever that happens to us. If we had to single out any human characteristic that distinguishes us from other animals, this is the one we would go for.

> Brian. The babe they called 'Brian',
> He grew, ... grew, grew, and grew - -
> Grew up to be – grew up to be
> A boy called 'Brian' - -
> A boy called 'Brian'.
> He had arms ... and legs ... and hands ... and feet,
> This boy ... whose name was 'Brian',
> And he grew, ... grew, grew, and grew - -
> Grew up to be - -
> Yes, he grew up to be
> A teenager called 'Brian' - -
> A teenager called 'Brian',
> (Internet reference 8)

And now the film really starts – in Judaea, thirty-three B.C., Saturday afternoon, at around teatime. A horde of people is on their way to a sermon on a mount. Those who pay attention can hear Reg (more about him and his associates later) saying that it is Jesus who is going to speak. Several of the listeners standing close to Brian and his mother cannot hear very well and spend most of the time goading each other. After a while Brian's mother wants to go to the stoning instead. After some more bickering that is what they do.

We cannot hear much of what Jesus says, but he says something like 'may God bless those who sorrow who shall soon find comfort, the tender who will soon inherit the earth, those who hunger and thirst after righteousness, the cheese makers (but here the source is unreliable), the Greeks who are clearly going to inherit the earth and the meek'. Francis, who walks by in the company of Reg and Judith, comes to the conclusion that all those interested in the status quo have been blessed.

The next reference to Jesus comes when an ex-leper beggar describes how he became 'ex'. Otherwise being cured was not a totally positive change. He had not asked for it and it is difficult to make a living now he is healthy. Leprosy was not much fun. Being a bit lame would have been all right.

The leader in this film is not Jesus. And it is also worth noting that this film is not about bosses, even though that is what Pilate and the Roman officers are, but about leaders. Nor is it a film about Jesus – he is somewhere in the periphery.

Reg – a leader who does not like acting

Reg is the leader of an anti-imperialistic group called the 'People's Front of Judaea' or 'PFJ'. A group consisting of Judith, Francis, Stan and Reg, who founded it, leads this front. They wander round discussing things or sit and discuss things. They have about ten or so members and they meet in their secret headquarters and hold formal planning meetings.

Even the everyday discussions among the leaders are formal, that is if Reg is in the chair and decides. We never find out anything about Reg's life outside the People's Front of Judaea. It is doubtful whether he has one. The others in the leadership group seem to take the place of his family and the struggle occupies his entire life. This is often the case even for leaders who officially have families and claim to have leisure interests.

One may ask why the People's Front of Judaea allows Reg to be its leader. He does a great deal of talking but evades any dangers. By referring to his back problems if necessary. Reg is a timid leader when physical action is required. In our postmodern period, as in the modern period we are in the process of leaving, lack of physical courage is no obstacle to leadership. But it is not so long since we were led by the strongest in the group, men who placed themselves in the front line. In some ways the strong men are still in place, but today press conferences are where you find the front line. Now that the microphone has replaced the sword, women are just as good at leading as men are. But as too many people in power still believe that the sword is what counts, there are too few women leaders.

Reg is fond of plans and formal meetings. Where small things are concerned he is not totally unrealistic. When Stan, biologically male, wants to be a woman called Loretta so that he can have a baby, Reg claims that this is fleeing from reality. On the other hand Francis and Judith consider it reasonable to support Loretta's right to a baby even though she lacks the necessary womb. And when there are no peanuts on sale, he buys 'a bag of otters' noses' from Brian.

But in the larger sphere, Reg talks about the People's Front of Judaea attaining mastery of the world within five years. 'We could reasonably overthrow the Romans within a year!' This is to some extent reminiscent of various left-wing groups before the Soviet Union lost its grip over Eastern Europe. Today business executives generally have visions that are only loosely linked to probable developments. For instance, the manufacturing industry in the west has traditionally been led by pessimists, like most major companies. Forecasts have been very cautious. The exponents of what is referred to as the new economy, on the other hand, have shown that an exaggeratedly positive image of the future attracts investment capital. Since then others have followed their lead.

The members of the People's Front of Judaea support Reg. Judith in particular is earnestly and honestly committed to what Reg claims is the group's cause and standpoint. She backs him energetically several times during the film. 'Yes, yes. Absolutely, Reg. Yes I see', are the first words we hear from her in the film. Sycophantic is the word. She does not do this to win promotion, though, but from conviction. Charismatic leaders often have this problem. When everyone gets carried away blindly, there is nobody in the organisation who can help by asking questions.

Apart from the total failure of a raid to kidnap Pilate's wife and an assignment given to Brian Cohen when he wants to join the group, the People's Front of Judaea achieves nothing. Even the job of organising the queue when Brian becomes the Messiah for a short time comes to nothing. There is only a bit of shouting while Brian leaves the building to be arrested by the Romans.

Reg is not only unwilling to take action himself. Proclamations instead of action seem to fascinate the rest of the group as well. When Brian is finally crucified, the People's Front of Judaea does not come as a rescue committee but to read out a statement. They then sing 'For he's a jolly good fellow'. Songs are not always out of place. In *The Bridge on the River Kwai* the lyric of a song that was never used fits very well (see chapter ten). Judith thanks Brian for what he is doing in allowing himself to be crucified. His mother rails away and says ' ... all I can say is go ahead. Be crucified. See if I care.' before turning on her heel and leaving.

When they talk and plan, Reg and the group emphasise the importance of wanting to act. Reg says that the movement needs 'doers', when Judith reports on the incredibly successful assignment Brian performed in order to join the group. His task was to scrawl 'Romans, go home' on the walls of the palace, but because his Latin is so bad he wrote instead 'Romanes eunt domus'. Stupid, wasn't he? As you know, this means 'Romans go to the toilet'. Brian was discovered by Roman soldiers who gave him a lesson in classical Latin. It finished with him having to write 'Romani ite domum' one hundred times on the palace walls. And by sunrise if he did not want his ... (OK – balls) cut off. He managed, some of it in really big letters. At the same meeting Reg asserts that there is no member (even though there is one) of the People's Front of Judaea who would not die to get rid of the cursed Romans.

The kidnapping of Pilate's wife included a plan to make demands. Pilate was to be given two days to overthrow the Roman state. If not, his wife would be executed. The People's Front of Judaea planned to cut off one of her limbs each hour. A really determined plan. And definitely not something to joke about ...

When the group are discussing domination of the world in five years, some members shout out that the '[People's Front of Judaea has] got to get up off our arses and stop just talking about it!' 'It's action that counts, not words, and we need action now.' 'We could sit around here all day talking, passing resolutions, making clever speeches. It's not going to shift one Roman soldier!' And 'So let's just stop gabbing on about it, it's completely pointless, and it's getting us nowhere.' Really fervent slogans take the place of action. If this had been expressed more moderately, some obligation to do something might have been felt.

We can learn from Reg something about the art of leading committed members. A common enemy, clear goals and structures are his instruments. The problem is that the leading does not go anywhere, and when nothing is made to happen the whole thing is anyway pointless. Why not resign?

However, the People's Front of Judaea is not the only group opposing the Romans without acting. The People's Front, which may also be called the Judaean People's Front, has only one member who is not particularly active. He is not even talkative.

The Judaean People's Front carries out a suicide attack, rushing up to the crucified in full armour and then killing themselves with swords hidden under their chain mail. This is definitely positive action. Things happen. The group dies – although their feet are still moving in time with the concluding song. And the Romans tidying up after the crosses have been erected hasten away. Even so the people of Judaea are not one whit freer because of it.

And the People's Front of Judaea come into conflict with a group called Campaign for Free Galilee in their attempt to kidnap Pilate's wife. The two groups go for each other, which costs all of them but Brian their lives. The Roman sentinels, who have been watching the freedom fighters attack each other, capture him. In addition to these groups there is also mention of a Front for Judaea in the film.

Brian – a reluctant Messiah

Not only Jesus preaches in the film. Here and there we see men (only men) standing preaching. They talk about things like the leviathan and the whore of Babylon, the sword of Satan with its nine blades, small things with raffia bases and a man beating a donkey. Often they have audiences, but one has only a solitary listener. One sequence shows us a sermon with the simile 'he comes to us like the ocean to the grave'. Nobody wants to listen and so the speaker stops talking and leaves. The preachers want not only listeners but also disciples and people to lead. They are leaders looking for their flock.

Brian was born at almost the same time as Jesus. For one brief moment the three wise men believed he was Jesus. His father is a Roman (which Brian usually denies) and his mother a grumpy old Jewess who lives off her Roman men friends. Brian supports himself by selling snacks at the Colloseum. During children's performances (with only adults in the audience) he sells 'dog's tongues, wren's livers, chaffinch brains, jaguar's earlobes, wolf nipple chips (they're lovely), dromedary pretzels, only half a dinar, Tuscan fried bats' and other 'imperialist tit-bits'.

When the Romans are pursuing him, Brian pretends to be a preacher and takes his task seriously. He uses a number of parables (lilies and birds) and wise saws 'you shouldn't judge others – then you can be judged yourself'. This does not sound very different from the words of Jesus as recorded in St Matthew's Gospel 'Pass no judgement, and you will not be judged' (Matthew, Chapter 7:1). Otherwise the parables founder before Brian has even tried to make any point. Nobody understands or can even be bothered to listen until the end. When the Romans leave an opening Brian stops preaching in mid-sentence. This arouses the interest of his audience. They want to know what he intended to say – the secret. They chase after him, interpreting signs. What can leaving a sandal mean? Brian has become a very reluctant leader. Is he a born leader?

At one moment during his escape from the Romans, Brian races up the inside of a tower from which there is no exit. Brian jumps from the top, or does he fall? As certain death approaches, a spaceship materialises and catches him in flight. They fly out into space but are attacked by other space creatures and crash not far from where he jumped. Brian steps out the craft totally unharmed. He seems to have what most people want and what we call luck.

Good leaders are often described as lucky. As we mentioned earlier (in chapter five) this is what is said of Martin Beck. Luck turns up in this film as well, even though it is something that does not exist. Luck is an expression of the great need we have to see connections in our environment. When these connections cannot be perceived, we ascribe what happens to what we call luck, if things turn out well, and misfortune, if they go badly.

Neither Brian nor good leaders are lucky, instead it is rather more a matter of situations being exploited by leaders. How well they manage can definitely not be attributed solely to the leaders themselves. A more recent example of exploitation of a situation like this can be found in the history of the LM Ericsson company. Not very long ago the company was facing a crisis as it had not kept abreast of developments in telephone exchanges. The management used this situation to invest in a totally new approach and the AXE exchange saw the light of day. This was to be a cash cow for many years. Perhaps you should not keep up with everything? Others can do some things better.

For the crowds following Brian he is the Messiah, the master, the chosen one and saviour. His shout of 'go away' is regarded as a benediction. And when the juniper bush he shows them turns out to have berries on it, this is felt to be a miracle and a gift from God. The blind man who believes he can see, like Simon who speaks after eighteen years of silence is also a miracle. In the second case even though Brian happened to tramp on his foot which hurt so much that Simon broke his vow of silence to shout 'Oh, my foot! Oh!' (cf. Matthew 9:32-34). His followers see what they want to see and want to be deceived – or rather they long to see the Messiah at last. One says that he has followed quite a few but this time it is the Messiah. Here the need for leadership arises and grows because of the restricted or even non-existent supply. There are quite a few that want to lead, but the crowd choose the one who is difficult to persuade.

Judith spends the night with Brian. Next morning the crowd salute their master. Brian is totally dismayed and gives a one-minute speech about the individual. This may be the very essence of the film. You know ... the one about all of us being individuals who ... 'You don't need to follow me. You don't need to follow anybody. You've got to think for yourselves. You're all individuals! You're all different! You've all got to work it out for yourselves! Don't let anyone tell you what to do. Otherwise ...' And that is where Brian's mother interrupts his speech. Here as well as there is lack of coherence between talk and action. This may well be why the crowd fail to accept the message.

On Golgotha just before his own crucifixion Brian returns to this message. He says: 'You don't have to take orders!' to the soldier. He hopes that a soldier that thinks for himself will not crucify him. Brian that is. The soldier answers that he 'like[s] orders'. And this fits in with modern institutional theory. We are all individuals who choose freely to conform to similar predictable patterns.

Roman officers

The Roman soldiers, or rather their officers, are highly action oriented. Soldiers are uncommitted but they do what they are told to. And what they do, at times they do intensively. They like orders and in some situations get a hell of a lot done. One good example is their search of the room in what seems to be Matthew's home, used by the People's Front in Judaea as its headquarters. They find nothing. But soon they return to find the ladle that the group has in fact been using as a gavel at its meetings. This small room contains so many people that it must have been enormously difficult not to find all of them.

In other situations the soldiers are totally passive. At a stoning we watch two bored soldiers who are not even moved when things go totally wrong and the official organising the spectacle is stoned. Rightly so, as he is the one who pronounces the most forbidden word. Do not ask what it is – watch the film.

The soldiers are undoubtedly well organised but in spite of this they are dreadfully ineffective. Even so the Romans control the community. Their savage punishments may be one explanation. These consist of more than threats of stoning, crucifixion, cruel dungeons and fighting wild animals in the Colloseum. But the threat of violence cannot alone explain the submissiveness. The people seem to want to be ruled by the Romans. Maybe for the simple reason that in spite of everything they have done quite a few positive things. The members of the People's Front of Judaea mention aqueducts, sewage collection (things were bad before the Romans), roads, irrigation, health care, education, law and order (the streets are safe at night) and peace.

Another reason for the acceptance of Roman rule is that the control is not very strict. Women are not allowed to take part in stoning, but false beards enable them to evade the rule with no difficulty. Indeed all of the participants seem to be women disguised as men. If the members of the People's Front want to avoid arrest, all they have to do is crawl under the table.

Pilate is a tricky case. He appears to be extremely feeble and to lack authority but is obeyed by his subordinates – especially the centurion. He wants to be governed by Pilate for reasons that we never find out. Pilate cannot pronounce the letter 'r', but says 'l' all the time, which the centurion ignores. The soldiers who find this impossible and end up giggling hysterically risk having to fight savage animals. This kind of punishment can admittedly put a damper on their mood.

The centurion goes so far as to try to cancel Pilate's speech to the people as it will make him a laughing stock. When this is what happens and Pilate asks if the people are mocking him, the centurion responds with a definite no. We tell lies to keep our bosses in a good mood.

Pilate's good friend, the brave warrior Biggus Diccus from Rome (married to Incontinentia Buttocks) also has a speech defect and arouses the people's laughter. Very droll. Idiotus Simplicissimus is something we remember from our own schooldays about 1932 years later.

Table 1. Actors, qualities and actions

	REG	BRIAN	PILATE	CENTURION
Qualities	Entrepreneur (founder of PFJ.) Structured (chairman) Sees talk as implementation	Messianic Brave, almost foolhardy Uneconomical Scared of his mother	Speech defect	Loyal Not stupid
Actions	Talks Allocates work 'Co-ordinates' Tells people off	Listens to others Works (sells sweets) Takes his punishment (writing on the walls) Protected by providence (space travel) Forced to preach Denies his role Sleeps at Judith's Crucified	Harasses staff Punishes Decides	Protects superiors Implements decisions

The end

And then the film ends with the crucified (Englishmen!) happily singing 'Always look at the Bright Side of Life'. This could well be the private song of all the leaders who are not yet burnt out. We can warmly recommend every leader to learn it before it is too late!

> If life seems jolly rotten,
> There's something you've forgotten,
> And that's to laugh and smile and dance and sing.
> When you're feeling in the dumps,
> Don't be silly chumps.
> Just purse your lips and whistle. That's the thing.

And ...
Always look on the bright side of life.
(whistling)
Always look on the right side of life,
(whistling)
For life is quite absurd
And death's the final word.
You must always face the curtain with a bow.
Forget about your sin.
Give the audience a grin.
Enjoy it. It's your last chance, anyhow.
So, ...
Always look on the bright side of death,
(whistling)
Just before you draw your terminal breath.
(whistling)
(Internet reference 8 and 9)

Reg as a leader

So far, this chapter on *Life of Brian* has not been burdened with very many references. But we will soon include some. We should admit that we came close to excluding the film about Brian from this book. It was easy to watch but all the more difficult to analyse. What does it really have to say about leadership? We still think it says quite a lot – but it is difficult to put a finger on what makes it great. Below we are going to highlight a few reflections about Reg's leadership.

In defence of the film we would also like to say that this book should not be seen as providing all the answers. There is no single film for which we have included all the interpretations or all the lessons that can be learned. One of the aims of the work is to stimulate viewers to make their own analyses of films.

Who can serve as a model?

Leadership depends on the context. Therefore good leadership varies over time. Sometimes the leader's personal qualities are important, sometimes it is their actions that count. Sometimes it is simply assumed that personal qualities are linked to their actions.

As can be seen from the table below, the actors in the film have relatively few qualities. This is characteristic of satirical comedy. As there are few characteristics they stand out more clearly. The actions in the film are more numerous than those we have listed. The distinction between characteristic and action is sometimes fluid. But who is the model?

Definitely not Pilate! In this context we note that he appears in a way we have never seen him before. Pilate is normally opposed to the crucifixion of Jesus but forced to make the decision anyway. Here instead the message is that those in power are defective, in other words that power causes defects. Both Pilate and his colleague have been affected. We are thinking about their speech. It would not hurt to have a warning sign POWER CAN EASILY CAUSE DEFECTS some way up the career ladder.

Reg does not have the kind of calibre that will make someone leave the cinema thinking 'that's what I want to be like'. The opposite rather – which is also a message. As researchers, we are drawn a little to his views on talking and its relationship to implementation. We are in the same branch – but we have our own models.

The centurion is a loyal character and obviously smarter than his boss without ever showing it. This is the kind of employee that management literature takes for granted. And if all members of the staff were like this, leadership would be simpler. Hiding your light under a bushel for whatever reason is hardly the thing nowadays. Today our models do the opposite. And if we have to choose one of these two plights, the second is preferable.

Undoubtedly the model in the table is Brian. From an analytical point of view, a number of messages can be found that it would be appropriate to adopt without thinking too much about them. One is that it is not at all clear who the Messiah is: it could be you or me (although that is more unlikely). Who will finally have to take the consequences is decided by the context.

Painfully rational

One of the two aspects displayed by leaders who function – the rational and the irrational (Sjöstrand 1997) – has gained the upper hand in this film. A leader who lacks one of these aspects will be limited and will fail in the long run. What makes Reg comic (and not tragic) is that for him rationality outweighs everything else. It is an old ideal of leadership and its consequences that the film describes.

If you do not want people to laugh at you, nowadays it is better to lean towards the irrational than to seem rational. Clear evidence of which way the wind is blowing is that the heroes in the 'guru tales' genre (Sjöstrand 1997, p. 178 ff.) are described as irrational. Many of the writers of these books are justifiably worried that their readers will discover that they have no clothes. Therefore they constantly hold one finger in the air to sense the slightest shift in conventions.

An ordinary organisation?

Finally one may ask whether the organisation we watch Reg leading in the film is not too zany. Is it so peculiar that there is nothing to learn from studying it? We do not think so. And moreover we are doubtful whether it is possible to divide the population up into organisations that are normal and those that are not. Emma Stenström's 'odd (because they are artistic) companies' (2000) seem for instance to be pretty ordinary.

In a short report Johan Hvenmark discusses burnout among managers in voluntary organisations (2001). The voluntary sector consists of 'organisations in that sector of the community between the market and the state' (Wijkström 1999, p. i). What makes Johan Hvenmark's study interesting for us is that he has interviewed executives in the Red Cross who have been asked to describe 'the fundamental reasons for burn-out in voluntary organisations in particular'. These causes can be read as a sample selection of the unsatisfactory circumstances associated with the characteristic nature of voluntary organisations. Although *Life of Brian* does not deal with the Red Cross, its organisation is a voluntary one. The executives interviewed gave the following reasons for burnout:

- vagueness and lack of clarity about operational roles, structures, objectives, areas of responsibility, authority and strategies,
- intolerance of different ways of thinking,
- unprofessional and ineffective leadership,
- being seized by an idea, too much commitment and voluntary work,
- passive, dependent and uncritical acceptance of traditions. (Hvenmark 2001)

Striking, isn't it? The text above could have been printed on the video box. Now it should be said in defence of the Red Cross that from a methodological point of view it is doubtful whether anonymous members of the organisation should be allowed to draw up lists of problems like this. Problems that one wants to describe for some reason, problems that one experiences and problems that actually exist in any real sense are different things. Carrying out the survey in the organisation in no way guarantees its results.

In his PhD thesis Lars-Erik Olsson (1999) is interested in the origin of voluntary organisations. He identifies three phases: the pre-phase, conception phase and maturity phase without going much further in developing these concepts. If we consider leadership in these three phases, it can be characterised in the following way:

> *Pre-phase*
>
> Entrepreneurs or firebrands with certain charismatic qualities. These leaders take risks and are innovative.
>
> *Conception phase*
>
> The leaders are organisers, in other words have their own experience of organising voluntary organisations.
>
> The leaders have certain charismatic qualities.
>
> The leaders have recourse to their own personal networks.
>
> *Maturity phase*
>
> The voluntary organisation is dependent on its leader, especially the founder.
>
> Leadership changes and becomes more institutionalised.
>
> Leaders are elected, for instance, at annual meetings.
>
> (Olsson 1999, p. 78)

Reg's organisation does not really differ in terms of its leadership from the voluntary movements described by Lars-Erik Olsson in his thesis – the Red Cross Noah's Ark Foundation, the 5 to 12 Movement and Moms and Dads in Town. The People's Front of Judaea is shifting from the conception phase to the maturity phase. The same is true of the other 'phenomena' in the analytical model proposed. Even so there can be no doubt that fundamental differences exist. What happens is that these are concealed as structure is dealt with separately from content. What is ridiculous about the voluntary organisation in the film is that it achieves nothing. Another difference can also be added, which is that what they seem to want to do cannot obviously be attained using means that we would appreciate. This is worth bearing in mind, for instance, when suicide attacks take place against civilians.

Satire always has something to say. It offers us action straight away that we can laugh at. We can only perceive a serious message if we reflect a little on what we have seen. One method of sifting out something other than that seen by tired bosses is to negate what is presented, roughly like putting a minus sign in front of every mathematical term – minus and minus make plus. Dealt with like this, *Life of Brian* is definitely not as amusing either to watch or analyse. Instead we see leadership types that function as figureheads, coordinate, supervise, filter and disseminate information (75 per cent of the time), allocate resources, manage work flows, come up with things, plan – on the run – and control, or in other words all that Colin Hales could see in the research records in 1986 already. How amusing is a description like that?

CHAPTER 9

The Godfather – an evil decision maker

Few films succeed in creating their own reality, but those that do establish genres. One such film is *The Godfather* (1972), directed by Francis Ford Coppola and based on the book by Mario Puzo (1969) with the same title (*The Godfather*). Many people are convinced that what is referred to as the Mafia in the USA more or less resembles what is described on the surface of the film. It is not surprising that the film gave rise to a great deal of protest from the Italo-American associations, senators and many others in the USA. The film offers a credible representation of the truth, no matter how fictional it may be. *The Godfather* was nominated for ten Oscars and won the award for best actor in a leading role, best photography and best script. This alone indicates that it was a remarkable film.

We will stick to the first film in the trilogy on the Godfather. Altogether the trilogy was nominated for twenty-nine Oscars and was awarded nine. The first of the films was premiered in 1972, the last as recently as 1990. We are using the version of the film included in the Saga box, which is slightly longer than the one first shown in the cinemas.

This film uses three key concepts – family, business and violent crime. Much of the film is based on keeping these three ingredients separate. When, nevertheless, this fails, the film often shifts direction. Tradition should be added to the three main ingredients. Respect for customs and practices is not merely a way of maintaining relationships but also a means of communication. If you receive a package with something that you know belongs to a good friend together with a dead fish, you know that your good friend is at the bottom of the sea. Clear and explicit symbolism.

One feature of the film is that most things happen very slowly, but, as it were, all the time. Francis Coppola is said to have described the rhythm of the film as 'legato, rather than staccato'. Very little is said in the film. In two hours and forty-seven minutes fewer than 14,000 words are uttered, which means that these few words have to be stretched to their full extent to suffice. (For the sake of comparison it can be pointed out that each chapter of this book comprises about 6,000 words. The words we use would therefore last for five films like *The Godfather.*) However, when murders or similar events take place the tempo becomes rapid, which has a marked impact on their effect.

Another feature of the film is the picture. There is a pale yellow tinge to the image all through the film – in other words it is not your video recorder that is faulty. This creates the impression that we are watching a documentary and could well have been part of the reason why the film, even though it is fictional, was considered to be realistic.

The first scene in the film presents the marriage of Constanzia, the daughter of the Godfather, Don Vito Corleone. While the celebrations are taking place in the garden, Don Vito (played by Marlon Brando) is giving audience, as it were, in his study. This room is gloomy and screened off from the rest of the world. Its doors are closed. There are windows of translucent concrete that you cannot see through and others with drawn Venetian blinds. Martin Johansson writes in his analysis of *The Godfather* (Internet reference 10) that the room 'resembles a prison'. 'However much Don Vito would like to free himself to devote more time to his family, for instance, and stop worrying about what may happen to them, in practice this is impossible.'

First we shape our environment and then it shapes us, as Winston Churchill would probably have put it (Internet reference 11). This room is therefore important for those who in a more limited sense of the word belong to the organisation. It is also important for those who encounter the organisation. There is a symbolism to the rooms and buildings in which organisations are based (see Yanow 1996, chapter six). This means that the furnishing and design of rooms, premises and buildings, etc. enables those running organisations to send signals to those who come into contact with them.

As his daughter is getting married, Don Vito is expected to be generous, even to those who seek audience with him. As the party continues, the important characters are introduced. In addition to Don Vito these include his sons Santino (usually called Sonny), Fredo and Michael (played by Al Pacino). Santino is very close to his father where business is concerned. Fredo is less well endowed intellectually than his brothers and is therefore assigned simpler tasks. But he copes with these really badly as well. When later in the film his father is seriously wounded, Fredo fumbles for his revolver and ends up dropping it without firing one shot.

When the film begins Michael has just returned from the war, where he has earned a number of citations, and he has no ambition whatsoever to take any part in his family's criminal activities. His remark to his fiancée Kay Adams from New Hampshire when an unpleasant but bloodless blackmail is referred to is 'That's my family, Kay. It's not me'.

Tom Hagen plays an important role. He is a lawyer, in the process of becoming what is known as the family's consigliere, i.e. councillor and advisor. Tom was adopted by Don Vito as a child and is considered to be almost a member of the family. The women in the film play relatively obscure roles. One exception is Michael's fiancée Kay, whose questions to Michael enable the audience to get some kind of picture of what is going on. Her dress at the wedding is, moreover, a bright orange, which means that she stands out among the other women.

After the festivities we see a number of scenes that deal with the fulfilment of the promises made by Don Vito at the wedding. One of these promises was to the crooner Johnny Fontane, who complained that he was not getting a part in a film that his career required. Don Vito's response has become a classic.

> I'm gonna make him an offer he can't refuse.

The offer is made to the film producer Jack Woltz. After a number of gambits the issue is resolved when Woltz finds the head of his favourite horse in his bed. Michael quotes the same expression when in response to Kay's persistent questions he divulges a glimpse of how the family operates. This was when Luca Brasi, the most eminent hired assassin in Don Vito's gang, offered a bandleader the choice between his signature and his brain on a contract. Santino also uses the expression on one occasion. This all suggests that offers of this kind are not too unusual in the Corleone family, and that the phrase is a classic one for them as well. When Michael eventually takes over as Godfather he also makes an offer that nobody can refuse. Not even Moe Greene, the owner of a casino – although he resists up until his violent death.

Moe Greene is murdered in his home with a bullet in the eye, just like Bugsy Siegel (1906–1947). However, the other characters in the film do not usually have any evident counterpart in or connection to the Mafia in the USA. The Godfather, Don Vito Corleone recalls certain features of Carlo Gambino (1902–1976) but the resemblance is not particularly close. Johnny Fontane could represent Frank Sinatra (1915–1998) or equally

Vic DeMone (born in 1928). For speculations like these see for example Internet reference 12). What is interesting is how the film and its successors have had such a strong influence on conceptions of the Mafia and its operations in the USA. They have probably also influenced the Mafia's own concept of the values that should typify leadership in the organisation. Mafia bosses also watch movies occasionally.

After some of the promises made during the wedding have been kept, the film shifts direction from everyday gangster behaviour to the war between the mafia families in New York. The background to this war is Don Vito's refusal to become involved in drug dealing. One of Don Vito's very valuable assets is that he 'owns' a large number of politicians and judges. These are not particularly opposed to crimes against drink laws, gambling or prostitution, but they are not, in Don Vito's opinion, going to like drugs.

Virgil Sollozzo is the one who suggests going into the drug business to Don Vito. To ensure the success of his business idea he arranges an attempt to murder Don Vito, who is seriously injured. Santino takes over management of the operations while Don Vito is recovering and a number of circumstances involve Michael increasingly in the family's criminal activities. He definitely becomes part of its operation with the cold-blooded execution of Virgil Sollozzo and the corrupt police chief of the city, McCluskey. One result of the execution is that Michael has to flee to Sicily. This is where he meets the virginal Apollonia. They marry but she is later killed by a bomb intended for Michael.

While Michael is in Sicily, things are happening in the USA. His brother Santino is murdered in an attempt in which his brother-in-law is one of the accomplices. This is unwise as strangulation can be meted out for less. Don Vito finally recovers and resumes power. To keep the peace, he attends a meeting with the other Mafia families where he accepts the launch of the drugs operation. During the meeting Don Vito understands who was behind Sollozzo. He also realises what has to be done. Michael returns to the USA and marries Kay. Don Vito prepares him for the assumption of power by increasingly taking second place. When Don Vito dies of a heart attack, while he is playing with one of his grandchildren (Michael's son Anthony), Michael is well trained.

When Constanzia's son is christened, Michael is the Godfather, and it is on his orders that various competitors are executed. The film ends with Michael denying to Kay that he is behind the murders. Isolated and inured, he survives as the undisputed Godfather.

There are a number of leader figures in the film. On first viewing Don Vito stands out most clearly, but as you watch the film again Michael emerges as an increasingly important leader. This is particularly noticeable in *The Godfather II* and *The Godfather III*. Both Don Vito (Marlon Brando) and Michael (Al Pacino) make a strong impression both during and after the film. The impact made by Santino (played by James Caan) is less distinct but his behaviour is also interesting from an analytical point of view. We focus below on the actions of these three leaders in the film.

Vito Corleone

There are not very many sides to Don Vito Corleone. A great deal is revealed in the following scene, which takes place towards the end of the wedding that starts the film. The crooner Johnny Fontane has requested a meeting with Don Vito Corleone and complains that he is not getting the part in a film that he wants.

VITO CORLEONE (to Johnny, after glancing to see Sonny enter):
You spend time with your family?

JOHNNY:
Sure I do.

VITO CORLEONE (to Johnny, but toward and about Sonny):
Good. 'Cause a man who doesn't spend time with his family can never be a real man. (then, to Johnny). Come're. (then) You look terrible. I want you to eat. I want you to rest a while. And in a month from now, this – Hollywood bigshot's gonna give you what you want.

JOHNNY:
It's too late; they start shooting in a week.

VITO CORLEONE:
I'm gonna make him an offer he can't refuse. (then) Now you just go outside and enjoy yourself, and ah, forget about all this nonsense. I want you to leave it all to me.

Here Santino has come directly from an encounter with his young and well-endowed mistress in the upstairs bathroom. This is something that Don Vito obviously disapproves of. His moral code is relatively predictable. Business is for men and men should take care of their families. Just before Don Vito dies he says the following when talking to Michael in confidence: 'I spent my life trying not to be careless – women and children can be careless, but not men.' A man should be happy with his family. Don Vito stresses this not only in the scene above but also several times during the film.

Bonds of friendship

Family, the private sphere, is one thing, business another. The separation is necessary, not least to enable decisions to be made rationally. The distinction between business and private life is merely one aspect of this. At the same time business is not done merely to make money, or even mainly to make money. Actions are motivated largely by friendship or indebtedness combined with respect. The money comes anyway.

During Constanzia's wedding reception the wealthy undertaker Amerigo Bonasera asks Don Corleone for justice. Bonasera is an elderly man. He and his family have lived an American life. Even though Don Vito's wife is the godmother of Bonasera's only child, he has avoided contact with them so as 'not to end up in trouble'. Don Vito claims to understand. Now Bonasera asks for justice. His daughter is in hospital with a broken nose and broken jaw – 'it's held together by wire' – after fighting off her American boy-friend and his friend when they tried to take advantage of her. They were condemned to three years in prison, given a conditional discharge and released on the same day.

Bonasera wants to see the men dead. This turns out not to be the kind of request that can be made offhand. 'I can't remember the last time that you invited me to your house for a cup of coffee', Don Vito snarls. He does not have people murdered for money. What Bonasera has to do is offer his friendship, kiss his hand, address him as Godfather and accept that a return favour may be requested in the future. This is what happens. When Amerigo Bonasera has left, Don Vito asks Tom Hagen to give the job to Clemenza. The problem will be handled without killing as 'blood is a great expense' as Sollozzo says in another scene. Towards the end of the film Don Vito asks his friend to return the favour. He is asked to tidy up Santino's corpse as it has been so shot to pieces that it cannot be displayed to his mother in the condition it is in.

Reflection and information

One obvious feature is Don Vito's reflective manner. Reflection seems to be an important instrument for a leader. Making people wait establishes respect. When Don Vito's reflection is interrupted, he is quick to reprimand. But only Santino makes this kind of mistake and he is made aware of this in front of everyone else.

Reflection also suggests decisions are calculated, in the sense that they are firmly grounded. Don Vito is not required to justify his decisions, but occasionally he does so. When he decides to help Bonasera to attain the satisfaction he seeks he says: 'Ah, give this to ah, Clemenza. I want reliable people; people that aren't gonna be carried away. I'm mean, we're not murderers, despite of what this undertaker says.'

After listening carefully to Sollozzo and deciding not to become involved in dealing with drugs Don Vito makes the following remark: 'I heard that you're a serious man, to be treated with respect. (then, after sitting) But uh, I must say 'no' to you – and I'll give you my reasons. It's true, I have a lot of friends in politics, but they wouldn't be friendly very long if they knew my business was drugs instead of gambling, which they rule that as a – harmless vice. But drugs is a dirty business.' After this the issue is dismissed.

Decisions are not made only in the light of reflection, they are also based on information. Don Vito seeks information from others, but most often he puts the pieces together himself to reach an irrevocable decision. Here, in other words, we have a combination of curiosity, reflection, calculation and also experience.

Experience

Several times during the film Don Vito displays an almost uncanny ability to interpret signs and move things in the direction he wants to. The way in which Don Vito talks to Bonasera, rebuking, accusing and forgiving, can lead to no other result than Bonasera's submission to his will.

Don Vito also realises in some way during a meeting that Don Barzini is really the man behind the attempt on his life. He knows things like how to recognise a traitor. To put it briefly, he knows his own operation – perhaps better than anyone else. In actual fact Don Vito makes only one mistake. This is when he does not realise that an attempt will be made on his life while he is buying fruit, the audience understand this much earlier.

Don Vito leaves behind him a clear line of wise, considerate, experienced, decisive and just leaders. He can even afford to let go. At the end of the film he becomes Michael's consigliere, providing him with support in every way. Don Vito is presented as a sympathetic individual – even though he is a gangster. But for this last feature, he would make an excellent President of the USA or the board of Mercedes Benz.

There was some criticism of the film for the links it made between criminality and Italians in the USA. Francis Coppola did not accept this criticism. On the other hand he does say in the forefilm (foreword but in film) to *The Godfather II* (1974) that he agrees with those who consider that he presented Don Vito as too sympathetic and admirable a figure.

Decisions – rational or irrational?

There are few phenomena as closely linked to leadership as making decisions. Leaders are expected to decide, but they do not spend a great deal of their time on the process. Well – that depends of course on what you mean by decisions. The Nobel Laureate Herbert Simon is one of those who have devoted some thought to this area. Sometimes things become difficult if you think too much. For Herbert Simon decisions are conscious or unconscious choices. With a definition like this deciding is everything, or in other words nothing. If we are to endow the concept of decision making with any meaning we need some form of definition or link. We use decision here to mean the kind of determination that is primarily intended to influence the actions of others.

Rational norms

In normal cases making decisions is relatively simple. Then rational patterns apply. There are divided opinions about what the decision-making pattern looks like in detail. A not infrequent version looks like this (it can be found for instance in Sharkansky 1978 and March 1994).

1. Identify the problem
2. Establish goals and rank them
3. List all conceivable alternatives
4. Evaluate the alternatives
5. Choose the alternative that best fits in with item 2.

Rational models of choice are fundamental to microeconomics when dealing with the allocation of resources, political theories about the creation of coalitions, statistical decision theory and many other models in the social sciences. The concept of rational choice is probably as old as concepts about human behaviour. (March 1994).

Criticism of rational theories

Even though the rational choice pattern is the norm, everyone is aware that is has not escaped criticism. The norm of rational choice may well quite simply be the most criticised norm we are blessed with. It is not particularly difficult to show that the goals of an organisation are often contradictory or not at all susceptible to ranking (see Rombach 1991). Even so we do not have to view the idea of an explicit goal as something logical and therefore paradoxical. It is considerably less frustrating to view it as something paralogical, i.e. something that is not linked to logic (Czarniawska-Joerges

1992). Social behaviour can be better understood if it is seen as essentially social rather than scientific.

Evaluating all the conceivable alternatives is even more unreasonable. In the fifties Charles Lindblom had already made the following comment. 'Limits on human intellectual capacities and on available information set definite limits to man's capacity to be comprehensive. In actual fact, therefore, no one can practise the rational comprehensive method for really complex problems ...' (Lindblom 1959, p. 84). Things become no better when the time available is usually restricted.

The criticism of the rational decision-making model can be made extremely extensive. Indeed, every book about decision making seems to begin with a chapter describing what is wrong with the model. Guy Peters (1988) speaks on behalf of many others when he asserts that the rational model lacks all contact with reality. Nils Brunsson and Sten Jönsson do not mince their words when they point out that it almost feels 'like kicking a man when he's down to criticise this decision-making model' (Brunsson and Jönsson 1979, p. 18).

Despite this massive criticism the rational model survives and thrives. One could well ask why. One explanation is that none, or at least few, of us feel particularly comfortable in describing ourselves as irrational, however apt it may be (see Brunsson 1985). Another explanation may be that when we say rational in everyday speech we do not mean rational but rather sensible just here and now.

A third explanation may be that we have just been to the cinema to see *The Godfather*. In movies decisions can be presented as rational. Take the scene when Don Vito goes to a meeting to listen to Virgil Sollozzo. The problem is clear. The subject is business and Sollozzo has qualifications in this area that he can refer to. Sollozzo presents the relevant information. Don Vito weighs the alternative of making a lot of money against the risk of losing the support he enjoys from politicians and judges. His decision seems to be a well-grounded one and follows the rational choice model. This is not a one-off occurrence. The way in which Don Vito makes his decisions concurs in all essentials with the rational model. Even so, we ask ourselves whether there may not be an alternative model that would be even more appropriate.

Three classics

For many years a decision-making model presented by Michael Cohen, James March and Johan Olsen more than thirty years ago (1972) has been classical. It is called the 'Garbage Can' model. Briefly, it states that decisions come about when the problem, solution, decision maker and options are all in the same place. One interpretation beneath the surface of the film could be that Don Vito was looking for an opportunity to state that he was against dealing in drugs and this was provided when Sollozzo raised the issue. This interpretation is contradicted by everything else that happened after the meeting.

It is not necessary to link the decision with what is subsequently done. A not-infrequent discussion in the literature on decisions is about the lack of any need for decisions and actions (in the sense of implementation) to relate to each other. There are examples of organisations where a decision is made, some other action taken and it is claimed that a third has been adopted. This is often referred to as decoupling (see Meyer och Rowan 1977; Rombach 1986; Solli et al. 2005). For Don Vito decision and action are linked to each other, where speech fits in is less clear. A gangster can hardly go round telling the truth all the time.

Another classical decision theory is known as 'Muddling through'. This states that decisions are not made in one go but result from struggling through a maze of obstacles, especially those posed by lack of comparison with the alternatives (Lindblom 1959). This is definitely an appealing description of how, in spite of everything, decisions are made.

In a later article (1979) Charles Lindblom has developed his ideas about 'Muddling through' and claims that it is not only a good description but also a good norm. Decisions are reasonable if they are muddled through. Don Vito does not share this opinion but endorses instead our preconception that strong leaders offer explicit decisions. There is definitely no muddling through in *The Godfather*.

Another theoretical school that seems to fit in with what we are discussing here involves dynamic decision making. The idea here is that the situation is continually changing and it is therefore obvious that new decisions must subsequently be made. This is in other words a decision theory that assumes no termination of the process and where counter decisions are frequent. If decisions are considered from this perspective, the time factor becomes important (Brehmer 1992). It is not only a question of what to do but also when.

One vital element in dynamic decision theory is the decision maker's ability to deal with feedback. Here complications of many kinds may arise. Inadequate information is obviously one of them but another is the decision maker's ability to see that old solutions no longer function (Kerstholt and Haajmakers 1997). It seems to us that this is one area where Don Vito has problems: the methods that served him during Prohibition no longer work as well in the new era of drug dealing.

Rational decisions

From whatever angle we consider Don Vito and his decision making, we have to conclude that the rational decision model provides an apt description of how he sets about making his decisions. One can wonder how the rational model can appear to be so unlikely and still serve to describe Don Vito's behaviour. The answer can be found in the desire that we all share to be rational. When we have made up our minds we can often retrospectively construct a sequence of events that does in fact seem rational. Post-rationalisation is the word! In films it is possible to post-rationalise before the event, then it looks a lot more sensible. Barbara Czarniawska (2001) sees this as the logic of representation, the rational way is the way to explain what we do, but it is not what we do.

Decisions – conscious or unconscious

The decision models we have considered up to now share one common feature. They presuppose a conscious decision maker. It is the methods of arriving at and viewing the decisions that differ. But no critical appraisal of decision making can allow this consciousness to stand unchallenged.

Tor Nørretranders (1999) has made a thorough study of whether decisions are conscious or unconscious. His primary point of departure is Benjamin Libet's experiment. This consisted of an attempt by Libet to describe minor phenomena in detail, like how the decision to move a finger is made. His conclusions are used to understand decision making on the level of principle. Just like the results of a lot of other micro-oriented research, Benjamin Libet's findings have considerable philosophical relevance.

One of the conclusions that Benjamin Libet came to on the basis of his experiment is that 'the consciousness that one wants to perform an action on which you decide yourself comes into being almost half a second after the brain has begun to implement the decision' (Nørretranders 1999, page 292). It is possible to challenge this finding and there is research that suggests it does not take as long as half a second before we become aware of what the brain is doing. It seems fairly certain that the brain does a lot of things before we are aware of what is going on. It can be objected that in the end we do become aware of what the brain is up to. But it is significant that there is some delay before this is the case.

To begin with, we can discuss what is meant by 'free will' if a decision is made before we know about it. This image of decision making totally contradicts a great deal of the research about decisions in the management sphere. Is it possible that decisions are something we normally make unconsciously? The answer according to Benjamin Libet is both yes and no. Yes, because it actually happens before we are aware of it. No, because we do nevertheless become conscious of our decisions and then our consciousness can veto the decision made by our unconscious.

Consciousness cannot initiate an action, but it can decide not to complete the action. Consciousness in other words says no. Another factor is that consciousness does not usually say no. It does not care, so to speak. When conflict arises between the conscious and the unconscious, the conscious prevails. All of this results in what is called in suppressed experiences the Freudian tradition. This means that the veto process is a fairly unpleasant phenomenon. Or to quote Tor Nørretranders on this point 'human beings feel best when they are merely taking action' (1999, p. 332).

Benjamin Libet gives us data on which we can base a model that clearly conflicts with the rational model. In our opinion, his contribution enables us to close the circle. We can better understand Don Vito's erroneous decisions. Almost certainly Don Vito decided unconsciously to extend operations to include drug dealing as well. A villain is after all a villain (and that is what Don Vito is, in case anyone has forgotten in the course of all this). When he becomes aware of his decision his veto machinery, in the form of his consciousness, swings into action and prevents it. And of course, in the long run, things screw up.

Santino (Sonny) Corleone

Santino's actions prompt thoughts about managers and leaders (see for instance Katz and Kahn 1978, Blom 1994). He takes over when his father is shot and wounded. This is natural as he is the eldest son. Santino is not a total failure as a leader. He gets others to do as he wants. His major problem is his temper. It makes him act quickly without reflection or at times without even telling his associates what is going on. The results are what can be expected. The enemy knows that he is hot-blooded and that he can easily be lured into an ambush. He takes the bait and is mown down.

Don Vito knows that his eldest son Santino is not a suitable successor and so do most others as well. This becomes clear when he is 'standing in' as Godfather. To be a leader it is not enough to think with your feet and fists.

The fact that Santino cheats on his wife emphasises his unsuitability to lead. Tom Hagen may smile when he hears evidence of his infidelity through the door at the wedding at the beginning of the film. But cheating his wife does not earn him respect. Santino does not even seem to realise that his behaviour is unwise, but carries on so openly that even his wife can see what is going on. On one occasion we see his bodyguards lined up waiting outside his lover's apartment while he is visiting her.

Neither Don Vito nor Michael could imagine being unfaithful to their wives. When a group of attractive young ladies and an orchestra (!) confront Michael in his hotel room while he is visiting Las Vegas, they are immediately sent packing. A leader needs to be respected if he is to impose his rules on his associates. Without respect there are only cudgels to turn to …

Under Santino's leadership business is mixed with emotion. He seeks revenge. And he talks about business at the dinner table. 'Papa never talked business at the table, and in front of the kids', as Connie points out. While Don Vito was leader, the only violence invoked was what was needed for business purposes. There was nothing personal. The attempt on Don Vito's own life was, according to Tom Hagen, also just business. Nothing personal.

Santino's role in the film is an important one: he provides a contrast. He represents the opposite to Don Vito's reflective manner and also to Michael's long-term planning. Santino's presence makes Michael's qualities even more inescapable. It is possible that this contrast is also what makes him an important part of the organisation. If everyone is similar it is more difficult to differentiate the good from the bad. Business intelligence also becomes more difficult in a homogenous organisation.

This contrast makes us recall an argument of Pierre Bourdieu's (with reference to Plato) that concerned 'fast-thinkers' and with it, in our interpretation, 'slow-thinkers' (for example 1998, pp. 44–46). In this era of economism admiration goes to the quick gains of stock traders and the conception of how quickly things are happening (Löfgren 2001). There is little appreciation of those who think slowly. *The Godfather* shows clearly that 'slow-thinkers' are superior in the long run, a conclusion that Plato, Pierre Bourdieu and we approve of.

Michael Corleone

Michael, the youngest son, has a major role in the film. If you count the minutes spent on screen it is doubtful whether Marlon Brando or Al Pacino has the leading role. But as the Oscar for the best leading role was awarded to Marlon Brando, he must have played the lead. If Don Vito ages in the film, Michael undergoes another transformation. At the beginning of the film he appears to be a brave young man who deliberately distances himself from the activities of his family. When he frankly tells his fiancée Kay what his family does and what methods they use he concludes by saying that he is different.

Michael behaves like a chameleon. As his role gradually changes so does the way he dresses, his haircut and his stance. From having been somewhat casual, slightly unkempt and relaxed, in the last frame he is wearing a suit, his hair is Brylcreemed and his back is as straight as a ramrod. In addition he lies like a Mafioso. In several respects he becomes more and more like his father. In Sicily, when he asks for the hand of the daughter of the innkeeper Vitelli in marriage he moves his hands in the same way as his father does.

Michael becomes the leader at a specific moment. When he is about to visit his father after the shooting he realises that a new attempt is going to be made on his life. By commandeering a nurse and persuading the peaceful baker Enzo, who has come to make a sick visit, to look like a guard, he effectively prevents the attempted assassination. Shooting Sollozzo and McClusky is then the logical development for someone who takes responsibility and command. What is interesting is the circumspection with which he plans the murder and how much he hates doing it.

Once Michael has returned from Sicily it becomes increasingly clear that Don Vito realises he is the one who must take over. Don Vito had really intended Michael to become a good governor or to attain some other respected post. As Michael assumes more and more responsibility he behaves like someone with long-term plans. All the time he says that the aim is eventually to enable the family to operate within the bounds of the law. His plans are often dramatic. All the murders that take place while he himself is becoming his nephew's godson are calculated, well timed and, not least, effective. We are then shown how difficult it can be to judge your allies. Tession (Sal) is a traitor and must die. We all thought it would be someone else.

Michael's assumption of the role of chief is remarkably painless. This certainly does not apply to all beginners. Linda Hill's (1992) study of managers in their first year provides an admirable comparison. She studied nineteen managers: fourteen men and five women. These new bosses were manifestly surprised by their new role. Their often romantic image of what leadership involved soon took a tumble. Even though this is a well-known phenomenon for researchers, the new managers were surprised by how frequently they were interrupted. They also found it difficult to shift from being popular to being respected. And they had underestimated the effort required to adapt from defending their own position to defending an entire organisation.

Other kinds of difficulties experienced by the new managers in Linda Hill's study involved the struggle not to be overwhelmed with tasks. Delegating sounds easy but is difficult. The managers who were unable to delegate not only ended up with a great deal to do but their staff interpreted it as meaning that their new bosses placed no confidence in them. The question 'how can I trust a boss that does not trust me?' is justifiable. Other difficulties for the new managers resulted from the realisation that not all of their staff could be treated in the same way – being fair involves acting in different ways to people.

Linda Hill concluded that on the whole managers learned what they had to learn, which is only to some extent what one wants to learn. Managers need problems if they are to learn. Professional expertise and training may help in this direction, but problems and surprises are needed as well. Linda Hill claims that the way to become a good manager is by simply being a manager. One way of putting this is that being a boss should be practised on a small scale before major tasks are confronted. Another piece of good advice from Linda Hill was that leadership should be based on the desire to become a leader combined with a realistic conception of what leadership involves.

Michael does not really offer support for Linda Hill's argument: for him things are too easy. Santino's failure is more apt. Santino can neither learn nor delegate, and that's why things end as they do. Michael does not want to be the boss, at least that is what he says, but he understands that he has to be. It is the organisation's unspoken norm system that more or less summons him. Instead of growing into the role, he is given proper support by his previous boss, i.e. Don Vito. This seems to provide a good substitute for his experience. Here there is almost certainly a great deal to be found in popular literature on mentorship in working life.

Michael has absolutely no problems with respect, on the contrary sometime the opposite is true. Even though he has earned some respect by being a war hero and demonstrating the capacity to act when his father is wounded, it is the organisation that confers respect. The organisation needs a respected leader and so it turns him into one. One conclusion that could be drawn from the argument presented here is that a leader's ability to learn his role is important. But that is not enough – existing norm systems (or institutions as they are called) also play an important role for whether leaders succeed.

Otherwise we can observe that efficiency is Michael's chief feature. He does not even eat unnecessarily, not even when offered food. The efficiency with which he murdered Sollozzo and McCluskey is seen in everything he does. Michael only really fails in two respects. One is when his Italian wife is murdered in Sicily, the other is that he never attains his explicit goal of running the operation within the bounds of the law.

Those who have seen the rest of the trilogy know that Michael never succeeds in attaining his primary objective. Nor does his transformation finish with the first film. Being efficient has its price – but that is another movie.

CHAPTER 10

The Bridge on the River Kwai – the curse of principles

Right and wrong are tricky gradations. Even so, we intend to devote this chapter to what the leaders in the film get right and where they go wrong. What behaviour leads to downfall and exclusion from the film? What provides success, security and creates heroes? The film we have chosen to illustrate this, or rather the film that invited this approach, is *The Bridge on the River Kwai* (1957). You must know it – it is the one where the soldiers march into the prison camp whistling.

The Bridge on the River Kwai is based on the novel written in 1952 by Pierre Boulle, *Le pont de la rivière Kwaï*. It is worth noting that the book differs from the film on a number of points. It describes a different kind of leadership from the film. Even though this is an interesting subject, the differences between the book and the film will not be examined here. This has been done well by others and does not belong to our analysis, where our starting point is that novels are not read while films are watched.

A great deal has been written about *The Bridge on the River Kwai*. The director who made the film, David Lean, never found the time, however, to write his memoirs. *David Lean*, a very readable presentation of interviews by Kevin Brownlow (1997), tells us a great deal that is amusing and interesting about the film. The DVD-version also contains worthwhile 'extra features'. Eddie Fowlie (Property Master) describes for instance what happened when they frightened thousands of birds in the scene in which Jack Hawkins is shot in the foot – about which more later. The magnificent impression this made on the viewers had its drawback for those standing around, who were drenched in a warm, evil-smelling downpour. However, we have not taken information of this kind into account, as few who have seen the film have read the book about it or had the energy to work through the extra material on the DVD.

There are a number of reasons for our choice of *The Bridge on the River Kwai*. It was the film that attracted most viewers in 1958 and this means that there is a good chance that most people born in the 1940s have seen it. Those of us who were born later have seen most films. The film won seven Oscars and one of the actors (William Holden) was paid more than had ever been paid earlier. If the million dollars he received is recalculated in terms of today's rates and added to the percentage of the gate he earned, you can still hire a relatively well-known actor for the same amount.

Yet another reason for choosing *The Bridge on the River Kwai* is that it is a film that presents many aspects of leadership. We see for instance ingredients like motivation, power, comradeship, leaders failing, leaders succeeding, situational leadership and ethics. After we had finished out analysis we discovered that *The Bridge on the River Kwai* is included in the *Hartwick Classic Film Leadership Cases*. These are intended for use at university level to enable students to watch films and then analyse and discuss leadership. This is definitely a film about leadership. Although Hartwick's teacher's guide was scanty, it still confirmed some of what we had discovered for ourselves.

Three leaders

The Bridge on the River Kwai offers us a clear presentation of three leaders: Colonel Nicholson who is in command of the remnants of the British battalion in captivity; Colonel Saito, commander of the prison camp and responsible for building the bridge over the river that will provide a link between Bangkok and Rangoon, as well as Major Warden from unit 316, who commands the small unit that blow the bridge up at the end of the film.

In addition, we are offered more restricted insight into the leadership exercised by Colonel Saito's superiors. The pressure they exert by radio to ensure that the schedule is adhered to is their sole form of contribution. We also meet Colonel Green who is in command of unit 316. Less successful attempts to lead are offered by Lieutenant Miura, who is in charge of the actual building work on the bridge until he is replaced and drives a dagger into his torso. Typically Japanese on film! The other British officers and the medical officer, Major Clipton, also exert some leadership. And there are sure to be others as well.

A relatively unknown film was also made in 1989 with the somewhat non-promising title of *Bridge on the River Kwai 2*. The sequel is based on the book written by Joan and Clay Blair in 1979 called *Return from the River Kwai*. In it they claim to tell a story that is more authentic than its predecessor. The preface tells us this: 'In February 1945 aircraft from the American 493rd squadron bombed the bridges over the River Kwai in Thailand, then occupied by the Japanese. This film is based on true events during this period.' It is not a continuation of the previous film nor is it a 'remake'. It begins by showing us the prison camp, the Japanese officers, the medical officer who now plays an important role, and the sun. Soon the bridge is blown up and the film tells us what then happens when the prisoners are transported to Japan. The film is not as bad as you might expect. It can teach leaders a thing or two as well.

A whistling start

As the title credits roll the whistling starts – of *The Colonel Bogey March*. The British soldiers are tired and ragged, but they radiate pride. The whistling helps. One may well ask why they are whistling on their way into a Japanese prisoner-of-war camp. The explanation can be found in the words that go with the tune. In 1956 it was perhaps impossible to sing them on film, and maybe not while entering a prisoner-of-war camp, but it was all right to whistle.

In the sources we have found on the Internet (among them the one below) *The Colonel Bogey March* can be dated to 1939–1940. This could well be true. There are various texts with minor differences but usually they are more or less the same as the one below (Internet reference 13).

Hitler, he only had one ball,
Goering had two but very small,
Himmler had something similar,
But poor old Goebbels had no balls at all.

Frankfurt has only one beer hall,
Stuttgart, die München all on call,
Munich, vee lift our tunich,
To show vee 'Cherman' have no balls at all.

Hans Otto is very short, not tall,
And blotto, for drinking Singhai and Skol.
A 'Cherman', unlike Bruce Erwin,
Because Hans Otto has no balls at all.

Sometimes, however, there is a different version of the first four lines. However, as far as we have seen, always as a second alternative. We have to imagine, in other words, that the British prisoners wanted to sing the text above but did not dare to: partly to save the blushes of the cinema audience and partly because of authenticity. Because we are told that British prisoners-of-war did in fact whistle the march as a form of protest against their captors during the Second World War.

Hitler, he only had one ball,
The other was in the Albert Hall
His mother, the dirty Bugger,
Chopped it off when he was small

(Internet reference 14)

The actual music for the march dates from 1914. It was written by Lieutenant Frederick Joseph Ricketts (1881–1945) under the pseudonym of Kenneth J Alford. It is said that Frederick Ricketts assumed the pseudonym because army officers were not supposed to earn money from other forms of work. The melody appears to have no military background even though a lieutenant at Fort George near Inverness in Scotland composed it. If we are to believe a widespread legend (see Internet references 15 or 16), an eccentric colonel whose nickname was Bogey used to whistle the first two notes of what was later to be the march before teeing off in golf (instead of shouting FORE!) and Rickets used to respond with the rest. In other words a golf march – if this is true.

What is somewhat amusing otherwise is that Malcolm Arnold (born 1921) received an Oscar for the music in the film. This included the River Kwai March, which is not the one whistled here. This is the music that takes over from the whistling, so that the score does not dominate the visual impact.

The prisoners arrive at the camp

We see a bird-of-prey in flight and then the jungle of Sri Lanka (which is made to serve for Thailand) from high above. We see it from the perspective of the bird-of-prey. Rapidly down to the treetops. Then slowly down to the ground where we see the simple crosses. A number of graves line the railway track. A train passes. It is carrying prisoners-of-war. Why otherwise would the machine guns be pointing at the passengers huddled in the open trucks?

At the railhead they dismount. Urged on by repeated Japanese commands, the group moves forwards. Alec Guinness, who plays the part of Colonel Nicholson is at their head, with a wand in his hand and bag over his shoulder. His wand looks magic.

The camera reaches the prison camp before the group from the train. Once there we witness a funeral, or rather a burial. William Holden (his face covered in stubble, his chest clean-shaven) and a fellow prisoner provide the grave with a simple cross among the many others. Shears (the role played by William Holden) tells the guard that he wants to go sick and then begs a cigarette end from him. Captain Kanematsu receives a lighter that belonged to the recently buried soldier (Herbert Thompson, who died of beri beri). Despite his appearance, Shears is hardly the hero type. Heroes do not wheedle sick leave when they are fit and do not trade what they have plundered from the dead for cigarette ends. As this is a film, we guess that Holden will get his chance to display heroism later on. In real life, off the silver screen, it is more difficult to take many steps up the status ladder.

The Japanese flag sways idly in the breeze. It is hot. The year is 1943. An elderly man who does not look European is sitting on the veranda of a house pulling regularly at a rope. In this way, he causes a large suspended sheet of canvas to move and circulate the air inside the building. This is a 'punkah', according to *Webster's New World Dictionary* 'pun|kah or pun|ka (pung'kê) n. in India, a large fan made from the Palmyra leaf, or a large, swinging fan consisting of canvas stretched over a rectangular frame and hung from the ceiling'.

Captain Kanematsu reports that the British prisoners have arrived. Colonel Saito thanks him and we hear the prisoners – whistling! Left turn! Stand at ease! A crate is carried out. Colonel Saito salutes Nicholson and climbs on to the crate.

COLONEL SAITO:

In the name of His Imperial Majesty I welcome you. I am the commanding officer of this camp, which is Camp 16 along the great railroad, which will soon connect Bangkok with Rangoon. You British prisoners have been chosen to build a bridge across the River Kwai. It will be pleasant work requiring skill. And officers will work as well as men. The Japanese Army cannot have idle mouths to feed. If you work hard, you will be treated well. But if you do not work hard, you will be punished. A word to you about escape. There is no barbed wire. No stockade. No watchtower. They are not necessary. We are on an island in the jungle. Escape is impossible. You would die. Today you rest.

Tomorrow you'll begin. Let me remind you of General Yamashita's motto: Be happy in your work. Dismissed.

COLONEL NICHOLSON (to Hughes, one of his officers):
Hughes, get the men to their quarters. See who's sick. I'm going to have a word with this fellow.

COLONEL NICHOLSON (to Saito):
Colonel! I heard your remarks just now, sir. My men will carry on in the way one expects of a British soldier. My officers and I will be responsible for their conduct. You may have overlooked the fact that the use of officers for labour is expressly forbidden by the Geneva Convention.

COLONEL SAITO:
Is that so?

COLONEL NICHOLSON:
I have a copy of the convention and would be glad to let you glance through it.

COLONEL SAITO:
That will not be necessary.

Then there is a thunderstorm and a downfall of rain. Nicholson and the officers inspect the men's quarters. One glance from Nicholson and – yes sir – the roof of this hut will be dealt with. Nicholson goes on to the sick bay. He greets the patients and talks to Major Clipton, the medical officer. Nicholson is also introduced to Shears, a captain in the United States navy. Apparently the lighter was enough to get him sick leave straight away. Clipton says that this is 'all that's left of the prisoners who built the camp'. Shears explains of the others: 'They died of malaria, dysentery, beri beri, gangrene. Other causes of death: starvation, overwork, bullet wounds, and snakebites. Saito. Then there were some who just got tired of living'.

That evening the (captive) officers have a meeting. At the end of the meeting Jennings raises the question of an escape committee. Nicholson responds straight away that there will be none. Even though Jennings has a plan. Even Clipton wants discussion of the idea. The talk continues for a while without the plan ever being disclosed to us.

COLONEL NICHOLSON:
I understand how you feel. Of course, it's the duty of a captured sol-

dier to attempt escape. But my men and I are involved in a curious legal point of which you are unaware. In Singapore we were ordered to surrender by command headquarters. Ordered, mind you. Therefore, in our case, escape might well be an infraction of military law.

COMMANDER SHEARS:
I'm sorry sir, I didn't quite follow you. You intend to uphold the letter of the law, no matter what it costs?

COLONEL NICHOLSON:
Without law, commander, there is no civilization.

COMMANDER SHEARS:
That's just my point. Here, there is no civilization.

COLONEL NICHOLSON:
Then we have the opportunity to introduce it ... I want everything to go off smoothly starting tomorrow morning.

Nicholson's ability to judge people turns out to be extremely limited. He considers that Saito is a 'reasonable man'. Nor does he understand that Shears has survived through cunning and dissimulation. Shears's experiences have turned him into a 'Queer bird. Even for an American' in Nicholson's eyes. But Nicholson is good with groups. It is interesting that this can involve two totally different things. This does not apply to all the leaders we have seen in the films. Tony D'Amato, for example, in *Any Given Sunday* (chapter two) was good at talking to groups and chatting with individuals.

COLONEL NICHOLSON:
And remember this: Our men must always feel they are still commanded by us and not by the Japanese. So long as they have that idea they'll be soldiers and not slaves.

Organisation seizes up

Next morning a low wooden table with steps behind it has been placed in front of the prisoners. Colonel Saito in a white helmet climbs on to it.

COLONEL SAITO:
English prisoners! Notice I do not say English soldiers. From the moment you surrendered, you ceased to be soldiers. You will finish

> the bridge by the May 12th. You will work under the direction of a Japanese engineer. Time is short. All men will work. Your officers will work besides you. This is only just, for it is they who betrayed you by surrender. Your shame is their dishonour. It is they who told you better to live like a coolie then die like a hero. It is they who brought you here. Not I. Therefore, they will join you in useful labour. That is all. Officer prisoners, collect your tools.

Huckley, one of the NCOs, steps forward: obviously about to obey the order. Nicholson immediately orders him back into the ranks. Saito climbs down the three steps from the wooden table and walks up to Nicholson, who again refers to the Geneva Convention (Article 27). He reads 'Belligerents may employ prisoners of war who are fit, other than officers'. After another brief exchange of opinions, Nicholson is struck severely across the mouth. His men move forward in anger but are stopped by Nicholson. 'Stand fast in the ranks!'

COLONEL SAITO (really angry):

> You speak to me of Code? What 'Code'? The coward's code! (Saito tosses Nicholson's booklet away.) What do you know of soldier's code? Of bushido? Nothing! You are unworthy to command! (Saito grabs Nicholson's wand, breaks it and throws it to the ground.)

Nicholson retrieves the booklet from the ground – as one would if a defiant child had thrown it there. He says: 'If you refuse to abide by the laws of civilized world we must consider ourselves absolved from our duty to obey you. My officers will not do manual labour.' Saito responds: 'We shall see', and turns to all the captives behind Nicholson. He gives the order 'All enlisted prisoners to work!' but there is no reaction at all. Saito then gives some orders in Japanese (which are not translated). The guards move, their rifles raised. Nicholson then turns round and orders the sergeant-major to lead the men to their work. He does. At the same time we hear a small truck approach. Two men are sitting on it with a machine gun.

The large group of British prisoners contains eight officers in addition to Nicholson. Their contribution to the daily work can hardly play a decisive role for Saito, and the whole thing is obviously a matter of principle. Both Nicholson and Saito seem prepared to go a long way to defend their principles. This may be British. The question is how it fits in with bushido. Bushido means the path of the warrior and is a system of rules of conduct that were primarily intended for the Samurai.

> The roots of bushido can be traced back to a number of sources. Buddhism provides the calm and resignation in the face of the inevitable, impassivity in the face of death. Shinto prescribes loyalty to superiors, reverence for the memory of our ancestors and respect for parents. The third source was Confucianism, with its various moral stances to others. Together with Zen Buddhism, bushido governed all the actions of the Samurai, in war and in peace. The most important Samurai qualities were integrity, courage, humanity, courtesy, honesty, diligence and a desire for honour. (Internet reference 17)

So far bushido fits in well with the British norms we recognise from other historical dramas. Before we leave this question, we would like to cite *A Book of Five Rings* by Miyamoto Musashi (born in 1584, 1974). This book is often referred to on the Internet and is a best-seller among devotees of the martial arts all over the world. What is interesting is that according to this publication the refinement and the principles apply to everything but the fighting. Then all that matters is effectiveness. At the beginning of the film Saito does not appear to have adopted this other interpretation but seems ready to sacrifice the bridge and, in the long run, himself for his principles.

COLONEL SAITO:
I will count three. If by the third count you and your officers are not on the way to work I will give the order to fire.

COMMANDER SHEARS (From the sick bay to the Medical Officer, Major Clipton):
He is going to do it! …

COLONEL SAITO:
One.

COLONEL NICHOLSON:
I warn you, Colonel … (You may well wonder – about what?)

COLONEL SAITO:
Two. (He raises his arm to give the order to fire.)

MAJOR CLIPTON (rushed forward):
Stop! Colonel Saito, I've been seen and heard everything. So has every man at the hospital. They're too many witnesses. You can't call it a

mass escape. Most of those men can't walk. Is this your soldier's code? Murdering unarmed men?

Saito glances up at the blazing sun and then walks into his hut. The eight officers, Nicholson and the Medical Officer (Major Clipton) are left standing in the sun. They stand motionless. The soldiers on the truck keep watch. The clock ticks on until it is time for lunch. There is a discussion in the sick bay about whether Nicholson's displayed courage. Shears claims that this is the type of courage that can cost the lives of all of them. Out in the sun one of the officers faints.

The sun begins to set and the captives return from their work. The Japanese soldiers come to life again. Clipton is allowed to look after the officer who fainted. All but Clipton and Nicholson are ordered to the punishment hut. The machine gun is driven away and Nicholson is given a going over with rods in Saito's office. Then he is placed in the 'oven' – a cramped metal box out in the sun.

It is dusk. Two men come running. We hear a cry and a shot. Weaver is hit and falls. Jennings continues but bumps into a Japanese soldier who shoots. Straight away he is knifed. It is Shears who continues to flee. We hear a shot and he falls or jumps into the river. The two Japanese soldiers can see nothing in the turbulent water. The guards' return with two dead prisoners and a dead guard. War is madness! In this context it is interesting that Lieutenant Jennings tried to escape against Colonel Nicholson's order and despite Colonel Saito's assertion that escape was impossible. Who is really in command?

Nicholson is sitting in the metal box. It appears to be unbearably warm. Clipton speaks to Saito and is given permission to visit Nicholson for five minutes. Saito claims that Nicholson is crazy. Clipton smuggles in some meat and a coconut. Nicholson's face is washed and he is told about the failed escape attempt. Nicholson says that he believes Saito to be crazy. Interesting! Two lunatics ...

Nicholson says that he realises that he will not be able to cope with much more and that the officers are finding captivity difficult. He can see that the reduced rations are an added burden for the captives and that the sick men now forced to work will never survive. But for Nicholson '... It's a matter of principle. If we give in now, there'll be no end to it. No.'

MAJOR CLIPTON:

Sir, we're lost in the jungle, a thousand miles from anywhere. We are under a man who'll stop at nothing to get his way. Principle! No one will ever know or care what happens to us. Give in, sir. Please!

COLONEL NICHOLSON:

I'm adamant. I will not have an officer from my battalion working as a coolie.

The Japanese guard reminds them of the time. Nicholson thanks those who have contributed drink and food. Bribing a guard will make it possible for Nicholson to get something to eat and drink later on as well. None of the British soldiers seems to object to bribing the guards. Honour and integrity have their limits. This is the cause of many of the scandals that have afflicted both the private and the public sector. Everyone does what all the others do and what is customary. It would not be until someone outside the culture revealed that 'British soldiers offer bribes' that there might be a scandal (cf. Johansson 2002).

Unharmed, Shears is swimming in the river. He has survived. Next time we see him he is in very bad condition. The vultures are sitting waiting for him. He is frightened by the colourful kite that a boy is flying when it lands close to him. Soon afterwards he collapses on the outskirts of a village.

Saito has lined the prisoners up outside his hut. In this way he can stand and address them from his veranda, which is reached by seven steps. He begins his address by upbraiding Lieutenant Miura, the engineer. In reality this means that he is now entitled to take his own life.

COLONEL SAITO:

English prisoners. Let us ask the question why does the bridge not progress? You know why, because your officers are lazy! They think themselves too good to share your burden. This is not just. Therefore, you are not happy in your work. Therefore the bridge does not progress. But there is another cause. I do not hide the truth. With deep shame and regret I admit to you the failure of a member of the Japanese staff. I refer to Lieutenant Miura. He is a bad engineer. He is unworthy of command. Therefore, I have removed him from his post. Tomorrow we begin again. I shall be in personal command. Today we rest. All work and no play make Jack a dull boy! As a token of regard for your efforts in the future I give presents to you all. (Emergency rations from the Red Cross). Let us be happy in our work. Company, dismissed.

When Saito concludes with his 'Company, dismissed' he looks extremely pleased with himself. Even so there is nothing to suggest that the shift of responsibility will solve the problem. And sure enough, the building work on the bridge progresses even more slowly next day. An entire section collapses into the water.

The way out of social deadlock

Under cover of darkness the Japanese guards take Nicholson away. His fellow prisoners believe that he is going to get another beating. They are wrong. Saito wants to talk to him. Now only twelve weeks remain before the bridge has to be completed. If it is not ready when ordered, Saito must take his own life. He offers English meat, Scotch whisky and cigars of unknown provenance. Nicholson politely refuses. Saito chats and tries to manoeuvre the two colonels out of the social deadlock. This is no easy task.

> Social deadlock is the opposite of organizational change. Deadlock occurs when a group of people have arrived at a situation which satisfies none of them but which they are unable to change. Instead their attempts to change things simply serve to reinforce the existing state of affairs. A social deadlock may be full of individual actions aimed at bringing about a change, but the situation as a whole does not alter. (Brunsson 1985, p. 97)

Nicholson claims that his men could build the bridge under the command of his officers. This does not mean, however, that he is able to make any concessions about physical labour for the officers. Saito offers to exempt the colonel and all with the rank of major and above from the work. The response is no. Not even the NCOs may be used for anything but administrative chores. After an argument in which Saito gets angry, Nicholson is taken back to the oven.

Saito's anger is certainly partly the result of the pressure he is under and Nicholson's refusal to begin any negotiations. He also finds it difficult to accept what Nicholson says about the importance of ensuring the men's respect. Saito's view of the situation is that they have no reason to respect Nicholson.

Saito has real problems. The bridge has to be finished and this will be impossible without the help of the captive officers. He has to find a way out of the social deadlock that has arisen between him and Nicholson. The organisation has seized up. Social deadlocks are tricky, financial deadlocks are much more tractable. Financial deadlock means resolving the equation of benefit and cost for a number of interests. Nicholson's adherence to principle and his incredible refusal to acknowledge Saito's position has managed to reverse the situation so that Saito is being punished. In Nicholson's eyes it is definitely not Saito who gives the orders. Johan Asplund (1987) refers to this form of power as micro-power. It is based on not seeing the other party in the way he or she requires. Lack of acknowledgement of who you are can be as painful a punishment as having to sit in the oven. The ball is not in Saito's court, as he must in some way propitiate Nicholson. If the unseen cannot find a solution he will disappear – this applies not only to Saito but to all bosses!

Now comes a scene from the village where Shears collapsed. He has recovered completely, is wearing a skirt and allows himself to be bedecked with what seem to be Hawaiian floral wreaths. The villagers give him a genuine canoe to travel in. But soon he is exhausted again and his drinking water is running out.

Back at the camp we see Saito's solution to the social deadlock. Salutes are fired. Japanese banners decorate the colonel's hut. Saito is making sure that 'the anniversary of our [Japan's] great victory over Russia in 1905' is celebrated. To honour the event, all of Nicholson's men have been given the day off. Saito has also announced an amnesty so that he can release the officers. The amnesty also means that the officers do not have to undertake physical work.

One explanation for the occurrence of social deadlocks is the predominance of ceremonial rather than instrumental values (see for instance Bush 1987). Another explanation is the existence of inconsistent organisational ideologies (see Brunsson 1985, pp. 109–118). Saito's solution conflicts with both these theses. He creates and institutes ceremonies to shift the organisation out of its deadlock. In addition, he creates ideological inconsistencies that did not exist in the organisation previously. One possible explanation is that his method works because it moves the organisation from one deadlock to another. Admittedly it eliminates the old obstacles but the new situation is at least as unyielding as the previous one. There has been no change in either the readiness to change or the possibility of doing so.

If we consider this to be a shift from one deadlock to another, we have to explain why discontent has been reduced in so many quarters. The large number of contented individuals in the new deadlock depends as far as the British are concerned on their disregard of overall objectives. They are strengthening the battalion by building a bridge that will assist their enemy in the war. Saito's superiors are presumably also content. They get their bridge 'just in time'. They would probably be much less happy if they knew the price paid in the loss of honour by the Japanese at the camp. Saito himself is more discontented after the resolution of the first deadlock. What the Japanese guards feel we never really know. It is possible that the pros make up for the cons as far as they are concerned.

The British captives are overjoyed when their officers are allowed to rejoin them. They consider that Nicholson has succeeded – 'he's done it'. Another interpretation is that Saito has done it. He has broken the social deadlock in an innovative way. Who wins victories is always decided by those who write history.

When the other officers are released Nicholson is there and they all shake hands. This seems to be an important gesture. Saito sits on his bed weeping. This was, by the way, a difficult scene to act credibly. In the end David Lean (the director) told Sessue Hayakawa (who plays the role of Saito) that he was a useless actor. Then he began to weep in earnest and the scene worked well. However tall this story may be, it enhances the film's representation of what is specifically Japanese.

Plans to build the bridge and blow it up

Next day Nicholson inspects the work on the railway lines and the bridge together with three of his officers. He can see that the captives are negligent, wasting time and protesting. He does not approve at all.

COLONEL NICHOLSON:
Reeves – ever built a bridge over a stream like the Kwai?

CAPTAIN REEVES:
Yes sir, half a dozen of them in Madras, Bengal …

COLONEL NICHOLSON:
If this were your bridge how would you get it under way?

CAPTAIN REEVES:
Get it under way, sir? First of all I wouldn't build it here.

COLONEL NICHOLSON:
Oh, why not?

CAPTAIN REEVES:
I was trying to tell you, the Japanese couldn't have picked a worse location. …

COLONEL NICHOLSON:
Hughes, if this was your bridge, how would you use the men?

CAPTAIN HUGHES:
Not the way they're doing it. It's chaos, as you can see. Uncoordinated activity. No teamwork …

COLONEL NICHOLSON:

> I say, gentlemen, we have a problem on our hands. Thanks to the Japanese, we command a rabble. There's no order, no discipline. Our task is to rebuild the battalion. ... Which isn't going to be easy. Fortunately, we have the means at hand. The bridge. ... We'll teach them a lesson in Western efficiency that'll put them to shame.

To get the organisation to work as it is supposed to, Nicholson needs tasks to give his men. The solution is to build a bridge. The work justifies establishing the hierarchy and imposing the regulations again. Nicholson and the officers make the necessary plans and arrange a conference with Saito 'and set him straight'. Even though Saito released the organisation from its deadlock, Nicholson has manoeuvred himself into a better position. He now has the chance to recreate a functioning organisation and he takes command of the Japanese.

Meeting and the hierarchies of meetings seem to be what Nicholson is good at. He makes the Japanese invisible. The technique is the same as the one used to render women attending meetings run by men. The key line is Nicholson's 'could we have a cup of tea?' Towards the end of the meeting Saito has been broken in. In response to several questions he merely repeats: 'I have already given the order'.

We rediscover Captain Shears in the pleasant atmosphere of Mount Lavinia Hospital close to Colombo, the capital of Ceylon (today Sri Lanka). Once out at sea a British air-sea rescue plane that brought him there picked him up. He is lying on the beach, fresh from a swim and about to be kissed by an attractive female lieutenant in a bathing costume. Major Warden interrupts their tryst. He turns out to belong to Unit 316, which has its headquarters in the Botanical Gardens close by. This is where commandos are trained. Warden is interested in the railway bridge that Shears escaped from.

Later Shears visits Warden. It turns out that Colonel Green has given him the task of blowing up the bridge over the river Kwai. The task has to be undertaken from the ground as the bridge is out of range for bombers. Parachutes and marching will be needed. Warden has only one question for Shears: 'How would you feel about going back?' Shears is considered to possess invaluable knowledge. The problem is that he really does not want to return.

Shears confesses that he is not a Captain in the navy – not even an officer. He is 'just an ordinary swab jockey, second class'. Warden then tells him about all the problems the false rank has caused the American navy. He is an impostor and a hero at one and the same time. The solution is to transfer him to Unit 316. In this situation Major Shears (as he has now become) volunteers, which pleases Green who has just arrived.

Work continues at the river. Some of the captives wonder and the

Medical Officer (Clipton) asks outright: 'Are you convinced that building the bridge is a good idea?' Yes, Nicholson really does think so. It never seems to occur to him that the bridge could benefit the enemy. For Nicholson the bridge over the river Kwai is merely an instrument. The morale of his men is high and discipline has been restored. Living conditions in the camp have also improved – the soldiers get better rations and are not mistreated any longer.

At the Botanical Gardens, they go on planning how to blow the bridge up. The unit assigned to the task consists of Warden, Shears, Chapman and Joyce. There is some doubt about whether Joyce is the right man to take. Chapman believes in him but Green is hesitant as Joyce has such a vivid imagination. He is a good swimmer – but can he really kill? And then we see the parachutes unfolding under cover of darkness. Three men land uninjured in the field outside the village that Shears got to know. One member of the group, Chapman, lands among the trees and does not survive.

Warden is soon out reconnoitring with one of the men from the village (Yai). He takes command and starts making progress. Shears is resting with a cigarette and Joyce is sitting beside Chapman's body. They are told that Yai will guide them through places where there are few patrols. Warden, who taught Asiatic languages at Cambridge, speaks the local language (Siamese according to the subtitles). Shears definitely feels that he could be spared. Warden's reason for bringing him along is that you cannot predict everything. It is unclear whether this refers to what has happened or future needs.

The three soldiers slash their way through the jungle undergrowth. Yai guides them. Six women porters carry their kit as all the men are forced to work on the railway. Circumstances are grim. The men struggle on and the women are charming.

Warden is neither pleasant nor clever. Shears wins hands down. Even so Warden is the group's natural leader. Joyce is too immature and Shears cannot abandon the slightly ironic distance he adopts. Leadership seems to demand presence.

The bridge is nearly ready. On May 13 the railway is to be inaugurated by a train 'with troops and VIPs'. Even though the officers are now working voluntarily on the bridge it looks as if the timetable will not be kept. Nicholson visits Clipton to discuss the lack of men. He cannot ask Saito for help as the bridge 'is ours'. On the other hand Nicholson hopes to be able to use some of the sick. 'There are always a few malingerers.' This is an assumption that does not sound so good today but was perhaps reasonable in the 1950s. About ten men, who are all seriously ill, go with their colonel to work on the bridge.

In the jungle it is time for a break. Someone is shaving and someone else washing carefully. The women porters are swimming. All is quiet and calm. Only Warden is armed and vigilant. Shears is having his hair washed. Then a scream rings out across the idyll. The men take their weapons and follow Warden. A group of Japanese soldiers is making towards them. Warden throws a grenade. Millions of bats fly up from the trees. The men shoot at the Japanese. When it is quiet again there are several bodies on the ground and the water is stained with blood. Only one of the ten or so Japanese soldiers is alive and he runs away between the trees.

Warden tells Shears to make sure that all those shot are dead. He and Joyce set off in pursuit. He says to Joyce: 'Use your knife or we'll be shooting each other', and then they split up. The Japanese soldier is running. Joyce gets close to him first but cannot bring himself to use his knife. Then Warden rushes up and stabs his knife into the enemy's chest. They fall and the Japanese soldier's rifle is discharged. Warden is hit in the foot.

The wound seems to be fairly superficial but Warden finds it increasingly difficult to walk. He throws away his shoes (which is probably not very clever) but still lags behind. Then the others carry Warden on a stretcher even though he has explicitly ordered them to go on without him. Under the command of Shears they reach the valley and see the bridge in the afternoon light. They approach the bridge and Warden takes command again.

Nicholson is strolling on his bridge – as always with a wand in his hand. After Saito broke the first one he uses the branch of a tree. Saito joins him. He too is carrying a wand. They are alone together on the completed bridge. Saito looks at the sunset and says 'beautiful' to which Nicholson responds 'a first-rate job. I had no idea it would turn out so well'. They are talking past each other, and it is Saito who saves the situation by saying 'yes, a beautiful creation'.

Nicholson makes a sentimental observation and drops his wand in the water. Then he and Saito each go their own way. Saito is sitting alone with a letter he seems to have written. A farewell letter? He cuts off a lock of hair and folds the letter round it.

The captives have arranged entertainment in the camp. This consists of simple music and men dressed as women – two things that seem to amuse many westerners. Then Nicholson makes a formal speech of thanks.

COLONEL NICHOLSON:

But one day, in a week, a month, a year … On that day when, God willing, we all return to our homes again you're going to feel very proud of what you've achieved here in the face of great adversity. What you have done should be, and I think will be, an example to all our countrymen, soldiers and civilian alike. You have survived with honour. That, and more. Here in the wilderness you have turned defeat into victory. I congratulate you. Well done. To the king.

Meanwhile Yai, Joyce and Shears are approaching along the river to attach the explosive charges. The river is in spate and they have difficulty in getting to the bridge clinging to a raft. Two soldiers guard the bridge, which means that the group have to work under the bridge in silence. They place the explosive charges a metre below the waterline. When all has been prepared a cable is led to a position downstream where a remote detonator has been hidden. Getting away will mean swimming across the river so Joyce is chosen to detonate the charges.

Resolution

The men who are going to blow the bridge up take their positions. The night passes and dawn reveals what they had failed to see. Nothing sounds right. The river has become quiet. The water level has sunk so that the explosive charges and cables are visible. Much of the river bed is dry. Joyce scatters sand on the cable to hide as much as possible.

Most of the captives trek across the bridge whistling on their way to the next camp. The symbolism that we attributed to the whistling at the beginning of the film no longer fits. Here they are merely whistling the tune because they like it. Nicholson and Clipton are left with the sick and they will be taken to the next camp by train.

The team that prepared the explosive charges is divided and they cannot communicate with each other. Joyce is on his own with the detonator. His orders are to wait for the train. Shears is sitting with Yai on the opposite bank. Warden and the two women have remained higher up on the slopes of the valley. Warden realises that it is too risky to wait for the train. At any moment someone might discover the cable.

Clipton chooses to watch the train arrive from the top of the slopes. He does not want to take part in the 'ceremony'. Nicholson does not understand but accepts his decision and walks contentedly out on to the bridge. There are quite a few Japanese soldiers on the bridge as well. Perhaps the inability to kill once again makes Joyce unable to act. Or he may simply lack any orders about when a previous order may be disobeyed. Anyway, he still waits before blowing up the bridge.

We hear the train's whistle. It should not be more than five minutes before it arrives. Joyce prepares the detonator. Warden prepares the mortar. At the same time Saito takes out his knife. Is he going to commit suicide now? If so, is this the outcome of bushido or the kind of reaction that often follows a successful project (see Blomberg 1995 or 1998)? This latter is sometimes referred to as 'post-project depression'. Before he can make use of the knife, Nicholson catches sight of the cable. He takes Saito down with him. They trace the cable towards Joyce. He cocks his rifle and places the detonator beside him.

The train will soon arrive. Nicholson concentrates fully on finding out what is going on. Saito follows him. They approach Joyce who rushes forward and drives his knife into Saito. Then Nicholson throws himself on Joyce, who tries to explain that he is a British officer 'here to blow up the bridge'. Instead of giving way Nicholson calls for help. The Japanese soldiers on the bridge realise that something is happening and Shears rushes towards the river to cross over to Joyce. Japanese soldiers start shooting and rush forwards. Yai shoots back and is hit. Warden begins to bombard them with mortar shells from above. When Shears has crossed the river he is hit in the leg but keeps moving and is shot again. Nicholson recognises Shears just before he dies. Joyce is shot dead as well. Nicholson sees the detonator and moves towards it.

COLONEL NICHOLSON:
What have I done?

A shell explodes close by and knocks Nicholson to the ground. Confused he stands up again. He takes his hat and then falls on the detonator so that the charges explode. The bridge collapses and the train follows it into the river.

Warden turns towards the women porters and has one final incomprehensible line. 'I had to do it! They might have been captured alive! It was the only thing to do!' He throws the mortar away and orders them to break camp.

Had to do what? The explanation can be found in the book. Nicholson does not fall on the detonator but the bridge remains in one piece. Nicholson, Joyce and Shears survive and are taken prisoner. Then Warden and the partisans shoot back with the mortar. He later reports to Green. 'Good results, sir. The first shells burst right among the group. A stroke of luck! Both our chaps were blown to pieces. I confirmed that by looking through my glasses. Believe me, sir, I didn't want to leave the job half-done either. All three of them, I should have said. The Colonel as well.

There was nothing left of him. Three birds with one stone. Not bad!' (Boulle 1958, p. 188).

In the film (but not the book) both Shears and Joyce had become intimate with two of the women, so it is not odd that they showed their disgust. After all, the men they were fond of had been blown to pieces by Warden. If this had happened in the film. Well ... that red herring can add little to our analysis.

The camera lifts and Clipton is seen from a bird's eye perspective. For him what has happened is madness. He walks past the bodies towards the bridge. And the last thing we see is the bird-of-prey we watched soaring at the beginning of the film.

And what can this teach us?

So far our analyses have led us to what lessons managers can derive from seeing each of the films. In this chapter we have tried to formulate our analysis as the advice given by the film to managers watching it.

An overall view leads to success

Colonel Nicholson's failure becomes increasingly apparent as the film continues. Too explicit. Admittedly he builds an excellent bridge in the time allotted over the river Kwai. But is this his main task? In the film's final scene the dying Alec Guinness falls very dramatically on the detonator. The bridge is blown up and the train with the high-ranking Japanese officers plunges into the river.

Colonel Nicholson took charge of the construction without realising the threat posed by the bridge to the British military interests. It is too late to shout 'What have I done?' once it has been done. The lesson is that success as a leader cannot be attained by following rules to the minuteness of detail. What is good for his men is not obviously good for the cause as a whole. Productivity cannot be the only goal and managers must see the overall picture. Richard Normann (1975) was one of the first to emphasise how important it was for business executives to keep their business concepts in view. Even if each nail is correctly driven home, and the work has been fast and relatively pleasant, it is pointless if the function of organisation does not involve nailing things together.

Major Warden succeeds in his assignment to blow the bridge up. The question is merely whether he will be able to live with his victory. He lost Chapman, Joyce and Shears. One of his shells probably also killed Nicholson. Warden could see his task clearly but not its consequences. Both form part of the total picture.

Leadership adapted to the situation is the only chance

To begin with Lieutenant Miura, who fails, leads the construction work. Then Colonel Saito takes over, but does not succeed in leading the building work either. Their failures are similar. Both attempt to command the British soldiers as if they were Japanese or as if they were captives. As is often the case, violence and punishment do not work. The leaders lacked the capacity to adapt.

Colonel Saito not only failed to manage the work. He then abandoned everything to get the bridge finished in time. Walking across the completed bridge he realised his mistake. He toyed with his dagger as the final solution to his little problem. He would probably have gone through with his plans if Colonel Nicholson had not suspected the explosive charges and dragged him off to find out. Saito's failure harmed his own side. In the film the British win at building bridges and would do so again, no matter who won the war.

Colonel Nicholson is not adaptable either. He confronts Saito in a struggle that one of them has to win. Nicholson gambles most and is prepared to lose most to win the kick-off. He wins and is able to choose the arena. Once there he is as cunning as a fox. During the meeting at which the construction work is planned he finally gains the upper hand over Saito. He has been leading men on a field he is in control of for so long he cannot fail.

The unsympathetic Major Warden is much more straightforward. A remarkable combination, or is it is perhaps always like that? If one method does not work, he tries another. When he wants Captain Shears to join the team he first uses persuasion and flattery. When that fails he confronts his bluff. The captain is really only a petty officer. When it becomes necessary Warden resigns command to the next best man. He protests but then allows himself to be carried against his will on a stretcher.

Adapting leadership to the situation is not infrequently recommended in the prescriptive literature in which highly simplified theoretical constructs have been presented that have done a great deal of harm. These models are based on the idea that there are only a few types of situations and that adaptation therefore merely involves opting for one of a few leadership styles. It is more reasonable to assume that situations can vary infinitely and that leadership styles therefore have to be adapted to suit.

Where the prescriptive literature is concerned there is not really much point in providing any references. One book is like another. These include works that explicitly claim to be handbooks in management or manuals for executives (such as Heller and Hindle 1998, Rosell and Lundén 1998). But many of the other titles found in bookshops on management shelves are prescriptive (cf. Rombach and Solli 1999).

Leadership demands the respect of subordinates

From our historical perspective, Colonel Nicholson appears to be pretty hopeless. He is a racist pettifogger, mired in British class stereotypes. Even so his firmness of principle has its attractions. Professional soldiers tend to be prepared to lay down their lives. The colonel comes perilously close to doing so, both in front of the machine gun and in the hot tin shed that is his prison. Under difficult conditions he perseveres, displays courage and earns his authority. And the prevailing norms mean that most of the members of his organisation consider it reasonable for Nicholson to put their lives at stake as well.

We often overrate the significance of formal hierarchies as a basis for leadership. Formal power can be given but authority has to be earned. It is virtually impossible to lead an organisation solely through formal power. Colonel Saito had total official power over the construction of the bridge and it collapsed. It does not get much clearer than that. But how is authority earned in contexts where military courage and tin shed are not available?

In his PhD thesis Erik Swartz (1994) writes interestingly about the role of earned authority in federations. There the 'joint representatives' had limited official authority. The 'fundamental basis' for acquiring earned authority was the 'trust of the member companies' (p. 254). Trust could be won either by factual argument or by demonstrating clearly that personal actions were based on the value system that governs the organisation. The word 'trust' sounds to our ears too intimate to fit armies, prisoner-of-war camps and savings banks. We prefer to replace it by 'respect', which anyway does not seem out of place in Erik Swartz's text either.

The film shows that leaders gain respect by being at the head of their men. If the leader leads, his subordinates follow. Colonel Nicholson marches at the head, in everyday situations as well. The others do not question the direction but follow behind him. Even Major Warden marches as far in front of his men as he can. It is a way of taking responsibility that gains respect. When Colonel Saito says that Lieutenant Miura is a bad engineer and not fit to command he is not only signing the Lieutenant's death-warrant. In refusing to take the responsibility himself Colonel Saito loses the respect of his own men.

Little by little Colonel Saito loses the respect of those around him and with it his leadership. He suffers just as much as the captive in the tin shed but gains nothing. His intention is totally transparent and his failures manifest. But not even predictability and honesty strengthen his official authority in the way they do for the already respected Colonel Nicholson. Firmness of principle, irrespective of what the principles are, appears in this film to be one way of earning the authority required for leadership.

Colonel Saito's posture reflects the waning respect he is given. The remedies he adopts do not make things better. When he speaks to the captives on their arrival he stands on a low crate, a little later he needs a higher table and then a veranda that is even higher. He enjoyed most respect when he was still standing on the ground.

The importance of listening selectively

Colonel Saito leads the building work in the wrong way and builds the bridge in the wrong place. It may be his elevated position that deprives him of the information he needs. He is so high up that he hears nothing. Other things are dealt with behind his back. For instance, there is at least one guard who can be bribed repeatedly.

Colonel Nicholson listens. His strength is that he asks experts with practical experience of similar activities and then does what they say. In the film the experts decide but they do not lead. Leading demands its own kind of expertise. Colonel Nicholson listens only to experts. In other contexts he allows people to talk and then disregards what he has heard. When no expert advice is involved, listening is a way of drumming up support and being obeyed.

Major Warden is an expert himself. He decides how and when the bridge is to be blown up. When circumstances change as the water level drops and the explosive charges become visible Joyce cannot take the initiative himself. It would have been better to separate the role of leader from the role of expert.

You have to put up with learning

If we disregard Colonel Nicholson's insight shortly before he collapses on the detonator and blows the bridge up, he learns nothing during the film. The action is, by no means, certainly deliberate. His tardy insight is not in anyway one that he will be able to benefit from as a leader. But that must not stop others from learning what to do when everything goes wrong!

The question is whether Colonel Saito learns anything. He seems to. However, he does not like what he learns but seems to suffer a great deal in the film as these new insights plague him. Towards the end of the film his new knowledge shows him that he has to commit suicide. This tells us a lot about the nature of knowledge. When we market higher education we always pretend that it is not only useful but also pleasant to know more.

Towards the end of the film Sessue Hayakawa (Saito) has learnt how a bridge can be built in an impossibly short time. The next time the Japanese can do it 'just in time' by themselves. For the British, however, this was an extraordinary measure. Their next bridge took the normal amount of time plus the customary delays. No wonder the Japanese car industry won its battle against the British. Hands down!

CHAPTER 11

The Ends

In our conception of a book there is a final chapter. And if researchers have written the book, at the end they are supposed to answer the question posed at the beginning of their work. The answer in itself, or a broader analysis, should make a contribution to the sum total of our collective theoretical knowledge. This book, however, does not permit the traditional kind of conclusion. The reason is that the films on which we have based our reflections are not cases in any kind of context but rather separate analyses in themselves. We in our turn have analysed the analysis of leadership behaviour we have discerned on the surface of these films. We have then used this meta-analysis to exemplify what the films teach us and also to probe for more knowledge about leadership. It must never be forgotten that the conclusions we can come to on the basis of this material will deal with the surface of the films and not with leaders in reality. For this reason the final chapter can best be described as a continuation of our reflections.

When you've fallen on the highway
and you're lying in the rain,
and they ask you how you're feeling
of course you say you can't complain.
If you're squeezed for information,
that's when you've got to play it dumb:
You just say you're out there waiting
for the miracle to come.

(Leonard Cohen 1992, *Waiting for the Miracle*)

We are not particularly bothered by the fact that the end of this book differs from what is traditionally offered. Nor that this is also true of the way in which the rest of the research has been planned. We do not believe that there is any set pattern for the way in which good research can be undertaken. This is demonstrated not least by the fact that all the patterns we know of have also generated bad research. Indeed that is all that some of them provide. Nor do we believe in standardising how research should be accounted for. Set patterns of this kind not infrequently make research results totally unreadable. Those who are looking for generally applicable causal statements in the final chapter are in for a disappointment. They will not find them here. General laws are extremely unusual, perhaps even impossible to formulate in the social sciences. We do not know of one single example. For that reason we have not been looking for any laws and are therefore not surprised not to have found any.

The final chapter has been given a number of endings. One ending has been constructed on the basis of the way in which the films end. It felt natural to deal with the endings of the film at the end of the book. It may be a little too post-modern to be really fashionable. But the ends of films are, like the ends of books, important.

'How does the film end?' is a frequent question. We all have abstract answers for those who ask. Our responses should preferably say a lot about the end of the film without disclosing in any way what it is really about. We say 'they get each other', 'he solves the case' or 'it ends with a fight'. It is very important not to reveal how a films ends to those who have not seen it. If we give the end away, we have 'ruined everything'. Some films are tested on audiences before the final version is released and sometimes different endings are evaluated in these popularity tests. The right ending makes it better box-office.

In our second ending we go through the assortment of themes dealt with in chapters two to ten of this volume. As we have pointed out earlier, the focus of the analyses is empirically determined to a large extent. The content of the films has, in other words, governed what we have analysed, which does not exonerate us entirely. On the one hand we have chosen the films ourselves, and also shown that it was possible to include the analytical themes we considered particularly important. Even so, there is some point to offering a survey of our analytical themes. To begin with, this kind of review enables us to summarise what we have been able to deal with on the basis of our view of the films. After all, analyses require data.

The other point of this second ending is just as important. Many people we know read non-fiction backwards. If they find the end interesting, they then read the book from the beginning. A summary of the themes we have taken up could rouse the appetites of readers who begin with the last pages. At the same time it is a reminder of what we have been through for those who started at the beginning.

The third and final ending deals with the continuation of the book. In it we talk about the continuation for you, dear leaders and leaders-to-be, for our fellow-researchers and for us as well. There are, in other words, at least as many conceivable continuations as there are endings. Then, as we know, it is not always the conceivable sequel that really gets filmed.

How the films end

After watching a film, brushing away the crumbs of pop corn and discarding the empty beaker that once held a well-known fizzy drink, something may have happened to the cinemagoer. Those who watched the film on television may have been drinking something else but even so the experience will not be as vivid. Afterwards one may wonder what the film had to say. Here we will ask no more than what impression did the end of the film make?

We cannot, by the way, take it for granted that the end of a film is what happens in the last few minutes. A film may well have several endings. When characters die or are phased out of the action, the film is over as far as they are concerned. For us the end may be what we remember when we get home from the cinema or next morning. The strong impressions, the peaks as it were, may also be the ending. We shall allow the question of what an ending is to remain open.

Any Given Sunday

Any Given Sunday really tricks the audience at the end. The penultimate scene seems to be the ending. We know that Tony is going to get the sack and are pretty sure that his profound conversation with Willie is the last thing that is going to happen. More than one member of the audience has stood up to leave after that scene. The owners will take over control of the team and we could possible envisage Tony being properly thanked before wandering off with a desirable woman. But that is not what happens.

Tony listens to all the farewell acclamation. When he gets a chance to speak himself, he amazes everyone by announcing that he is transferring to a rival team and taking the best player with him. Everyone is surprised. Those of us rooting for Tony like what we see, money is not everything and power can be defeated. Tony shows us that we have a choice, we can develop or start afresh and that life is to be lived.

That is how the film ends. One of the American dreams is realised. The two men (Tony and Willie) wander (symbolically) hand in hand towards the sunset and new shared successes. The older hero has become young again, told the young woman where she belongs and simply arranged his succession himself.

It is not our job to alter how the film ends. Here, however, we have to make an exception. We cannot avoid feeling disturbed at once again seeing a man victorious at the expense of a woman. Christina loses her best player, the owners have all their prejudices confirmed and Nick, the male strategist, gets what he wants. Is what really happens that a woman manager gets rid of a worthless old stick-in-the-mud trainer with an attitude to woman that should be kept out of furnished rooms? And players come and go, do they not? The managers can create a successful team without Willie Beamen.

Matrix

Some films make the end we see into a prologue. Instead of making an impact on the audience they create expectations. *Matrix* is one example of a film that could just as well have ended with the text 'To be continued' rather than 'The End' – in fact it has neither.

Neo's emphatic speech to AI, those who rule, on the telephone (Call trans opt: received. 9–18–99 14:32:21 REC:Log>) could be a group call to the world. The king declares war on the oppressors. It inspires hope.

The leap straight up into the air made by Neo in the final scene also signals hope and power. Our new superhero will make life difficult for the oppressors. The impression is that with the right leader the organisation can achieve great things, real feats. But the choice of leader is not easy when there is only one individual in the entire world who is suitable.

> Still knee-deep in the system's shit
>
> ...
>
> Whadda I have to do to wake ya up
>
> To shake ya up, to break the
>
> structure up
>
> (Rage Against The Machine 1992, Wake Up)

Elizabeth

Elizabeth finishes with a highly visible change that is used to indicate a long-term inner transformation. The queen has her long hair shorn. She allows herself to be daubed in white and dressed in something that looks like a wedding dress. While this is happening, she daydreams briefly of her less responsible youth. With her altered appearance Elizabeth then makes her entry as a virgin before her court.

As she slowly progresses through her humbly kneeling courtiers, she stops and announces to Lord Burghley that now she is wed to England. She then ascends the throne. Distance and power are manifested. For safety's sake, the director makes sure that we learn that Elizabeth ruled England with exceptional success for another forty years.

Beck

In the end Martin Beck clears everything up. The Prime Minister is told what happened and that the security service has kept him in the dark. Beck is the final victor in the eternal battle in the film between the evil and the somewhat less evil, and also between detectives and the intelligence service. Beck sorts out the remaining loose ends in a confidential conversation with the funeral undertaker. He also talks to Benny Skacke and persuades him that it would be a good idea to try a new job.

Everything that Martin Beck does at the end provides clarity and is correct. He knows what he wants and gets it. At the very end we see him after a brief conversation with his neighbour. He is on his own, staring out into a pitch-black Swedish night. Even so Beck seems pleased. And a sequel will obviously be provided in the next film. When films come one after another like this they remind us of television series. Nothing wrong with that. The most illuminating detective stories we have seen were made for television.

Nixon

Nixon has an ending and an epilogue. The end contains the high-flown speech he made before his resignation. It sounds most like a victory speech. The viewer is bombarded with rhetoric of the highest standard. Here there is definitely nothing to be sad about. The speech is rather a demonstration of how to resign with colours flying. When Nixon finally climbs into the helicopter after making a V-sign with his arms stretched into the air, the last thing we remember is that Nixon is 'Tricky Dick' and we see him rather as a great statesman that we did not understand at the time. When it was released there was some criticism of the film for going too far in its hagiography of Nixon.

In the epilogue Nixon is dead and there are five presidents attending his funeral. The epilogue adds to the effect of the final scene. The viewer is left with a feeling that it is not easy to accomplish difficult things. It is not certain that the staff will like their boss at the time. Only later are we rewarded for our efforts, when the staff realise that the boss was right. Leaders in every country – endure!

The Mozart Brothers

While the cast accept the plaudits of the audience, in *The Mozart Brothers* the director walks away alone along streets slippery with rain. Those who see the film may feel this is unfair. We want people who make sure that things turn out well to be praised for their efforts. But there are many things this final scene can teach us. When the party begins, the boss should leave – his employees need time to themselves. The intensive development process abrades the relationship between the leader and those he leads. When they no longer have to sit round the same table, the director leaves his cast to their own devices.

Bosses who are almost never on their own also need time to themselves, time to reflect. Something tells us that as he walks away the director is considering his next feat, in other words another production somewhere else. He does not want to waste time on a project that has already been brought to fruition.

It could also be thought that the director has made a different assessment of how the glory should be divided. Glory and praise are a form of remuneration. The director has put a lot of pressure on the cast. When he leaves, it is to make room for others to take the glory that would otherwise have gone to him. Devising remuneration systems is typically one of the tasks of managers.

Life of Brian

You cannot avoid the end of *Life of Brian*. Happy and exalted they hang there on their crosses singing 'Always look on the bright side of life'. Even if it were not a satire, the end of this film is fairly pleasant. There are worse things to think about than the song, for example crucifixion or other dramatic ways of losing one's position. The death of a leader is not unusual in films, but if seen from the bright side perhaps it is not the worst thing that one could imagine.

We ourselves are struck by how difficult it was to analyse this particular film. This is because the Monty Python gang have really skewed their analysis of leadership. Our analysis has involved skewing the representation back to make it more realistic. The question is how to do so with a group of happy singing Brits who have just been crucified. Oddly enough, we can still learn a thing or two about leadership.

The Godfather

In *The Godfather* the horse's head is an *aber*, difficult to free us from. If it had been a human head, we would probably not have been as upset. This tells us a lot about the world of film and its values. Perhaps part of the effect is that the horse's head we see has actually come from a horse (see Internet reference 18) while human heads in films are artificial.

The line 'I'm gonna make him an offer he can't refuse' will not go away either. Almost everyone knows where it comes from. On the other hand the final minutes of the film pass us by as it were, they are far too logical. What then is totally logical. That's right, after one leader comes another.

Don Vito is allowed to die, an old man playing with one of his grandchildren among the tomato plants – it is natural. Even the succession has been arranged. Michael has already taken over and the new broom is sweeping in its own way.

Michael demonstrates the ability to act and a talent for running a mob of gangsters when during the christening of his nephew, where he is the Godfather, we see how five individuals are terminated and a few others along with them for good measure. For the viewers it is a stroke of luck that Michael seems up to his task, it invites a sequel. In addition Michael shows us his genuine personality by lying to his wife. He denies convincingly that he is involved in the murders – Michael is definitely no longer sympathetic, but he is a leader. His colleagues like what they see and swear their fealty to him and then the door of his office shuts. More ill deeds are definitely being planned. And not all bosses find it so easy to take over.

The Bridge on the River Kwai

'Madness, madness', says the Medical Officer in the final scene of *The Bridge on the River Kwai*. He is quite right! Apart from this line and the famous whistling, it is Colonel Nicholson who has made his mark. Firmness of principle is what stands out. A leader should not only stand at the front, march at the head and speak with a loud voice but must also stand for what he says. Quite simply he has to be a decent chap, in the old-fashioned meaning of the term.

If you have a good memory, you may also remember that it is better to have a project to collaborate on rather than nothing to do. What the project is matters less, as long as it is one that involves action and seems to lead somewhere. Nicholson can teach us a lot about how bosses should behave, for example walking with a straight back – that can be imitated.

Table 2. Important themes raised in the analysis of each of the films.

FILM	IMPORTANT THEMES IN THE ANALYSIS
Any Given Sunday	Apologies, challenges, cohesion, enthusiasm, humility, injustice, intrigues, motivation, ownership-perspectives, power, recovery, relationships, respect, rhetoric, role of experts, self-assurance, solidarity and values.
Matrix	Alice in Wonderland, conceptions of reality, cooking, doubt, inertia, leadership qualities, organisational culture, planning, possibilities, post-modernism, redemption, social construction, training and learning and visions of the good.
Elizabeth	Abruption, action, assassination, becoming a virgin, change of leader, diplomacy, espionage, female leadership, formal mandates, fusion, gender systems, groups, image, intrigues, lockable cellars, loyal opposition, loyalty, marriage, metaphors, popular appeal, power to act, power, procedures, scope for action, shared objectives, survival and thinking.
Beck	Chance, diminution, disobedience, ethics, giving orders, influence, informal leadership, institutions, middle-level managers, need of control, objectives, official position, perspective, population ecology, private life, profession, quick-thinking, rasing pyramids, success, teams, translation and truth and falsehood.
Nixon	Balanced justice, burnout, contact with reality, dependence on staff, responsibility, restitution, scapegoats, scope for action and the attractions of leadership.
The Mozart Brothers	Anxiety, artistic production, change, charm, conspiracy, conventions, customers, demand for leadership, discipline, fragmentation, glory, groups, ignoring, implementation problems, informal leaders, insight inertia, manipulation, millstones, opposition, profession, redefinition, reform, reputation and structure
Life of Brian	Action-orientation, cowardice, creativity trap, defects, formal models, individuals, institutions, meetings, non-profit organisations, noteworthiness, pessimism, plans, rational, sanctions, secrets, unwillingness to act, yes-men and control.

The Godfather	Choice, contrast, decisions, decoupling, delegation, dynamic decision making, effectiveness, experience, family, 'garbage-can' model, information, legato, muddling, planning, problems, rational choice, reflectiveness, respect, separation, slow-thinkers, ties of friendship and unconscious.
The Bridge on the River Kwai	Arena, bribes, bushido, ceremonies, courage, earned authority, hierarchisation, holistic approach, judging people, learning, madness, micro-power, mistakes, obeying laws, presence, principles, right and wrong, role of experts, selective listening, situation-adapted leadership, social deadlock, trust and work.

A fragmentary concluding theory

In films, leaders may easily die. In two of our stories the leader dies during the film (Don Vito, Nicholson), one is about to die (Brian) and another two die in the epilogues (Nixon, Elizabeth). There is nothing remarkable about this as everybody dies if we follow their fate for long enough. And the intervention of death in the end is not the point either. Leaders die after achieving what they set out to do, and that is the point. Death is not necessary, but it is one way of bringing a story to an end.

Nearly all the leaders in the films we have studied have been successful in the end. The only doubtful cases are really Brian, Reg and Nicholson. Brian and Reg are successful, however, within the confines of their individual ideas about what leadership comprises. Brian's own choice leads him involuntarily to become the Messiah – and we do not usually regard the end of Jesus' life as a failure. In the same film Reg succeeds in keeping his resistance group together so that it is still strong when the film ends. Nicholson restored courage and dignity to his men. When they leave the bridge they are a functioning battalion. Nicholson's misreading of the situation could be due to the heat or to his age. And its consequences are not too serious when the bridge is nevertheless blown to pieces.

In the end, all the leaders in the films we have analysed are abandoned. Their solitude is a feature that arouses our sympathy. In research publications we rarely see solitary managers, on the contrary they seem always to be surrounded by others. Solitude comes after the leader has finished acting for the people's, or his employees', best. Solitude offers time for contemplation. This is definitely somewhat thankless but it is lonely at the top and 'a man's got to do what a man's got to do', even if the man is a woman. There is a promise of new major feats in the solitude. The director, Warden, Nixon and not least Beck are only going to reflect while they are alone before going on to deal with the next task. Elizabeth uses aloofness as a trick to ensure that she is alone.

Promise is also offered by a third category of ending, in other words the endings that are really the beginnings of the next films. The three films that deal with the life and death of a specific leader have no sequels. All of the others display this potential. As *The Bridge on the River Kwai* is so old, we know the outcome. There is admittedly a number two but it presents a totally new version of history and does not continue where this leaves off. Major Warden never got a sequel.

The end can make the film we watch an introduction to the next. The new leader is recruited and will quite certainly do something great, she has already indicated which course events are likely to take. Neo puts his shades on and lifts like a rocket to an unknown but paradoxically obvious goal. Michael has initiated modernisation of the operation. After turning into a virgin Elizabeth is well placed to rule the country with unusual success, and for safety's sake the credits tell us how things turned out in the other reality.

The highlights of the films

In our readings we have been looking for clear lessons that can be learned by managers or managers-to-be as they watch the films. Obviously you cannot become a fully-fledged leader by watching and analysing nine films. Leadership is learnt by exercising it; this is true both in films and in reality. However, this does not prevent films from having a lot to tell us. Even if what we learn from a film is fragmentary in relationship to everyday reality, in certain respects it is very explicit. The recipes provided by the films we have studied can be put into words.

We would like to see these as lessons offered at three levels. At the first level there is learning that may not be omitted under any circumstances if we are to consider a film to deal with leadership. Nor can we do without this first-level learning in practice, if there is to be the slightest drama in our everyday experiences.

We have grouped lessons that are merely relevant but not vital in every situation in what we call the second level of learning offered by leadership films. There is nothing to suggest that a manager must have mastered all these lessons at the second level, but it is possible to go a long way by being good at some of them.

The third level comprises some reflections of a meta-nature that we have considered interesting. Presumably leaders are already familiar with these lessons.

Let us begin with a table (Table 2) of the more important themes that have arisen in analysing each of the films. The word 'important' suggests that we are allowing ourselves to forget some of them. This has not, on the other hand, prevented us from including some that obviously must or should be less important.

First level lessons

Crisis management is an obvious ingredient in the films. Even so, this theme is touched on only indirectly in our analyses. The reason is that leadership in films deals with crises rather than crisis management. Drama demands something tangibly hazardous, risky or at least extraordinary. The leaders we have seen in films have been exposed to demanding tests. At times during the films they take the wrong course, kill the wrong person or end up in some other way in complicated situations.

Crisis means a turning point. Once this has been reached things only become better and better. In taking advantage of the situation leaders are created, or is it merely the hero of the film that is created? Be that as it may, the message is a hopeful one. A good leader turns a setback into an advantage and therefore no situation is totally hopeless.

In films a crisis is the leader's best friend, but not only there. The list of changes that have been inspired by the threat of crisis could be a long one. One example is the dismantling of the welfare state that took place in Sweden at the beginning of the 1990s. It would hardly have been possible to reduce child allowances without reference to the country's deplorable economic predicament. After September 11, 2001, the aviation industry got rid of more than 100,000 employees all over the world. Would it have been possible to dismiss such large numbers but for the events in New York? Crises obviously provide scope for change. Is it possible that our leaders have learnt their leadership skills by watching films?

Closely linked to crises come convincing speeches – rhetoric. None of the leaders in the films we have analysed have suffered from speech defects or anything else to prevent them from giving brilliant speeches. The exception that confirms the rule in two senses is Pilate in *Life of Brian*. This is an exception both because Pilate has a severe speech defect that makes him difficult to listen to and also because in satire the obvious is turned upside down. And for this second reason, this is just the kind of exception we expect.

The turning point of the crisis comes after the great speech. Speech has many different functions. One is to provide leaders with an opportunity to show that they are leaders. Another function is that major speeches to large audiences enable leaders to define the situation and the solution that is most suitable. Speeches also offer excellent opportunities to motivate staff: this is an almost obligatory element. Where motivation is involved it is not merely a case of speaking well to many, leaders must also be able to speak to one individual at a time. Leaders need the chance to speak. This is a reasonable message in films and it also fits closely with the tradition that the important leaders speak first and the less important after them. Films depict reality – or is it the other way round?

Second level lessons

Crises and speeches are two phenomena that are as closely linked as chickens and eggs. It seems difficult to lead without a crisis and without speech leading would be impossible. But dealing with crises and speech are not the only lessons that have to be learnt. In our analyses we have indicated four other lessons, although it is not likely that they all have to be learnt; on the other hand one or two could come in very handy, especially in combination.

Closely linked to both crisis management and speech is the ability to define the situation. If we acknowledge that reality is a social construction, we have also admitted that it is possible for us to form perceptions outside an objective reality. In fiction this is close enough to objective reality. That is why we knowingly enter into the fiction of the film. This means that we accept the perception of reality depicted in the film. Those who see merely zeroes and ones on the screen will soon fall asleep.

What determines what we can be expected to do, or at least agree with, is our perception of the situation. Defining a situation involves determining the problem, time, location and tempo and also being able to present it convincingly. Definitions of problems seem particularly important for the leaders in films. It is helpful to have an evident enemy or some other clear and easily argued problem.

There is something special about experts in films. Leaders cannot do what they have to do on their own. In cases where someone does everything on his own we are not talking about leadership. Apart from crises and speech, the other workers are the most important resource for leaders. If the project is a difficult one, experts must be available. Experts are not leaders, not in films at least, nor should they be. Leaders must have the ability to choose good experts who in addition to their expertise can accept a leader who listens to what they have to say but at times overrules them. Experts have to be kept on a tight rein!

In chapter six we have reflected quite a lot on the concept of responsibility, so no further comment on this issue seems necessary. But it should be listed as one lesson for leaders. In films the responsibility of leaders is indisputable. Assuming responsibility is one of the ways of showing that one is a leader. The belief that taking responsibility means assuming personal liability for the outcome may well derive from films. In drama, this accountability is obviously dramatic – and can even lead to the loss of life or limbs. And if that is what happens in films, it could in practice as well. The lesson in this context should be that it is a question of being sure to appear to take responsibility but ensuring that the personal consequences are avoided. One way of reducing the impact of responsibility is to quit when you are ahead. Leaders! Leave the organisation with your head high and look as if you were on your way somewhere where another great deed is to be accomplished.

In the films making decisions plays a central role. The decisions are clear and are not misunderstood – circumstances that are hardly frequent in real life. How decisions are really made could be discussed. In fact we do in chapter nine. The lesson to be learnt concerns communicating decisions in situations where they are heard and noticed. People who watch a lot of films expect clarity.

Third level lessons

Table two demonstrates that leadership involves many different things. Therefore a good leader must have a broad area of expertise. The film analyses we have made, like studies of leadership, also show that leaders find themselves needing knowledge in many areas at the same time, and usually permanently. Being a boss is tough.

This image of leadership may almost certainly make it more difficult to recruit them. Being a pop-star or a professional athlete seems to have fewer drawbacks, at least from the superficial impression provided by the media. Those who still nurse hopes that the surface presented by the media depicts reality can see their beliefs challenged in the *Black book on the media* (2001) by Maria-Pia Boëthius.

In spite of all this, the films still do not present a hopeless image of being a leader. Their message is rather that while it is difficult to manage groups and organisations it is by no means impossible. Nobody can attain complete mastery of the entire range of skills required. It is therefore natural that some things work better for managers than others. Despite a few misses, one can still be the right woman for the job.

Different demands are made of the leaders in the different films. This too inspires hope. Bosses may get their fingers burnt. Not only CEOs are discarded with 'defective' stamped on their brows. Considering that you do not fit in one situation, or being considered unsuitable by others, does not mean that you will not fit somewhere else. The successful leaders in these films would do much worse if they swapped films with each other.

Life after the end

Leaders and leaders-to-be who have read this book and watched or watched again several of the films we discuss have hopefully learnt something about leadership. That at least is the kind of knowledge we have wanted to convey. We hope as well that we have been able to communicate something about how films can be watched. Watching for pleasure is not something we want to get involved in. If you go on doing it your way, we will carry on as we do. But as films make an impression on us, it can at times be valuable to take a more active stance to what is being conveyed. Next time a leader appears in a film – think about what she is really doing and what you can learn from it.

Our presentation of our data and of our analysis is of necessity fragmentary. More can certainly be found in the nine films we have dealt with that is interesting for leaders. The analyses could be extended and made more profound. Even more obviously there are a lot more good films that depict leadership. But there is no room in this book for more and we do not intend to write a sequel. On the other hand, we would be glad to see someone take advantage of the opening offered for more books that deal with leadership in films. We would love to read a book about leaders in Russian, German, French films – or why not Asiatic ones? We would also like to read a book entirely devoted to deeper analysis of one leadership theme on the basis of a scene in a film or perhaps one hundred scenes from just as many films. We have done our bit – now it is your turn to write a book.

But now we intend to celebrate the end of our project in the garage of a friend of ours – a genuine cineaste. He has converted the garage into a real home cinema with a screen on one wall, a DVD player, a ceiling-mounted projector and loudspeakers all over the place. Facing the screen are three reclining leather armchairs with footstools and a table for beer and popcorn. We thought we would watch a film with no thought of leadership whatsoever. But first we have to get a pizza each and rent a film. Perhaps we can find something decent about researchers …

References

Articles and books

Abrahamsson, Bengt and Jon Aarum Andersson. 2000. *Organisation: att beskriva och förstå organisationer.* Malmö: Liber.

Adams, Douglas. 2002 (1979–1984). *The Hitchhiker's Guide to the Galaxy. The Trilogy of Four.* London: Picador.

Aggestam, Rolf and Gunnar Harding, editors. 1974. *20 unga poeter.* Stockholm: FIB:s lyrikklubb.

Albran, Kehlog. 1974 (1973). *The Profit.* Los Angeles: Price/Stern/Sloan.

Aldrich, Howard. 1979. *Organizations and Environments.* Englewood Cliffs, NJ: Prentice-Hall.

Altheide, David. 1996. *Qualitative Media Analysis.* Thousand Oaks, CA: Sage.

Alvesson, Mats and Per Olof Berg. 1992. *Corporate Culture and Organizational Symbolism.* Berlin: de Gruyter.

Alvesson, Mats. 1998. 'Kritisk organisationsteori'. In: *Organisationsteorier på svenska*, editor Barbara Czarniawska, pages 105–128. Malmö: Liber.

Asklöf, Kajsa. 2001. 'Vem i hela världen kan man lita på?' *GU Journalen*, number 6, pages 16–17.

Asplund, Johan. 1987. *Om hälsningsceremonier, mikromakt och asocial pratsamhet.* Göteborg: Korpen.

— 1989. *Rivaler och syndabockar.* Göteborg: Korpen.

Axelrod, Alan. 2000. *Elizabeth I CEO. Strategic Lessons from the Leader who Built an Empire.* Paramus, NJ: Prentice Hall.

Bandura, Albert. 1986. *Social Foundations of Thought and Action: a Social Cognitive Theory.* Englewood Cliffs, NJ: Prentice-Hall.

Bang 2000. Tema: Film. *Bang.* Number 3.

Barbuto, John Jr. 2000. 'Influence triggers. A framework for understanding follower compliance.' *Leadership Quarterly*, volume 11, number 3, pages 365–387.

Barnard, Chester. 1938. *The Functions of the Executive.* Cambridge, MA: Harvard University Press.

Bass, Bernard. 1985. *Leadership and Performance beyond Expectations.* New York: Free Press.

Baudrillard, Jean. 2000 (1981). *Simulacra & Simulation*. Ann Arbour: University of Michigan Press.

Bauman, Zygmunt. 1997. *Postmodernity and its Discontents*. Oxford: Blackwell Publishers.

Berger, Peter and Thomas Luckman. 1991 (1966). The *Social Construction of Reality*. London: Penguin Books.

Berggren, Curt, Lars Gillström, Lena Gillström and Barbro Östling. 1998. *Praktiskt ledarskap. En bok om hur man gör när man leder människor*. Malmö: Liber.

The Bible, Exodus, XXI

The Bible, http://www.biblegateway.com

The Bible, Matthew IX.

The Bible, Matthew VII.

Björklund, Cristina. 2001. *Work Motivation – Studies of its Determinants and Outcomes*. Stockholm: The Economic Research Institute (EFI) at the Stockholm School of Economics.

Blair, Clay and Joan Blair. 1979. *Return from the River Kwai*. New York: Simon and Schuster.

Blake, Robert and Jane Mouton. 1964. *The Managerial Grid: Key Orientations for Achieving Production through People*. Houston, Texas: Gulf Publishing Company.

Blom, Agneta. 1994. *Kommunalt chefskap: en studie om ansvar, ledarskap och demokrati*. Lund: Dialogos.

Blomberg, Eva. 2001. 'Vett och vetande, hut och hållning. Magister Film i folkbildningens tjänst'. *Häften för kritiska studier*, volume 34, number 1, pages 33–50.

Blomberg, Jesper. 1995. *Ordning & kaos i projektsamarbete. En socialfenomenologisk upplösning av en organisationsteoretisk paradox*. Stockholm: The Economic Research Institute (EFI) at the Stockholm School of Economics.

– 1998. *Myter om projekt*. Stockholm: Nerenius & Santérus.

Blomquist, Tomas and Johann Packendorff. 1998. *Ekonomisk styrning för förändring. En studie av ekonomiska styrinitiativ i hälso- och sjukvården*. Umeå: Umeå School of Business, Umeå University.

Boëthius, Maria-Pia. 2001. *Mediernas svarta bok. En kriminografi*. Stockholm: Ordfront.

Boli, John and George Thomas, editors. 1999. *Constructing World Culture*. Stanford, CA: Stanford University Press.

Bonazzi, Giuseppe. 1983. 'Scapegoating in Complex Organizations: The Results of a Comparative Study of Symbolic Blame-Giving in Italian and French Public Administration.' *Organization Studies*, volume 4, number 1, pages 1–18.

Borg, Frank. 1995. 'Fascistisk estetik och degenererad konst.' *Ny Tid*, number 8, pages 10–13.

Boulle, Pierre. 1958 (1952). *The Bridge on the River Kwai*. London: Fontana Books.

Bourdieu, Pierre. 1998 (1996). *Om televisionen*. Stockholm: Symposion.

Brehmer, Berndt. 1992. Dynamic decision making: human control of complex systems. *Acta Psychologica*, volume 81, pages 211–241.

Brint, Steven. 1996 (1994). *In an Age of Experts. The Changing Role of Professionals in Politics and Public Life*. Princeton, NJ: Princeton University Press.

Brodin, Bengt, Leif Lundkvist, Sven-Erik Sjöstrand and Lars Östman. 2000. *Koncernchefen och ägarna*. Stockholm: The Economic Research Institute (EFI) at the Stockholm School of Economics.

Brownlow, Kevin. 1997. *David Lean*. London: Faber and Faber.

Brunsson, Nils and Johan Olsen. 1993. *The Reforming Organization*. London: Routledge.

Brunsson, Nils and Sten Jönsson. 1979. *Beslut och handling. Om politikers inflytande på politiken*. Stockholm: Liber.

Brunsson, Nils. 1981. *Politik och administration*. Malmö: Liber.

— 1985. The Irrational Organization. Irrationality as a Basis for Organizational Action and Change. Chichester: Wiley.

— 1989. *The Organization of Hypocrisy. Talk, Decisions and Action in Organizations*. Chichester: Wiley.

— 1990. Deciding for responsibility and legitimation: Alternative interpretations of organizational decision-making. *Accounting, Organizations and Society*, volume 15, number 1/2, pages 47–59.

Burke, Kenneth. 1969 (1950). *A Rhetoric of Motives*. London: University of California Press.

Bush, Paul. 1987. 'The Theory of Institutional Change.' *Journal of Economic Issues*, volume 21, number 3, pages 1075–1116.

Carlson, Sune. 1991 (1951). *Executive Behaviour*. Uppsala: Acta Universitatis Upsaliensis, 32.

Carroll, Lewis. 1990 (1865/1982). *The Complete Illustrated Works of Lewis Carroll*. London: Chancellor Press.

Cohen, Michael, James March and Johan Olsen. 1972. 'A Garbage Can Model of Organizational Choice.' *Administrative Science Quarterly*, volume 17, number 1, pages 1–25.

Cohn, Dorrit. 1999. *The Distinction of Fiction*. London: The Johns Hopkins University Press.

Collinson, David and Jeff Hearn, editors. 1996. *Men as Managers, Managers as Men. Critical Perspectives on Men, Masculinities and Managements*. London: Sage.

Cregård, Anna. 1996. *Skolchefers arbete: Om chefskap och styrning inom skolsektorn*. Göteborg: Centre for Public Sector Research (CEFOS) Göteborg University.

— 2000. *Förvaltningschefers styrning: En studie av praktik och representation i skolans värld*. Göteborg: Centrum för forskning om offentlig sektor (CEFOS) vid Göteborgs universitet.

Crozier, Michel and Erhard Friedberg. 1980 (1977). *Actors and Systems*. The Politics of Collective Action. Chicago, Ill: The University of Chicago Press.

Cyert, Richard and James March. 1962. *A Behavioral Theory of the Firm*. Englewood Cliffs, NJ: Prentice Hall.

Czarniawska, Barbara. 2001. 'Is it possible to be a constructionist consultant?' *Management Learning*, volume 32, number 2, pages 253–266.

Czarniawska-Joerges, Barbara and Pierre Guillet de Monthoux. 1994. *Good Novels, Better Management. Reading Organizational Realities*. Chur: Harwood Academic Publishers.

Czarniawska-Joerges, Barbara 1988. *To Coin a Phrase*. Stockholm: The Economic Research Institute (EFI) at the Stockholm School of Economics, The Study of Democracy in Sweden.

— 1992. *Styrningens paradoxer. Scener ur den offentliga verksamheten*. Stockholm: Norstedts.

Dagens Nyheter. 2001. 'Brittisk mördarjakt i blindo'. TV-guide August 1–7. *Dagens Nyheter*. page 3,

Drucker, Peter. 1969 (1968). *The Age of Discontinuity. Guidelines to Our Changing Society*. New York, NY: Harper & Row.

— 1986 (1954). *The Practice of Management*. New York, NY: Harper & Row.

Dunbar, Robin. 1996. *Grooming, Gossip and the Evolution of Language*. London: Faber and Faber.

Ekman, Gunnar. 2001 (1999). *Från text till batong: Om poliser, busar och svennar*. Stockholm: The Economic

Research Institute (EFI) at the Stockholm School of Economics.
Eriksson-Zetterquist, Ulla (2002) 'Construction of Gender'. In: Czarniawska, Barbara and Höpfl, Heather (eds.) *Casting the Other*. London: Blackwell
Etzioni, Amitai. 1988. *The Moral Dimension. Toward a New Economics*. London: Collier Macmillan.
Fayol, Henri. 1949 (1916). *General and Industrial Management*. London: Pitman.
Foucault, Michel. 1998 (1974). *Övervakning och straff. Fängelsets förödelse. (Surveiller et punir)*. Lund: Arkiv.
Gibson, William. 1994 (1988). *Mona Lisa Overdrive*. Stockholm: Norstedts.
– 1995 (1984). *Neuromancer*. Stockholm: Norstedts.
Girard, René. 1986 (1982). *The Scapegoat*. Baltimore, Md: Johns Hopkins University Press.
Girard, René. 1987 (1985). *Job the Victim of his People*. London: Athlone Press.
Glassy, Mark. 2001. *The Biology of Science Fiction Cinema*. Jefferson, NC: McFarland & Company.
Gleick, James. 1999. Faster. *The Acceleration of Just About Everything*. New York: Pantheon Books.
Gorey, Edward. 1980 (collected edition 1972, originally published 1963). 'The Wuggly Ump.' In: *Amphigorey*, no page numbers. New York, NY: Perigee Book, The Berkeley Publishing Group.
Granath, Gunilla. 1996. *Gäst hos overkligheten: En 48-årig sjundeklassares dagbok*. Stockholm: Ordfront.
Grint, Keith and Peter Case. 1998. 'The Violent Rhetoric of Re-engineering: Management Consulting on the Offensive.' *Journal of Management Studies*, volume 35, number 5, pages 557–577.
Gustafsson, Claes. 1988. *Om företag, moral och handling*. Lund: Studentlitteratur.
Hacking, Ian. 1999. *The Social Construction of What?* London: Harvard University Press.
Haldén, Eva. 1997. *Den föreställda förvaltningen: En institutionell historia om central skolförvaltning*. Stockholm: Dept. of Political Science, Stockholm University.
Hales, Colin. 1986. 'What do managers do? A critical review of the evidence.' *Journal of Management Studies*, volume 23, number 1, pages 88–115.
Hallberg, Margareta. 1992. *Kunskap och kön: En studie av feministisk vetenskapsteori*. Göteborg: Daidalos.
Handy, Charles, 1990, *The Age of Unreason*. Cambridge, MA: Harvard Business School Press.
Hedberg, Bo and Anders Ericson. 1979. 'Insiktströghet och manöverteröghet i organisationers omorientering.' In: *Från företagskriser till industripolitik*, editors Bo Hedberg and Sven-Erik Sjöstrand, pages 54–70. Stockholm: Liber.
Heller, Robert and Tim Hindle. 1998. *Essential Manager's Manual*. London: Dorling Kindersley.
Herzberg, Frederick, Bernard Mausner and Barbara Bloch Snyderman. 1999 (1959). *The Motivation to Work*. With a New Introduction by Frederick Herzberg. New Brunswick, NJ: Transaction.
Hibbert, Christopher. 1991. *The Virgin Queen: Elizabeth I, Genius of the Golden Age*. Reading, MA: Perseus Books.
Hill, Linda. 1992. *Becoming a Manager: How New Managers Master the Challenges of Leadership*. New York: Penguin Press.
Hirdman, Yvonne. 2001. *Genus: om det stabilas föränderliga former*. Malmö: Liber.

Huxley, Aldous. 2001 (1932). *Brave New World*. London: HarperCollins.

Hvenmark, Johan. 2001. *Varför slocknar elden? Om utbrändhet bland chefer i ideell verksamhet.* Stockholm: The Economic Research Institute (EFI) at the Stockholm School of Economics.

Hörnqvist, Magnus. 1996. *Foucaults maktanalys.* Stockholm. Carlssons.

Höök, Pia. 1998. 'Kvinnligt ledarskap: en helt hysterisk historia.' In: *Ironi & Sexualitet: Om ledarskap och kön,* Anna Wahl, Charlotte Holgersson and Pia Höök, pages 85–106. Stockholm: Carlssons.

Ivarsson Westerberg, Anders. 2004. *Papperspolisen: den ökande administrationen i moderna organisationer.* Stockholm: The Economic Research Institute (EFI) at the Stockholm School of Economics.

Jacobsson, Bengt and Björn Rombach. 1999. 'Hip Hop meets Classic'. *Svenska Dagbladet*, 3 oktober.

Jimenez, Jacques and Timothy Johnson. 1998. *Metaphors at Work. The Unseen Influencers.* Rowayton, Connecticut: Helix Press.

Johansson, Patrik. 2002. *Vem tar notan? Skandaler i svensk offentlig sektor.* Göteborg: Förvaltningshögskolans rapporter 39.

Johansson, Ulla. 1998. *Om ansvar: Ansvarsföreställningar och deras betydelse för den organisatoriska verkligheten.* Lund: Lund University Press.

Jonsson, Peter. 2001. 'Järnhästen i biomörkret. Motorcykeln i svensk film.' *MCM,* number 2, pages 60–66.

Jönsson, Sten and Rolf Solli. 1995. *Anatomy of Decision: the Engendering Meeting.* GRI-rapport 1995:5. Göteborg: Gothenburg Research Institute.

Jönsson, Sten. 1988. *Kommunal organisation: från programbudgetering till kommundelsnämnder.* Lund: Studentlitteratur.

— 2004. *Product Development: Work for Premium Values.* Malmö: Liber & Copenhagen Business School Press.

Katz, Daniel and Robert Kahn. 1978. *The Social Psychology of Organizations.* New York: Wiley.

Kelman, Herbert and Lee Lawrence. 1972. 'Assignment of Responsibility in the Case of Lt. Calley: Preliminary Report on a National Survey.' *Journal of Social Issues*, volume 28, number 1, pages 177–212.

Kerstholt, José and Jeroen Haajmakers. 1997. 'Decision making in dynamic task environments.' In: *Decision Making. Cognitive models and Explanations*, editors Rob Ranyard, Ray Crozier and Ola Svensson, pages 205–217. London: Routledge.

Kotter, John. 1982. 'What Effective General Managers Really Do.' *Harvard Business Review,* volume 60, November–December, pages 156–167.

Krauss, Lawrence. 1997 (1995). *The Physics of Star Trek.* London: HarperCollins.

Källström, Anders and Rolf Solli. 1997. *Med takt och taktik: Om den ekonomiska krisen, våra kommuner och det kommunala ledarskapet.* Göteborg: BAS.

Kärreman, Dan. 1996. *Det oväntades administration: Kultur och koordination i ett tidningsföretag.* Stockholm: Nerenius & Santérus.

Legge, Karen. 1978. *Power, Innovation, and Problem-Solving in Personnel Management.* Maidenhead: McGraw-Hill.

Levin, Carole. 1994. *The Heart and Stomach of a King: Elizabeth I and the Politics of Sex and Power.* Philadelphia: University of Pennsylvania Press.

Lewin, Kurt. 1959 (1958 eller tidigare). 'Group Decision and Social Change.' In: *Readings in Social Psychology*, third edition, editors Eleanor Maccoby, Theodore Newcomb and Eugene

Hartley, pages 197–211. London: Methuen.
Lindblom, Charles. 1959. 'The Science of Muddling Through.' *Public Administration Review,* volume 19, spring, pages 79–88.
– 1979. Still Muddling, Not Yet Through. *Public Administration Review,* volume 39, November/December, pages 517–526.
Lind Nilsson, Iréne. 2001. *Ledarskap i kris, kaos och omställning: En empirisk studie av chefer i företag och förvaltning.* Uppsala: Acta Universitatis Upsaliensis, 98.
Lorin, Peter. 2001. 'Historisk drottning förebild för ledare.' *Svenska Dagbladet,* 18 mars.
Lundquist, Lennart. 1998. *Demokratins väktare.* Lund: Studentlitteratur.
Löfgren, Orvar. 2001. 'Urbana koreografier: rum och rörelse i 1900-talets städer.' In: *Modernisering av storstaden:Marknad och management i stora städer vid sekelskiftet,* editors Rolf Solli and Barbara Czarniawska, pages 15–34. Malmö: Liber.
Maclagan, Patrick. 1983. 'The concept of responsibility: Some implications for organizational behaviour and development.' *Journal of Management Studies,* volume 20, number 4, pages 411–423.
Maltin, Leonard and Mårten Blomkvist (also Lars Axelson, Leif Furhammar, Jannike Åhlund and Gunnar Bolin). 1999. *Bonniers stora film & videoguide.* Stockholm: Bonniers.
March, James and Thierry Weil. 2005 (2003). *On Leadership.* Malden, MA: Blackwell.
March, James. 1994. *A Primer on Decision Making: How Decisions Happen.* New York: Free Press.
Maslow, Abraham. 1954. *Motivation and Personality.* New York: Harper & Row.
McClelland, David. 1985. *Human Motivation.* Glenview, Ill: Scott, Foresman.
Meyer, John W. och Brian Rowan. 1977. 'Institutionalized organizations: formal structure as myth and ceremony.' *American Journal of Sociology.* 83(2): 340–363.
Mintzberg, Henry. 1973. *The Nature of Managerial Work.* New York, NY: HarperCollins.
– 1983. *Structures in Fives. Designing Effective Organizations.* Englewood Cliffs: Prentice Hall.
Moss Kanter, Rosabeth. 1993 (1977). *Men and Women of the Corporation.* New York, NY: Basic Books.
Mozart, Wolfgang Amadeus. 1974 (1792 eller 1793). *Don Giovanni.* Don Juan. (Swedish text Erik Lindegren). Stockholm: The Royal Opera.
Mumford, Michael, Fred Dansereau and Francis Yammarino. 2000. 'Followers, motivations, and levels of analysis. The case of individualized leadership.' *Leadership Quarterly,* volume 11, number 3, pages 313–340.
Musashi, Miyamoto. 1995 (circa 1600/1974). *A Book of Five Rings.* London: HarperCollins.
Nadolny, Sten. 1983. *Die Entdeckung der Langsamkeit.* München: Piper Verlag.
Nørretranders, Tord. 1999. *Märk världen: en bok om vetenskap och intuition.* Stockholm: Bonniers.
Ohlsson, Östen and Björn Rombach. 1998. *Res pyramiderna.* Om frihetsskapande hierarkier och tillplattningens slaveri. Stockholm: Svenska Förlaget.
Ohlsson, Östen and Björn Rombach. 2000. *Organisationspyramiden och Buridans åsna: en lagom teori.* Göteborg: Förvaltningshögskolans rapporter 27.
Olsson, Lars-Erik. 1999. *Från idé till handling: En sociologisk studie av frivilliga organisationers uppkomst och fallstudier av: Noaks Ark, 5i12-rörelsen,*

Farsor och Morsor på Stan. Stockholm: Almqvist & Wiksell.
Osten, Suzanne. 1986. 'På olika stolar.' In: *På tredjebänk: ett antal besökare förklarar sig besatta av biograffilm*, editors Eric Fylkeson and Ellinor Fylkeson, pages 147–151. Uppsala: Janus förlag.
Perelman, Chaïm. 1990. *The New Rhetoric and the Humanities*. Dordrecht: Reidel.
Peters, Guy. 1988. *Comparing Public Bureaucracies: Problems of Theory and Method*. Tuscaloosa: University of Alabama Press.
Pfeffer, Jeffrey and Gerald Salancik. 1975. 'Determinants of supervisory behaviour: A role set analysis.' *Human Relations*, volume 28, pages 139–153.
Piltz, Anders. 1999. 'Fångarna på nätet.' *Moderna tider*, årgång 10, number 109, pages 44–46.
Postman, Neil. 1986 (1985). *Amusing Ourselves to Death. Public Discourse in the Age of Show Business*. London: Heinemann.
Powell, Walter and Paul DiMaggio, editors. 1991. *The New Institutionalism in Organizational Analysis*. London: University of Chicago Press.
Puzo, Mario. 1998 (1969). *The Godfather*. London: Arrow Books.
Ransom, John. 1997. *Foucault's Discipline: the Politics of Subjectivity*. Durham: Duke University Press.
Rawls, John. 1999 (1971). *A Theory of Justice*. Oxford: Oxford University Press.
Rhinehart, Luke. 1972 (1971). *The Dice Man*. New York: Pocket Book.
Rombach, Björn and Karin Svedberg Nilsson. 2000. 'Kejsare i kortbyxor.' *Svenska Dagbladet*, 28 maj.
Rombach, Björn and Rolf Solli. 1999. 'Vad vi vet om ledarskap.' *Nordiske Organisasjonsstudier*, volume 1, number 2, pages 105–110.
Rombach, Björn. 1986. *Rationalisering eller prat*. Lund: Studentlitteratur (Doxa).
— 1990. *Kvalitet i offentlig sektor: Att mäta och förbättra kvaliteten i landstingets verksamhet*. Stockholm: Norstedts.
— 1991. *Det går inte att styra med mål! En bok om varför den offentliga sektorns organisationer inte kan målstyras*. Lund: Studentlitteratur.
— 1997. *Den marknadslika kommunen*. Stockholm: Nerenius & Santérus.
Rosell, Lennart and Björn Lundén. 1998. *Ledarskap. Praktisk handbok för företagare och chefer*. Näsviken: Björn Lundén Information.
Savage, Mike. 1998. 'Discipline, Surveillance and "Career": Employment on the Great Western Railway 1833–1914.' In: *Panopticon to Technologies of Self*, editors Alan McKinleay and Ken Starkey, pages 65–92. London: Sage.
Scott, John and John Meyer (and Associates). 1994. *Institutional Environments and Organizations. Structural Complexity and Individualism*. London: Sage.
Scott, Richard. 1995. *Institutions and Organizations*. London: Sage.
Selznick, Philip. 1984 (1957). *Leadership in Administration*. London: University of California Press.
Sharkansky, Ira. 1978. *Public Administration: Policy-Making in Government Agencies*. (Fourth edition). Chicago, Ill: Rand McNally.
Simon, Herbert. 1997 (1947). *Administrative Behavior. A Study of Decision-Making Processes in Administrative Organization*. Fourth Edition. New York: Free Press.
Sjöstrand, Sven-Erik, Jörgen Sandberg and Mats Tyrstrup, editors. 2001. *Invisible Management. The Social Construction of Leadership*. London: Thomson Learning.

Sjöstrand, Sven-Erik. 1997. *The Two Faces of Management. The Janus Factor*. London: Thomson Business Press.
Sjöwall, Maj and Per Wahlöö. 1993 (1965). *Roseanna*. New York: Random House.
Solli, Rolf, Peter Demediuk och Rob Sims. 2005. 'The Namesake: On Best Value and other reform marks.' In: *Global Ideas: How Ideas, Objects and Practices Travel in the Global Economy*, editors Barbara Czarniawska and Guje Sevón, pages 30–46. Malmö: Liber & Copenhagen Business School Press.
Solli, Rolf. 1988. *Decentralisering i kommuner*. Lund: Studentlitteratur.
— 1999. *Lågmäld styrning: Perspektiv på kommunala ekonomers yrkesroll*. Stockholm: SNS.
Stenström, Emma. 2000. *Konstiga företag*. Stockholm: The Economic Research Institute (EFI) at the Stockholm School of Economics.
Stok, Danusia. 1995 (1993). *Kieslowski on Kieslowski*. Stockholm: Norstedts.
Strömwall, Leif. 2001. *Deception Detection. Moderating Factors and Accuracy*. Göteborg: Dept. of Psychology, Göteborg University.
Sumari, Anni. 2000 (1998). *Mått och mängd*. Lund: Ellerströms.
Summers, Anthony. 2000. *The Arrogance of Power: The Secret World of Richard Nixon*. London: Victor Gollancz.
Swartz, Erik. 1994. *Ledning och organisering av federationer*. Stockholm: Nerenius & Santérus.
Swedish National Encyclopaedia 2000. Höganäs: Bra Böcker.
Svens, Christina. 2002. *Regi med feministiska förtecken. Suzanne Osten på teatern*. Hedemora: Gidlunds förlag.
Tarde, Gabriel. 1962 (1900/1903). *The Laws of Imitation*. Glocester, MA: Peter Smith.
Taylor, Frederick. 1967 (1911). *Principles of Scientific Management*. New York: W W Norton.
Tengblad, Stefan. 2005. 'Is there a "new managerial work"? A comparison with Henry Mintzberg's classic study 30 years later.' *Journal of Management Studies*. Forthcoming.
Thomas, Jane Resh. 1998. *Behind the Mask: The Life of Queen Elizabeth I*. New York: Clarion Books.
Thompson, James. 1992 (1967). *Hur organisationer fungerar*. Stockholm: Prisma.
Verne, Jules. 1994 (1870). *Twenty Thousand Leagues under the Sea*. London: Puffin Classics.
Virilio, Paul. 1980. *Esthétique de la disparation*. Paris: Balland.
Wahl, Anna, Charlotte Holgersson, Pia Höök and Sophie Linghag. 2001. *Det ordnar sig: Teorier om organisation och kön*. Lund: Studentlitteratur.
Wahlberg, Maria. 2002. 'Företagsdoktor. Städgumma. Samma jobb. Vem vill du vara?' *Svenska Dagbladet*, 24 januari.
Wahlberg, Rickard. 2001. *Konst och marknad: en studie av resursanskaffningens inverkan på konstnärlig produktion*. Luleå: Luleå University of Technology
Waldersten, Jesper. 2002. *Tack för senast din jävel!* Stockholm: Max Ström.
Weiner, Gena. 2001. 'Hjälte, bov eller förförare. Läkarnas roller på bioduken stereotypa men fascinerande.' *Läkartidningen*, volume 98, number 15, pages 1814–1820.
Wijkström, Filip. 1999. *Svenskt organisationsliv: framväxten av en ideell sektor*. Stockholm: The Economic Research Institute (EFI) at the Stockholm School of Economics.
Yanow, Dvora. 1996. *How Does a Policy Mean? Interpreting Policy and Organizational Actions*. Washington: Georgetown University Press.

Yukl, Gary. 1998. *Leadership in Organizations*. Englewood Cliffs, NJ: Prentice Hall.

Zander, Lena. 1997. *The Licence to Lead: An 18 Country Study of the Relationship between Employees' Preferences Regarding Interpersonal Leadership and National Culture*. Stockholm: Stockholm School of Economics.

Öijer, Bruno K. 1974. *Fotografier av undergångens leende*. Stockholm: Wahlström & Widstrand.

Films and television serials (by year)

Leagues Under the Sea. 1916. Stuart Paton.

The Passion of Joan of Arc (La passion de Jeanne d'Arc). 1928. Carl Theodor Dreyer.

Triumph of the Will (Triumph des Willens). 1935. Leni Riefenstahl.

The Great Dictator. 1940. Charles Chaplin.

Leagues Under the Sea. 1954. Richard Fleischer.

The Bridge on The River Kwai. 1957. David Lean.

Psycho. 1960. Alfred Hitchcock.

The Good, The Bad, and The Ugly. 1966. Sergio Leone.

Patton. 1970. Franklin Schaffner.

The Godfather. 1972. Francis Ford Coppola.

The Godfather, Part II. 1974. Francis Ford Coppola.

Alien. 1979. Ridley Scott.

Monty Python's Life of Brian. 1979. Terry Jones.

Fitzcarraldo. 1982. Werner Herzog.

Aliens. 1986. James Cameron.

The Mozart Brothers (Bröderna Mozart). 1986. Suzanne Osten.

Return from River Kwai. 1989. Andrew McLaglen.

Nikita. 1990. Luc Besson.

Prime Suspect. TV-serial produced by Granada Television 1990-96.

The Godfather, Part III. 1990. Francis Ford Coppola.

Prime Suspect 1. 1991. Christopher Menaul.

Absolutely Fabulous. TV-serial produced by BBC 1992-96; 2001.

Alien^3. 1992. David Fincher.

House of Angels (Änglagård). 1992. Colin Nutley.

Lady Boss. 1992. Charles Jarrot.

Point of No Return. 1993. John Badham.

GoldenEye. 1995. Martin Campbell.

Nixon. 1995. Oliver Stone.

Barb Wire. 1996. David Hogan.

Eddie. 1996. Steve Rash.

The Associate. 1996. Donald Petrie.

Alien Resurrection. 1997. Jean-Pierre Jeunet.

Beck: Decoy Boy. 1997. Pelle Seth.

Elizabeth. 1998. Shekhar Kapur.

Any Given Sunday. 1999. Oliver Stone.

Matrix. 1999. Wachowski brothers.

The Messenger: The Story of Joan of Arc (Jeanne d'Arc). 1999. Luc Besson.

Internet references

1 anygivensunday.warnerbros.com/
2 www.cmgww.com/football/lombardi
3 www.theunholytrinity.org/movies/matrix/docs/matrixscript_97.htm
4 www.starwars.talkcity.com/transcripts/WarnerBros/11-23-1999.1-1.htmpl
5 www.google.com/intl/sv/
6 www.eb.com/
7 http://www.waywardintellectuals.com/1930841736_DON%20GIOVANNI%20E%20Libretto.pdf
8 www.mwscomp.com/movies/brian/b-script.htm
9 www.mwscomp.com/movies/brian/b-lyrics.htm
10 www.ihu.his.se/filmvet/johnssonmartin/thegodfather/inledning.html
11 www.winstonchurchill.org/bonmots.htm

12 www.sicilianculture.com/godfather/i.htm
13 ingeb.org/songs/hitlerha.html
14 www.acronet.net/~robokopp/english/hitlerha.htm
15 hem.passagen.se/truelove/marsch/bogey.html
16 www.mvdaily.com/articles/1999/04/bogey.htm
17 www.algonet.se/~shogun01/introduktion.html
18 www.jgeoff.com/godfather.html

Music

Cohen, Leonard. 1992. Waiting for the Miracle. On: The Future, track 2. CD: Sony Music.

Marley, Bob & The Wailers. 1980. Zion Train. On: Uprising, track 1. LP: Wea Music.

Rage Against the Machine. 1992. Wake Up. On: Rage Against the Machine, track 7. CD: Sony Music.

Index

Industrial Patterns in Deregulated Industries

When national common services become international service companies

by

Henrik Blomgren

When national common services become international service companies, new strategies and structures are needed in order to become competitive.

It challenges companies. It challenges how we perceive these businesses.

Not the least it challenges the way we assume that government can influence these former 'top-down controlled markets'.

New tools are needed both for management of these companies as well as government interested in influencing 'the name of the game'. However, in order to see this, the companies' way of acting is important to study. Which is exactly what is done in this book.

The pattern that evolves concerns, i.e. how the value chain is being split up in pieces, how former 'monoliths' is becoming more of open networks, and how focused but international strategies threatens the strategies of former 'full-house' monopolists.

Business-Industrial, 219 pages, soft cover, published September 2006

ISBN 10: 91-7335-001-x

ISBN 13: 978-91-7335-001-3

Santérus Academic Press Sweden

www.santerus.com

Printed in the United Kingdom
by Lightning Source UK Ltd.
117283UKS00001B/285

9 789173 350020